# Tech Smart Parenting

# Tech Smart Parenting

## How to Keep Your Kids Happy & Safe Online

### Catherine Knibbs

VERMILION

UK | USA | Canada | Ireland | Australia
India | New Zealand | South Africa

Vermilion is part of the Penguin Random House group of companies
whose addresses can be found at global.penguinrandomhouse.com

Penguin Random House UK
One Embassy Gardens, 8 Viaduct Gardens, London SW11 7BW

penguin.co.uk
global.penguinrandomhouse.com

First published by Vermilion in 2025

1

Copyright © Catherine Knibbs 2025
The moral right of the author has been asserted.

Penguin Random House values and supports copyright. Copyright fuels creativity, encourages diverse voices, promotes freedom of expression and supports a vibrant culture. Thank you for purchasing an authorised edition of this book and for respecting intellectual property laws by not reproducing, scanning or distributing any part of it by any means without permission. You are supporting authors and enabling Penguin Random House to continue to publish books for everyone. No part of this book may be used or reproduced in any manner for the purpose of training artificial intelligence technologies or systems. In accordance with Article 4(3) of the DSM Directive 2019/790, Penguin Random House expressly reserves this work from the text and data mining exception.

Typeset in 11.9/14.2pt Fournier MT Pro by Six Red Marbles UK, Thetford, Norfolk

Printed and bound in Great Britain by Clays Ltd, Elcograf S.p.A.

The authorised representative in the EEA is Penguin Random House Ireland,
Morrison Chambers, 32 Nassau Street, Dublin D02 YH68

A CIP catalogue record for this book is available from the British Library

ISBN 9781785045707

Penguin Random House is committed to a sustainable future
for our business, our readers and our planet. This book is made
from Forest Stewardship Council® certified paper.

# Contents

Introduction   1

### PART 1
### Your Kids in an Online World

1. Exploring the Online Landscape   21
2. To Ban or Not to Ban – Should We Ban Tech for Kids?   35
3. Addiction or Attachment?   61
4. The Effect of Tech on the Brain   87
5. Love, Respect and Belonging – The Importance of Connection and Communication   107
6. What Are the Risks That Children Face Online?   125

### PART 2
### Your Practical Guide to Keeping Kids Safe Online

7. The Early Years – Ages Zero to Five   159
8. 'But All My Friends . . .' – Middle Childhood and Tweens: Ages Six to Twelve   185
9. Teenage Tensions and Time Alone   221
10. Boundaries – How to Create and Implement Them   275
11. Let's Keep Talking   297
12. Troubleshooting – How to Respond When Things Go Wrong   311

Conclusion   333

## CONTENTS

*Glossary* — 337
*Notes* — 341
*Further Resources* — 347
*Acknowledgements* — 353
*Index* — 355

# Introduction

In an age of ever-evolving digital technologies, the challenge of keeping our kids safe online has never been more pressing or complicated. And with so little balanced and nuanced advice out there for parents and guardians who are concerned about children and tech, my hope is that this book will become your go-to manual, whatever stage you are at in your parenting journey.

In fact, I wish a book like this had been available when my own kids were smaller, at the start of the millennium, when we were only just beginning to realise how quickly the online landscape can change. My parenting around tech was based on my professional knowledge in information technology and cybersecurity, dealing with issues of IT support, cybercrime, internet use and helping people to navigate this space. But as this was still such a new area at the time, there was little general parenting advice to support me because it simply didn't exist for parents in a way that was accessible.

I mainly navigated my role using a framework of 'the city park'. In essence this is a metaphor I use, comparing the online world to a park you might take your children to, and how you would navigate that space with them in an age-appropriate way. We'll look at this idea more a bit later in the book, but it's a great tool for helping you and your children to approach the internet in a safe and empowered way. Back then, I understood how the internet worked, and I knew that people from all over the world were 'on it', so I educated my children about who they could game with on their consoles and the computer and how to do this safely. I also taught them how to spot potential scams, crimes and hackers (real cybercrime hackers, that is). I used 'filtering' software (now called parental controls) and kept technology in the living room, and they were only allowed to have mobile devices when I felt they were responsible enough to use them. This was a trial-and-error process because children aren't wholly safe with flip phones that can text or that have screens, as I'll explain later. Moreover, working directly in schools with young people helped me learn more about the use, challenges and, sadly, the pitfalls that can be encountered when using technology.

While many of us today may be familiar with some aspects of the tech landscape, it is advancing at an incredible rate and we may not always feel able to keep up when it comes to protecting our kids. To make matters even more confusing, the worldwide debate about children and technology appears to suggest that parents have messed up an entire generation or more of kids by allowing them access to this demon called the internet, with its evil social media, gaming, ever-changing technologies, smartphones and devices. I'm not surprised many parents today are scared and confused and just want phones, tablets, social media and the whole caboodle of the internet to go away. You've likely been told on social media (oh, the irony!) that this is the only solution to protecting our kids, and, given the severity of some of the issues, of course it can seem like the correct line of attack. But although banning kids from things like smartphones and social media may seem like a good idea, the answer isn't straightforward for a number of reasons, as we'll see in the course of this book.

It's in children's natures to take risks; the problem is that the internet wasn't designed with them in mind, and we can't rely on the tech industry to protect them, so it's up to us. That's why, amid all the noise and bluster out there, I'm here to guide you through the ages and stages of childhood in the world of technology – from babyhood to the teenage years – and to support you with easy-to-follow principles, science-based facts and a balanced viewpoint. I'll also be offering you a tech-smart approach – which is not

INTRODUCTION

about becoming a technology master or guru but, rather, being smart about tech when it applies to parenting and child development. Like the approach of a parent who knows which foods are nutritionally sound for a growing child, this is a style based on building trust and a strong, supportive connection with your child, which can be adapted to meet any digital developments that the decades ahead may bring. It draws on what I call 'the needs (body- and brain-based) model of online safety', which threads through this book. It's based on meeting the needs of our children in the real world, so they don't go looking to fulfil them in risky places online where they could fall foul of 'bad actors', as dangerous individuals are often called. Secure children have many more tools with which to navigate life and, as we'll see, you can help your child to feel secure by adjusting how you to speak to them about the space online. This tech-smart approach isn't about imposing inflexible rules and bans; instead, it involves educating ourselves about the world online to better guide our children through their early tech use.

Given all the different opinions about parenting in a world of tech, you might be wondering if I've an agenda of my own. I'll tell you a little bit more about myself in a moment, but just to reassure you now that I've no axe to grind or banner to wave here I want to stress that I am pro-child, family and technology working together, with the knowledge of how to do this safely. As the research suggests all the way back from early attachment theorists such as Bowlby, Ainsworth and Klein to more recent specialists such as Fonagy, Sroufe, Panksepp, Delahooke, Bryson and Siegel, the most helpful way to do this is to understand child development and how to connect with your child as they mature and grow. That's why I'm going to help you become even more attuned to your child and to form a secure relationship with them that will help them navigate both the real world and the one online.

For a child to develop the skills of socialisation, self-development and maturity, they need to feel connected to their parent or guardian deeply and for many, many years. The 'self' in self-esteem comes from children being looked after when they're tiny by a caring adult who acts as their emotional and psychological thermostat and enables them to manage their emotions and behaviours as they grow. This is known as 'co-regulating', and we do this with our children when they are young so they can self-regulate in adulthood.

So as the adults in our children's lives and the regulators of their emotional lives, we are helping to build the architecture of a good-enough brain – one adapted for today and tomorrow's world, whatever that might look like (and no one really knows the answer to this). We therefore need to consider what messages we want to pass on to them through 'our script': what we say and our own habitual behaviours with technology. To do that, we need incremental, age-appropriate, consistent and regular messages that empower the maturing child and create space for more conversations. And for that, in turn, to happen, we need to consider the messages we ourselves take to heart without question – the ones we were exposed to in our own childhoods, in school and on the TV, in the media and online, for example. These messages were (and still are) often delivered as the incontestable 'truth' – as facts that can't be challenged – and, over time, they've become ingrained. (The ones I hear being spoken about by adults in therapy include: children should be seen and not heard; children shouldn't speak up and be part of the 'equation' when we make the rules; children don't understand the world, so can't possibly have an opinion; and, of course, tales about how the TV will make your eyes square if you watch it too much or get too close to the screen.) It's up to us now to question what we swallow unthinkingly about the online space when we hear scary stories, so that we don't unwittingly pass on misinformation to our own kids or bury our heads in the sand when it comes to keeping them safe. It's our job to create a space in which to have balanced conversations with them about technology, not to react to it from a place of misunderstanding or a lack of awareness, but to communicate with them so that, for example, they understand the reasons for putting in place age-appropriate boundaries designed to protect them from harm, while still respecting their thoughts and feelings. And, yes, I do believe in setting boundaries, which is why I'll be talking you through how to do this in ways that will encourage your child to engage with them, rather than reject them out of hand.

With this in mind, my aim here is to support you and your children, whatever their ages, to be truly 'connected'. You need tools and solutions to be able to do this, rather than criticism and being told how awful the whole situation is. This book gives you ways to parent and be connected with your child, so they will come to you with the expectation that you can help, whether this be listening to a problem, solving their issues or even helping a friend, rather than worrying that you'll block and ban everything instead.

Your connection with your child will be your superpower in protecting them from harm, whatever their age. So I'll be emphasising throughout this book why age-appropriate, open dialogue with your child is necessary, not only for online safety reasons but also to create a secure connection with you, which is the ultimate aim of this book, alongside keeping them safe. And I'm here to give you helpful tips to be able to do that – and also to remind you that you won't always get it right (I should know, as I've got it wrong before), and there is advice for those times, too.

All the research and my own practice as a therapist have consistently shown me that open dialogue is the way we feel that someone 'gets us'. It creates the golden healing thread of feeling understood and empathised with and having a deep sense of rapport and connection. And while it might sound almost magical that to create open dialogue all we have to do is listen, the real crux of 'getting' your child and who they are, how they think and what concerns them is through truly listening and hearing, and this is a thread that will be running throughout this book.

There will be some parents reading this book whose child has additional needs or difficulties or neurodiversity And I'm aware that, if this applies to you, you may feel you can't have or provide a neurotypical connection with your child or engage in conversations with them as suggested above. You may feel that trying to reason with your child isn't appropriate, whatever age they are. That's why I'll also be touching upon the areas of trauma, specific needs and neurodiversity throughout the book, as this cohort of children may – and often do – call for differing approaches and thinking applied to their friendships and connections through technology, and the risks they face can be complicated by their vulnerabilities, which I don't want to approach as a one-size-fits-all topic, given the broad spectrum of behaviours, needs and considerations of each of them. However, I do want to say here that these children do, at times, require much more in the way of real-world connection with you to enable you to keep them safe in their online interactions. You know your child and I know that you can take the advice in this book and adapt it uniquely and appropriately for them.

## A Bit About Me

I'm an evidence-based practitioner and clinician with many years of experience in the field of child mental health and wellbeing, online safety, cybertrauma (any trauma that occurs because of the internet, online spaces or digital technology) and online harms, and over thirty years of technology-based employment. I've also carried out academic research in this space, too. I have, as they say, been on the scene for some time and can attest to the many issues that can arise.

In fact, you could say that I've been working with issues around technology and human behaviour in kids and with families since the internet first began. I've been there with families in all

INTRODUCTION

sorts of ways since before the start of this millennium, when I often had to explain to people what the internet actually was and how it worked. That all seems light years away from the speedy space we now find ourselves in, with portable devices, internet on the go, a constantly switched-on online life and, of course, new and ever-emerging technologies.

As I mentioned earlier, as a mum myself I raised my own children in a world of technology, which I introduced to them when they were around eighteen months to two years old. Before that, it was mainly about redirecting them away from technology due to their offerings of biscuits, toast and toys that would have broken the video recorder or CD tray when they were perceived as 'hungry' and needing to be fed, or wanting to 'share the drink'. (In my clinic nowadays small children pull at disc drawers as though they're foreign objects, given that many devices are CD-/DVD-free!) Then, when they were around two to three years old, I let them play a computer game designed by the toy manufacturer Tonka.

They'd watched me and my parents using a PC at home and wanted to join in – just like all small children, who want to do what adults do, and to have what they have. So in a way that was appropriate for their ages, I brought them into a world of screens. Through songs, (gaming) activities and being able to use and direct the mouse and type gibberish, they could feel like they were participating in the 'computer', too. And so I watched them grow up with IT. I'll be sharing stories to help you see that I wasn't always the best tech-smart parent, so this is not about me sitting on my high horse and pontificating.

While I was raising my boys, I trained as a child psychotherapist, and learned many lessons about my not-so-great parenting style, which I'd inherited from my own parents and their parents in turn, and which often resulted in me feeling shame and offering profuse apologies to my children. However, the training ultimately helped me become a better, more connected parent and that is a priceless skill.

I now wear many different 'hats' at work, but for the last fifteen years or so I've specialised in cybertrauma and I now train organisations globally about this issue.

My professional background includes information technology, the gaming industry, cybersecurity and data protection. During the course of my career, I worked in the area of relationship education for children and young people, just as the dreaded iPhone and Facebook were becoming the behemoths of the early tech revolution (around 2007 onwards), so I've seen first-hand how the young actually used these environments when they emerged.

Today, I work with parents and children in the therapy room, schools and other settings, and regularly teach courses to therapists about the safe use of technology with children. I've been using technology in the therapy space for over a decade to support children who've suffered cybertrauma. This includes the use of gaming, virtual reality (VR) and something called biofeedback (gaming using physiological responses such as heartbeats), because some cybertrauma events, such as being groomed online, seeing violent content or self-injury imagery, can affect the nervous system's response.

I'm both excited and a bit wary about this technology and what we can now use it for, such as learning about ourselves, communicating in new ways and, of course, being able to do our work on the go (as I was when writing this book on trains, planes and in lots of conference centres). And I'm intrigued by how artificial intelligence (AI) can help us tackle many of the different issues that will affect the children of today and tomorrow through its advances in climate solutions, financial problem solving and developments in education, science and even productivity. There are also incredible emerging technologies in medical science and advances that will help us understand the world in more depth, which may include evolution and how we as humans can live longer – and heck, maybe even become an interplanetary species. But mostly, I'm personally and professionally excited about the use of technology for mental-health interventions in my and other clinicians' practice, because I'd like to see a reduction in the distress that people suffer or subject others to.

As part of my work today in the therapy room, I often see the effects of the most extreme online harms. I've worked with children who've experienced things they should never have to deal with as a result of the idiocy, egos and greed that have created a space that never seemed to consider that children would enter it. So I'm passionate about teaching parents and professionals how to navigate the ever-changing world of tech, and this has led to me setting up my own social media channels to share this education for free (including on TikTok and Instagram), where some of my videos have amassed millions of views. (My now grown-up children find this simultaneously cringeworthy and sort of bragworthy, as some of this content has led to me meeting some awesome and famous people along the way.)

I'll be drawing on my clinical approach of 'interpersonal neurobiology', which makes use of multiple disciplines of theory and practice and collates this into a 'best-evidenced' guide. There are, of course, many different ways to parent, many different cultures and many individual circumstances to take into consideration that will affect any kind of guidance I might give you. But what I can offer, I guess, is a unique perspective that is the culmination of years spent working in a therapeutic setting, discovering firsthand what makes for a good connection between children and parents, *and* working in the technology sector and knowing how best to protect children or mitigate harms when they are using technology. With a foot in either camp, I am perfectly placed to share some of the very best advice out there with you.

That said, what do I or any other professionals really know about your personal situation? Unless we're in dialogue, unless you share with me the issues you specifically face as a family, which I cannot do on social media or in this book, I can only offer you general guidance, not tailored support. And while there are plenty of influencers online who will likely tell you they know you better than you know yourself, I don't claim to be one of them. This isn't that kind of book and I'm not that kind of therapist and consultant. And in the end, only you can make those decisions, because you know your child best. However, the guidance in these pages, backed by my teaching, writing and lots of research about behaviours of people on the internet, social media and gaming, will provide you with the assistance and scaffolding you need to help make the informed choices that you feel work for you and your family.

We now live in an age where we understand somewhat more the effects of technology, social media and gaming. However, because this is so complicated to measure and track, given that very little stays the same over time, we can't compare it from one year to the next accurately. Instead, we can look to established theories of human behaviour and try to use these to support our claims and thinking, and for discussion of the threats and dangers of technology and spaces online, as well as the positives and progressions, and how we are changing – or not. But ultimately, parenting is about . . . well, parenting. We're moving to a place of better regulation and protection online, globally, but, as I've said already, the most important thing in helping to keep your child or teen safe online has little to do with 'cybersecurity' – rather, it's about you and your relationship with your child.

I want to help you see that what we need to do as parents is rarely about technology itself; it's about us as humans. It's what I spend much of my clinical work addressing, which is why this is a guide to how to be the best parent you can be in a world of technology – and that is something *you can do*.

## About This Book

Whenever concerned parents and guardians come to me for help, I ask them what they'd like to talk to me about. They might say

INTRODUCTION

something general along the lines of, 'Everything that is technology, Cath!' Or, 'They know more than me; they're better at this than I am, and I can't do it. I just don't get it!' However, their worries can often be more specific. They might ask:

- 'Is my child addicted to the internet?'
- 'Will it melt or rot their brains?'
- 'Why do they always need to buy the latest version of games?'
- 'What about all the bullies and peer pressure?'
- 'What do I do about them seeing sexual content?'
- 'How long is too long online?'
- 'What about inappropriate content and language they're exposed to?'
- 'What about the risk of criminals online?'
- 'What about the damage it can cause to their self-esteem?'
- 'What about all the other kids on there?'
- 'What about the adults on there?'
- 'At what age is it ok for them to go online and for how long?'

We don't have the scope here to address every single issue that exists online – not least because they can and do evolve rapidly alongside tech systems and apps – but this book is here to help you think about the reality of what can occur in and through technology. This means that you'll be equipped with that knowledge and a raised awareness of what your child might be exposed to. This could include what they might happen upon when they search online or when they are directed to sites by algorithms (computer programs that use our behaviours online to point us towards content they think we want to see), or what other children or adults might show them deliberately, or what they might even be doing themselves in these spaces.

We need to care, as the adults in children's lives, when and where technology is present, and we can only do that when we have all the information we need to make balanced decisions as parents, carers or guardians. This book will help you to be aware of the dangers and pitfalls, so you won't feel isolated, in the dark or too frightened to tackle them if your family does encounter them, and also to give you strategies to help prevent them from occurring in the first place, based in the strong connection you have with your child.

Heartbreakingly, in the aftermath of a serious problem, parents will often say, 'I just didn't know', meaning they had no idea about the situation their child was caught up in. That is why this book is going to provide answers and address situations you might not know about yet. I'll be giving you the tools with which to make your own parenting decisions, because *you're the parent to your child and not me*. And when you have the full picture, you can make those decisions based on the facts and find ways to talk to your child about them comfortably. Ok, maybe not always comfortably, but I'll give you pointers on how to have important conversations and at least *look like* you're comfortable doing so.

As well as helping you to have important conversations about life online with your child, this book will provide you with facts taken from research on both sides of the debate about technology's impact on children, as well as my own direct experience of working clinically and in other settings with children and young people aged between two and twenty-five. It's also informed by my years of working with and supervising other clinicians and professionals in roles where they work with children who're affected by things online. I personally and professionally may or may not agree with some of the viewpoints I'll share with you, but I feel it's my duty to present *all* the information to you where possible, so that you can make up your own mind.

INTRODUCTION

## A Word on the Science

As I've touched on already, at the time of writing the amount of research into technology and children is very limited compared to other disciplines and domains. I once compared research parameters on an academic journal site about technology and children's mental health with research conducted into broccoli, and found there was more of the latter by a ratio of approximately 1000:3.[1] This gives you an insight into how slow research in this area is, as well as hints as to how complicated it can be.

Trying to gauge or 'measure' technology is a bit like trying to measure the weather; there are so many different ways to approach it and, moreover, the time it takes to carry out the research means that the landscape has often changed by the time we're ready to share the results. I've been going deeply into the existing research for over a decade and, while there are some good studies, they're mostly focused in one small aspect of human behaviour – because, as I've suggested, we cannot robustly measure anything to do with technology, despite the claims on social media. For example, we can't measure social media as though it were one single thing or entity. Each channel, application or platform – such as WhatsApp, Snapchat, YouTube, Discord and Pinterest – does something different and allows for different things to happen.

Also, I don't want to overload you with academic research terms, but I will use the academic groupings where possible, to help you understand the vast range and types of issues in play. (At the time of writing, up to around seventy different types of cybertrauma have been defined, so keeping these in general groupings like 'bullying', rather than separating them out into, say, fifteen specific versions, prevents the overwhelm.)

The book is divided into two parts. Part 1 will give you an overview of the online world and the challenges it presents to parents, while Part 2 is your handbook – a practical guide to addressing those challenges.

In Chapter 1 we take a look at the landscape of tech and what it means for children at different ages. Chapter 2 explores the question of whether or not to ban tech for our children, while Chapter 3 is all about addiction – what it is and, importantly, what it isn't. In Chapter 4 we'll discuss the effects of tech on the brain and how it does (or doesn't) impact things like developmental milestones, language acquisition and empathy and learning. Chapter 5 is all about the importance of connection and communication and their role in keeping children safe. And to end Part 1, in Chapter 6 we will look at the 'dark side' of tech, including algorithms, inappropriate images, cyberbullying and more.

Chapters 7, 8 and 9 will take you through the issues arising with children in the early years, middle childhood and teenage years, respectively, and how to address them from a practical perspective. In Chapter 10 we will go deeper into boundaries and how to present and implement them at different stages. Chapter 11, 'Let's Keep Talking', is another look at communication, which is the cornerstone of parenting with tech. And we end with Chapter 12, which gives you troubleshooting advice for particular scenarios when things go wrong.

Throughout Part 2 you will find tips, providing small, actionable steps, as well as food for thought, including the viewpoints of children themselves in case studies and comments (in which all identifying details have been changed to protect the anonymity and privacy of my clients and the children I spoke with while researching my book and my PhD). There are also carefully placed 'self-care breaks' in Part 2, where you can choose to put the book down for a while and engage in an activity to nourish yourself and support your own mental health, giving you some space in which to take it all in (of course, you can do this at any point, not just at the designated breaks). Many of the issues that children face will also be discussed through case studies or little vignettes (in which all identifying details have been changed to protect identities whilst remaining true to the recurring issues I encounter), so you can get a sense of the risks and dangers you need to be aware of. Finally, a summary at the end of each chapter will give you an at-a-glance review of the key points or takeaways within it.

In an era of technology that isn't going to stop evolving, it's very much our job as the adults in our children's lives to ensure they can navigate online spaces safely – something this book will help you to do. It will cut through the conflicting advice and noise about technology and what it's really doing to our brains, and give you a north star to follow so that you can make your own decisions about what works best for your family. This might mean that you choose to go down the no-technology route, or perhaps you'll make other decisions around screens for toddlers or teens. While these may sometimes go against what your friends or family think, you can feel reassured that you'll be making informed choices based in tech-smart parenting. You'll show your child how to use tech as a tool in a responsible manner, supervising their use of that tool until this no longer needs to happen – just like teaching a kid to ride a bike or a teenager to drive.

As you read, I hope you'll feel empowered and reassured that I'm not lecturing or chastising you for what you've already done. There are times when I look back and realise I could have done so much better as a parent – and that can be painful to think about; but when I look at the toolbox I had at the time, it was nigh on empty at times. There is a saying that if all you have is a hammer, then every problem looks like a nail. But that just reminds me of childhoods of the past, where the most common tool, as reported to me in therapy, was a slipper or belt. And I think we can safely say that parenting in that style is not what this book aims to put in the toolbox!

## You've Got This!

There isn't enough support for parents or recognition that parenting is the hardest job on the planet, especially when it concerns the technology that we're now expected to master. But I hear you and see you are doing a great job – the fact that you are here, reading these words, tells me you are trying to be a super-duper parent, and I am cheering you on as parents who are doing your best to raise, connect with and support your own child or children.

It can be difficult to know whether we're up to the task of keeping our kids safe when they access online spaces, especially when we feel shame and inadequacy or are hugely confused by the numbers of experts and social media posts telling us that there's no 'good' side to social media or gaming. In a world of terrifying clickbait that tells us 'it's impossible', that we should 'ban and remove it all' and that 'you're out of your depth', I am telling you: you *can* do this, and I believe strongly that you will – because you have the intention to help your child and that makes you their greatest ally.

I want you to think of this book as your guiding light – something you can dip into whenever you need to during the course of raising your family. I'm going to be at your side as we explore the issues, perils and pitfalls of life online. And in the same way that I'll be there for you I suspect that, after reading the information in these pages, you may well find that you are there for others, passing on details of what you've learned. By adopting the approach in this book, you'll be in an even stronger position to continue being a great parent in the world of technology as it advances, because the principles here are all about parenting and connecting with your child, and that goes way beyond all the technological innovations in the world as *the* most important connection in your child's life.

I often give out little cards to people when I'm running training

INTRODUCTION

sessions, reminding them that they are awesome, and I would like you to have an affirmation, too, so here it is, loud and clear:

> *You are an awesome parent who can and will learn how to be more skilled in a world of technology for your child. And your child will notice – they will know this, and it will plant a seed in their heart.*

Of course, they might not tell you till they reach adulthood, but that's ok, I guess. I'm sure you can wait!

So remember, you've got this – and you really aren't alone in this process: I believe in you. Now, let's get started . . .

# PART 1

# Your Kids in an Online World

In Part 1 we're going to start exploring the world online and how to help kids navigate it safely. Along the way, we'll consider the debate about banning children from accessing things like social media and whether children are really at risk of becoming addicted to their devices or developmentally impacted by them. I'll also be explaining why communication with your child holds the key to protecting them and will guide you through the very real dangers that are lurking out there.

CHAPTER 1

# Exploring the Online Landscape

There seems to be a narrative that parents today are the first generation to raise children who are surrounded by technology, but this isn't quite true, as the internet has been with us in one form or another since at least the turn of the millennium. However, parents today are probably the first to be told (even scolded) that they 'ought to know how to protect their children online' – because, in all truth, my peers and I were mostly unaware of the need for this when we were bringing up our kids.

Yet the difficult truth to swallow is that it isn't just down to companies, organisations and people in power to keep our kids safe; it's our responsibility as adults and parents to know where our children go online and to teach them how to keep safe there – just as we do when it comes to navigating the real world. Exploring the world online and the real world share the same underlying principles, yet many of us may feel that the former is somehow too big for us to cope with, which is why a tech-smart parenting approach is now necessary – to help us feel confident in guiding our kids through digital spaces.

Gen Z (born between 1997 and 2012), otherwise known as 'digital natives', are technically the first cohort of children to grow up in the information age. While the oldest members of that generation are now approaching their late twenties, the youngest are still in their teens. Sadly, the older members of this generation were failed on many levels around technology, because of a lack of knowledge about the possible risks.

The fact is that the sorts of problems and harms we're now discussing have been happening to children and teens in internet spaces since the worldwide web first began to go mainstream, near the end of the 1990s, although this mainly went unnoticed and many people didn't necessarily understand it. What is so different now is the public response to digital technology, social media and gaming that's emerged over the last few years. However, just as we were starting to get some proper research findings that could help us really understand the issues around what children were doing online and how this was impacting their everyday lives and other aspects of their health and wellbeing, the worldwide Covid-19 pandemic occurred, and our technology use changed during the lockdowns in 2020 to 2021. There was a huge increase in our need to be online for work and play, which really highlighted the problems in this space but also somewhat skewed the baseline results about what constitutes 'normal' digital use for each age and stage of childhood. The pandemic period is now talked about as having highlighted lots of developmental issues in children, as there has been nothing like it before or since. It represents a major blip in the timeline of human history and, as we are only a few years on from it, we still don't have the clarity with which to assess its impact on the human species writ large. Moreover, given the rapid rise of AI models, we likely won't get the chance to study this in isolation again, as there may be more pressing matters that will need our attention.

Needless to say, many of the parents and professionals who are now vocal about banning devices have learned about these issues slowly in comparison to the speed with which technology itself has developed. The current climate of devices and online harm has become muddled up with blaming the big-tech industry for not doing enough (which is true in some cases), and pathologising language (such as the terms 'addicted', 'attention deficit' and 'depressed') used by non-clinical professionals, the mainstream media and even some parents. Tech has become embroiled in scare stories, often with little robust research to back this up (the blue-light myth, for example), resulting in the need for books like this one to help parents understand the real situation on- and offline.

This is absolutely not to say that there aren't some very real dangers out there, which include the kind of content that our children can encounter online and also some of the individuals who can be found there. And similar to the threats we warn our children about in the real world, on rare occasions things can go terribly wrong. The awful reality is that in the past children have tragically died from interactions connected to the world online, such as buying drugs or taking part in challenges that have proved fatal, while high-profile cases in the news have highlighted the dangers of grooming and viewing content relating to self-harm. However, once we are aware of these sorts of risks, we can educate our children about them by discussing them with them in age-appropriate language and taking steps together to prevent those sorts of dangers ever becoming a reality. By prioritising your own connection with your child through the sort of tech-smart approach we're going to be considering in these pages, you'll be in a much stronger position to protect them and to help them navigate the online world safely.

## Let's Take a Walk in the Park . . .

I mentioned in the Introduction that, when I talk to parents about navigating the world online with their child, I sometimes compare it to taking them to the park. And if I were to list the sorts of risks and dangers that can exist in a real park (such as unsafe equipment, strangers, people using bad language and behaving badly, cyclists going too fast, skateboard accidents and so on), you'd think that no one would ever want to visit one, let alone allow their children to do so.

And, if I were to list all the risks and dangers in the online world, it would probably sound even scarier. But what tends to happen is that we talk about or get overly fixated on particular issues, such as kids spending too much time on screens, or coming across adult content like swearing, sex or violence, while forgetting these things exist on TV and in cinemas, too, and that children have access to them there.

There's a lot to think about. Which is why I'd like you to imagine taking your child to a city park now. When they are little, you hold their hand tightly, you support them when they wobble on the swings and you steer them away from that dodgy-looking character lurking by the bins – and you *talk to them about it*. As they get older, you still keep a watchful eye, but you gradually give them a little more freedom to roam, making sure you always know where they are and that they can call out to you if they need to – and, again, *you talk to them* about tricky people, and you tell them not to take sweets from strangers or stroke dogs without asking first and so on.

We can take a similar approach online: when your child is small, you hold their hand as you both enter that space and, as they grow, you teach them how to engage with it safely, before letting them go it alone.

So the first thing to say here is: I'm not anti-technology for small children (or children of any age), and, yes, I'm aware that's going to shock a lot of people, because they might jump to conclusions and think I'm suggesting that babies and toddlers should be let loose with technology. But I'm not saying that at all (and I'll be explaining why later, in Chapter 7 on parenting and the early years).

## Why *Do* Kids Take Risks and How Can We Protect Them?

Coming back to our city-park metaphor, the dangers we teach children about tend to be the same ones that have existed since time immemorial, which often involve strangers or risky behaviours. We educate our kids about the things they will feel in their tummies (such as a feeling of dread, butterflies, sickness and so on); these are their gut instincts, and we teach them where to run or who to run to when they feel them, such as to adults in uniform. And, of course, we show them how to cross the road safely when we're not with them. But we also know that children *will* still run into the road unexpectedly, and they *will* still make mistakes and take risks in the city park and online (where there are often no safeguards in place to stop or prevent this), which we probably wouldn't take as adults. It's in their nature – it's biology – and non-thinking risks such as running out into the road or even doing-it-on-purpose-type risks, for dares, are generally more common in children than adults. They will (and do) talk to strangers in the park, and most certainly to the other children who're playing with them when they're there. And they'll look for thrills, such as scaling heights that would terrify most adults.

The difference is that while not all children today will have access to or want to climb trees, run around in parks, throw the moves on trampolines or play games of 'dare' or 'spin the bottle', they're doing versions of this behaviour online. They will explore dangerous territory, they will experiment with new things, talk to strangers and compete with each other in risky ways. In fact, they take many more calculated and emotional risks in online spaces than in the real world, as we'll see. But online, there aren't a lot of protective measures to take care of them before or after these experiences.

Humans engage in all sorts of activities, including in 'invisible spaces' online, which aren't engineered to be particularly safe for anyone using them – least of all a child in an environment that was created and originally designed for adults, such as the internet. While parts of that environment are designed by well-meaning adults (such as chat forums for children with disabilities), some are not so well meaning (such as adult sites with sexual content), while others may have no concept of how children actually can and do use these spaces (such as forums about special interests, like music and fashion) – or of where children themselves might also create spaces for fun, for bullying, for harassment, for chills, for clicks and engagement and, of course, where children can encounter harm in myriad ways.

The most difficult aspect of being a parent (and I know – I am one) is to think that your child can be hurt in so many ways and you're powerless to stop it or to stop them from hurting – and this can result in you beating yourself up for being a failure when things do go wrong. Please try not to do this. The fact is that we can only be as good as the knowledge we have and that we impart to our children – and even then, the baddies can still hurt them. That is the ugly possibility we often hide from, burying our heads in the sand like ostriches, when we need to face up to it (also, apparently ostriches don't bury their heads – this too is misinformation).

Scary stories about the harms that some children face in the online world are shared on the news and on social media with such great gusto and emotion that they can cause outrage and/or emotional shutdown, leading us to do what scientists call a cognitive reframe in order to shield ourselves from our own fears of, for example, losing a child, which might entail thinking, 'That would never happen to me or my child.' Our brains are master manipulators of information and can make it seem that, although a terrible tragedy might befall others, we'd never allow that to happen to our child, because we're 'good parents' or because our children do exactly what we tell them – and we would really, truly believe it. This is a process that helps us feel more in control, because the truth is that the world can be a scary place, and we'd rather not think about that.

But while I know it can make you sick to your stomach, facing the very real dangers out there is precisely how you can have the most impact and prevent many of the issues arising in the first place. It's also how we can learn the most about our children and strengthen our connection with them in ways to help to keep them safe.

## Conversation, Conversation, Conversation

Parenting in a world of digital technology is mostly the same as parenting was before IT existed. It's about communication, observation and *checking in, not checking on* (which is a way to observe and protect, while refraining from intrusion, as a sense of intrusion can cause disconnect between children and parents, which I'll be speaking more about later). It's about what American clinical professor of psychiatry Dan Siegel calls the 4Ss, which all children need: to be *s*afe, *s*een, *s*oothed and *s*ecure. We'll look at this idea more in Part 2, but essentially it means that all our behaviours in parenting can impact whether our child feels safe with or around us, feels truly seen and understood by us, feels soothed when things go awry and not punished harshly, and secure in the knowledge that we are there and understand them and have time *for them*. I won't be pointing to each of these behaviours in each example in this book, as that would become tiresome and repetitive, but as you read through the strategies, interventions, case studies and stories, allow yourself to think about how *your* child feels *'in relationship to you'* and whether it would meet these 4Ss.

The truth is that scare stories, bans and hiding the 'forbidden fruit' just don't work in terms of online use – either for you or for children. I have seen seminars and keynotes delivered in the realms of e-safety with messages such as 'ALL kids are playing Grand Theft Auto!!' 'Your child's self-esteem and body image have been COMPLETELY eradicated because of social media', 'ALL children under thirteen see porn' or 'YOUR child's images are ALL over the internet!' This style of speaking is called grandiosity and involves the use of value-laden words like 'all' and 'everyone' and so on. It's also a form of victim blaming, humiliating and shaming both parents and their children. Children often communicate in this way when they want to make a point that they want you to take seriously. For example, they might claim, '*ALL* the kids have one' and '*NO ONE* likes me', or, 'It wasn't my fault; *THEY ALL* did it first – I just copied!' I expect you've heard those sorts of arguments, too, at some point.

Instead of getting caught up in this kind of hyperbole and the scare stories that use it, we need balanced and ongoing tech-smart conversations with our kids about the things that might just possibly happen at all ages and stages of their development and the tools, strategies and solutions with which to manage and parent around those potential harms.

I'm not advocating that you non-stop question your child to avoid missing something. Instead, it's about creating the space for age-appropriate dialogue with them, in which you talk to each other openly and honestly about the online world and create workable boundaries for you and your family around the use of technology to keep everyone happy and safe.

But boy, does talking calmly feel like a superpower when taking a device away from a screaming toddler or dealing with a teen who's furious about losing their winning Snap streak! So to enable a productive two-way conversation, it is up to us as guardians and parents to take the first steps and find a way to communicate with our children, whatever the obstacles, not the other way round. It's also up to us to become observant and compassionate detectives and tune in to our knowledge of our children through the Wi-Fi of human-to-human connection, creating a space to talk – and not to lecture, have a go at them or intrude. It's about what in psychotherapy language we call 'co-created interpersonal communication', which really just means that there are two of us in dialogue, and in between us there's a space into which we can either invite collaboration and connection or push the other away through power and domination. I'm sure you can work out which is the winning parent strategy, and yet I'm guessing that some readers may want to opt for the latter, or won't want to be seen as being 'equal' to their child. But when we 'meet' our children in this way the approach is far from soft parenting. So please keep reading to find out the how and the why of this method. If it's so successful in therapeutic settings and can help a client to change their behaviour, surely this is a great recipe for stress-free parenting?

Successful communication is the very cornerstone of how we relate to our children, and should always be prioritised, rather than taking a more authoritarian approach. We will be looking at this again a bit later in the book (see pp. 107–8).

## Identifying Online Risks – The 4Cs

The risks that children face online have been distilled into what's known as the 4Cs by CO:RE (a pan-European knowledge platform consisting of academics, consultants and policy makers, which aims to keep children safe). They are as follows:

- *Content*: types of material (like those which have an age rating in cinemas, such as sex, violence, war and graphic imagery).
- *Contact*: who can contact children and who they, in turn, can contact (such as whether adults can talk to children and send them content and vice versa).
- *Conduct*: how children and others behave online (this is about how we 'talk' to each other online, in games and social media – are people using anonymous accounts, for example?).
- *Commercialism*: exposure to adverts, sales and marketing (and we could include a subdivision here, to do with 'contracting', by which I mean the terms and conditions dictating how children's data can be used when downloading or

playing games, updating an app or agreeing to those cookie pop ups on websites).

As we'll see, some of the above categories are about the people 'in there', such as groomers, criminals, people who will bully from afar or share inappropriate content, while others will be about the kinds of material encountered online or the platforms, websites and businesses who want to collect data to sell their products to children. In addition to these concerns, I think it's important to consider two more Cs, because they relate to how the original 4Cs can impact on a child and cause cybertrauma:

- *Context*: this applies to where the child is when using the device, who they're with, why they're using the online space and what they're doing 'in there'.
- *Child development*: this can help you to understand the use and impact of the digital devices and the internet on your child at the age and stage of their development.

While the dangers online are similar to those in the real-world city park in some respects, there's a stark difference in terms of speed and quantity or volume of exposure. For example, in the real world children might not have previously been exposed to other children and adults selling illegal drugs at the rate they are online. However, on the internet it's likely they will stumble upon these kinds of things very quickly on certain platforms, although not all. To date, US court cases reported in the news suggest that, tragically, between 2018 and 2021 over sixty children aged between ten and sixteen were exposed online to either illegal drugs or a legal variant (such as the opioid fentanyl), obtained them and then took quantities of them that resulted in death.[1]

This is why having an awareness, along with the language with which to be able to talk to our children about it, can help us meet them in their space or world and enable us to listen out for the dangers. Being able to talk to your children about illegal and 'killer' drug use may not have been on your radar as part of your parenting role so early on in their lives, and it may come as a surprise, but, as you'll see, there are going to be many challenging conversations that need to be had openly in order to raise awareness of issues and protect them. (I will be giving you examples to help you do this throughout the book.)

Of course, it's sad that we need to think about these issues with children under the age of ten, but there are children in this age group who game online and have access to social media, so we need to pre-empt them encountering sexual content, war and graphic images (in games or on the news that is shared on social media). They may also hear or see abusive, racist and sexist language, and be exposed to adults online and other children whose values may not reflect yours. Today, the ills of society are readily accessible at the press of a button, in the palm of their hands, on screens and even on the TV they use in your home. That's why filters (a form of internet and parental controls that are discussed more in Part 2) relating to the 4 (or 6) Cs outlined above are now everybody's concern and responsibility. You may even find you have to learn a whole new vocabulary as part of the process (for example, you might think the word 'hacker' refers to a cybercriminal who can get into bank accounts and government websites; however, it can also mean 'cheater' when used in a game such as Fortnite).

All that said, I'm not going to name *all* the issues out there because that would be information overload (and the book would be too big), but we will consider some of the more pressing risks in more detail in Chapter 6 – those that are concerning and those that have led to the most harm and affected children in my clinical practice, including grooming, intimate sexual imagery and violence, to name a few. Because sometimes, even with the best will in the world, stuff happens and things get through any filters or precautions we put in place. (To give you examples of this, I'll be sharing stories throughout the book of mishaps and muddles, including something *I* wasn't prepared for as a tech-savvy parent myself.)

> ### *A Note on Children with Social, Emotional or Educational Needs, Neurodiversity and/or Trauma*
>
> With a special nod to those children with vulnerabilities, trauma or neurodivergence, consider the sixth C of child development (see p. 30) as being centred on your child's unique needs, how they learn, what they understand about everyday experiences and how you apply that to the general advice in this book. For example, if you know your child has a specific learning or social need, this could mean you'll want to dip into the sections of the book about younger children for guidance. While this doesn't mean you have to talk to your child in a babyfied voice or manner, you may have to phrase things differently if discussing topics relating to online harms. The advice I always give in clinics and with parents and carers is that we don't want to scare, terrify or traumatise children, or make them reticent to use technology, but we do want them to know what to do and who to turn to for help and support. I have much more information about this on my website for parents with children who meet the criteria for additional support, as this cohort may require specialist interventions to which I may not be able to do justice in this book.

## Tech at different ages

The principles of 'age and stage' are often used in child development theory and practice as a way to understand what is happening for a child, their adaptation to the world and how they're progressing and maturing. For example, when a child is moving towards the toddler stage, the standard expectation is for them to reach milestones such as talking and walking, and we'll be approaching tech-smart parenting in much the same way in this book. You'll see that Part 2 is divided into age ranges. However, these aren't fixed, as although there are general trends, each child develops differently compared to their peers. You may see sections in the chapters either side of your child's age that could be of help, but this doesn't mean your child isn't meeting their developmental milestones. It means, in practice, that some children develop emotionally or cognitively (in their thinking) at a different rate to their growing body. So, they may be able to climb competently but be less skilled at reading the facial expressions of their peers or they may frequently fall out with them. This book is aimed at all aspects of child development. And yes, that means the whole book will be useful for you!

In explaining issues to the public online, I'm both intrigued about where technology is going and saddened by the harms that can be encountered, especially by the fact that they will affect more children worldwide if we don't lean in to learning about what we can do to protect them. This requires us to work together and leave our egos at the door. It's about taking a holistic approach – meaning that it involves all of us, working together. Besides parents, I know some readers will be professionals supporting or working with children, and the guidance in this book can easily transition into those spaces, too. So let's take a walk together.

## Summary

- It's our responsibility as parents to help children navigate online spaces safely.
- We can take a similar age and stage approach to teaching our kids about staying safe online as we do in the real world.
- Remember to keep 'checking in, not checking on' – so that your child doesn't feel that you are intruding on their privacy, yet still feels safe, seen, soothed and secure.
- The 4Cs of risk can be loosely categorised as content, contact, conduct and commercialism. Two additional Cs are: context and child development.
- Be aware that there is a real difference between the speed and volume of exposure to danger online compared to the real world.

CHAPTER 2

# To Ban or Not to Ban – Should We Ban Tech for Kids?

Given that technology isn't going to go away any time soon, we need to prepare our children to survive and thrive in a digital age. As we saw in the previous chapter, using the analogy of the city park, many children, with their natural curiosity, will find ways to take risks and break any rules that we seek to impose upon them when it comes to accessing the internet and smartphone use. So how best can we approach this difficult area?

Before going any further, I'd like to add my tuppence ha'penny-worth right now by saying that I believe the whole idea of banning anything to do with technology just won't work practically, because there are so many issues and complexities that are going to be difficult to manage, monitor and maintain our knowledge about.

- The internet is global and there aren't any borders with which to enforce bans – and we know this from countries where access to the internet is highly restricted, such as North Korea, China and Cuba.
- There are issues around who would regulate bans and how to confirm which users they apply to. For example, ID, passports, user images, email confirmation, parental approval and the like can all easily be faked.
- There is a lack of clarity around which 'social media'

would be banned or permitted. And how do we actually define it – exactly what is or isn't considered to be social media? How do we tackle forums and websites?
- Kids can use other people's accounts, such as other family members, parents in separated households or other individuals in institutions or care.
- There would have to be some means of tackling proxy networks (VPNs – virtual proxy networks – a way to disguise or hide where the computer or phone is connected to the internet) and public access points.

In fact, there are so many issues that, as someone who works in technology, I find it bewildering that anyone can think banning access to it is easy. If the internet had been designed with safeguards in place at the outset, then we might have some processes, policies and protocols we could employ, but that wasn't the case. As things stand, I'm not holding my breath to see where any attempt to impose bans might end up.

On a related note, I recently saw a clip on social media in which the actress Drew Barrymore described how any children who visit for playdates with her daughters place their phones in a 'phone box' for safekeeping, the idea being that they then 'play nicely' without them. I laughed hard at this, mainly because I work with children and know – and love – how clever they are. Of course, many of them carry a secret second phone! (This also happens in educational settings and is complicated by the fact that hidden phones can play a part in issues such as exploitation, which we'll cover later.) This means that, while it may look on the surface as if they're abiding by a 'no-phones' rule, they could have a 'burner' phone stashed away somewhere that they can use when they're out of sight from adults.

When children do resort to measures such as this or others, breaking the rules we have put in place around technology, it means that if they do run into difficulties they might be reluctant to tell us about their problems, for fear of possible punishment.

As a therapist who works with children in this area, I've also seen how the current momentum to ban tech for kids until their mid-teens has been creating anxiety in children themselves about the threat of having their online lives taken away from them. It seems to them like it's the ultimate punishment – a bit like being grounded for no reason till you're sixteen. At the time of writing, the movement to remove this technology from their lives hasn't yet offered any alternative solutions as to how we might then expect our children to be educated about technology if they're banned from using it, or what's supposed to happen when they're older and are given access to it. The age of sixteen, for example, doesn't have any particular correlation with the sort of life skills needed for socialising online (or otherwise) or being active in digital spaces. It seems to have been plucked from the air (although it's the age at which teens can legally engage in sex, so perhaps that is a factor).

Moreover, how are parents and guardians to be expected to keep their child away from websites or social media once they are outside the confines of home? Are they supposed to keep them locked up to prevent them ever seeing or encountering any online content? For those who think this might be the answer, perhaps they should watch the episode of the TV series *Black Mirror* called 'Arkangel' to see how that panned out for a parent who imposed restrictions on what her daughter could see (and they might also like to read my blog about why dragon or helicopter parenting rarely leads to a great relationship with your child later in life).[1] Moreover, inside the family unit, how are we meant to ensure that older siblings, cousins or grandparents won't give our kids access to content online? Who says the children need to use their own account at all anyway, given we don't know what social media platforms are in development right now? Will it still look the same in the near future as it does now?

Also, we need to have a think about exactly what content we're banning kids from accessing. I ask this in all seriousness, because child mental-health issues and 'trends' existed long before social media, and many of the 'fads' (as they've been referred to) or social-contagion harms such as self-harm, eating-related issues, suicide and sexual activity resulted in children requiring mental-health support.* We wouldn't have the services that have become household names in the UK, such as CAMHS, if this were not a fact.

## Is This a Government Problem . . .

Even though the UK government is currently under pressure from lots of activist groups, it's not calling for a ban of social media or smartphones at this stage, but instead wants big-tech companies to do more to protect children or for the regulation bodies to enact the Online Safety Act. It's delegated the regulation of this approach to a service called Ofcom, which is trying to do the impossible and hold big tech accountable. This mainly concerns social media and websites that host 'adult material' and, while the laws in place are relatively tight, there are still many loopholes because, as we've said, the internet is not easily regulated, despite efforts being made globally.

Instead of relying on governments, corporations and institutions to look after our children in the online world, I view keeping children safe online as being a multifaceted societal issue that involves *us, as their parents*, as well as those of us who work with children and those of us who know them. It requires robust ethics, morals, values and evidence and, above all, the desire to protect

---

* For those who respond that this is a social media phenomenon resulting in increasing self-esteem issues, self-diagnosis of mental health disorders and labels etc., then why have other issues not increased upon more visual exposure like altruism, pet ownership or zoo donations (given our love of cats and quokkas) or the 'positive' viral influence of kindness acts? Why is this only a 'negative' skewed relationship? To read more about the research here and to understand why we only report in one direction, read my book *Managing Your Social Media and Gaming Habits*.

children from being hurt. And it requires us to take this approach in all we do, especially when we are online, too.

## ... Or Can We 'Just' Get the Tech Industry to Fix it?

Many of those who've spoken out in favour of bans (some of whom have trolled me on social media) will say things like, 'Well, it's easy, isn't it? Just put in place age-assurance tests or facial-recognition software; or prevent children from using those sorts of platforms in the first place.' I even hear some of them say, 'AI can just sort this out.' But unfortunately we cannot 'just' set up, use or employ technology (such as facial-recognition checks) without a trade-off of some sort.

This might relate to the collection, storage and even 'ownership' of personal data about our children and their online behaviours. We've all seen how targeted adverts and social media feeds become curated and personalised because companies collect our data and sell it, even though we, the adults, have not necessarily consented to this. This is just one reason why we have to think carefully about the use of technological 'solutions' to ensure that children can or cannot access online spaces. It's not as simple as just designing a system (such as verifying the age or faces of users) to prevent, stop and remove all of the 'bad stuff', or using AI to detect and prevent the uploading of it, or even removing the stuff when it's located or reported as an 'online harm', according to the criteria of the Online Safety Act in the UK. There are major issues with this sort of labelling, which is why we're also looking in this book at how to tackle the stuff not classified or as a 'harm'.

You may also have seen the narrative in the news, on TV and social media that big tech simply doesn't care, and has a 'get-out clause' in the form of a law (called Section 230), which suggests they aren't responsible for any content uploaded by users, i.e. the people or systems created by people who post what is called 'user-generated content'.[2]

And the truth is that it's complicated. Much more so than many people realise.

It seems nigh on impossible to design a complete system that is simultaneously able to respect the rights, freedoms and privacy of people using technology and also provide them with complete protection while using the internet without monitoring them in some way – which would then infringe on their freedom to roam online, and invade their privacy rights in many cases. As an example, think about your text messages to your partner. Besides asking them what they want for dinner, these might sometimes include things like sexual banter or images. If, say, you'd shared photos of yourself in your underwear, would you want those text messages to be monitored by the phone provider, or would you want them to reassure you that your information is secure and private and that they don't monitor them? Likewise, any email communications between you and your doctor about, say, a sensitive medical issue: wouldn't you like that to be kept confidential, too – especially if it concerned something embarrassing?

And here's the dilemma that I deal with professionally: that the privacy rights of my clients and the need to keep communication with them confidential can sometimes be at odds with my wish that phone manufacturers and social media platforms undertake more careful monitoring.

So to those who wonder why technology programs or companies can't just be programmed to act as gatekeepers to keep kids safe: it is not that straightforward. While facial recognition and even age recognition are already present in everyday spaces such as the supermarket, with checkouts that have cameras overhead, it's a different story when it concerns kids accessing the internet.

That said, at the time of writing there are some companies working on the age-assurance issue globally, as are social media companies (because they are being forced to by political and public pressure). But let's pause briefly to consider another question: who would run the app, platform or software that scans a child's face? How would this work and would AI be involved? As we touched on above, who might then keep that data and what could or might it be used for in the future? What ethical issues might arise? What security measures would be put in place to stop the data being exploited in any way, now or in the future? Would there be a global version, or would it be used by one country? But could the data then be shared with other countries? What privacy rights would a child have concerning their data, now or in the future?

Another question is can we really trust the tech industry to create accurate and safe age-assurance checks? And, assuming checks are put in place, more questions arise, such as what happens then to children who change their gender (in countries where this occurs) and how would the system allow for this or detect it? What about children with facial scars, injuries or congenital disfigurement, or who those who undergo plastic surgery or wear lots of make-up? I ask this as there are many faults still with facial-recognition software that has been designed by humans, such that there are intricacies we can detect as humans that AI isn't yet nuanced enough to pick up. But that doesn't mean it won't become adept at this in the future.

And what about those children who are clever enough to find a way round all these verification processes – like children do in the real world when it comes to purchasing things like vapes or alcohol that are age restricted? Smart cookies will always find a way.

All these questions are exhausting enough to consider, let alone resolve, but at the centre of it all has to be the drive, above all else, to provide children with safety, security and preventative care with respect to the online world, for all of their childhood. We need a careful, ethical debate and process to prevent data brokers, social media companies and even governments having information about us and our children and using it in ways we wouldn't be comfortable with. As well as including us as parents, academic and professional bodies also need to be involved to assess how this space affects children's development, changes society, assists and supports kids and interacts with all the other complexities about childhood we can measure.

The rights of children in the digital space are now reflected in the United Nations Convention on the Rights of the Child of 2021, with General Comment 25 suggesting they should have access to a safe digital life online. How we do this globally and while placing the rights of children in the centre is part of the ongoing work of digital spaces and the conversations taking place on an international scale today.[3] It's tough and requires lots of connectivity between authorities, countries, big tech and governments, which is now starting to happen. Hopefully, we will get there sooner rather than later, and the online city park will be a space with 'safety by design' at its core.

## The Cycle of Blame and Shame

Perhaps inevitably, the lack of research, or of a shared vocabulary or consensus about the best approach to take, has meant a lack of clarity around how best to respond to children's behaviours around digital technology and to protect them. News headlines proclaim that parents are failing to protect their children online, or that they don't care about their activity there, while we are also being blamed by well-meaning professionals and campaigns saying that we're overprotecting children in the real world but under-protecting them online, which is the argument of Jonathan Haidt's book *The Anxious Generation*. The argument has been that we give kids devices but don't supervise them (yet some parents do), or that we're snowflake parents who mollycoddle them in real life (a description that can make us feel less than great). To which parents then respond by wanting to remove the wretched thing that created the problems in the first place and to ban children from accessing it. Because if we've been told that this is the problem, rather than us, then of course we want it to go away! The most difficult thing to hear is that we are in some way responsible, because that can hit hard and hurt.

The solution that's offered to the hypothetical issue of overprotection in the real world is to tell parents (and I'm summarising here) to allow their children out unsupervised more often and at younger ages, like children used to do in the 1970s and 1980s. With respect to technology, on the other hand, the recommendation is to delay kids accessing social media (but not gaming or the internet per se, or streaming TV media), yet with no clear directive on how to do this. A couple of major questions concern how this would work within blended families or care settings, and which social media platforms would or wouldn't be accessible to children and why.

In the meantime, internet providers and mobile-phone providers argue we already have the protective and safety tools we need, but parents don't use them, or children circumnavigate them. Parents respond by saying that this situation isn't their fault as they don't understand the tech or the controls themselves, so the tech industries and government should do more to protect children, too. However, governments and the tech industry then argue that parents and educational settings should be the ones responsible for this supervision and safety provision. Hard-pressed education services respond saying parents and government are responsible, their argument being that they are busy enough and teach academic subjects, not internet safety, as a rule – nor do they know enough to teach it competently.

And round and round it goes . . . In the middle of all this, when asked in surveys, mostly in schools (lots of these have been carried out, by internet safety companies, Ofcom, The Cybersurvey and smaller services delivering training in schools), children say they want education and help to navigate this space but that parents, schools and websites etc. won't help them. Which ricochets the issue back to internet-safety companies, who do try to provide this sort of education, but it can seem overwhelming for both children and parents.

Sadly, among all the recrimination and finger-pointing, many children end up in the middle, finding themselves exploited, attacked or abused and generally going it alone online while the adults carry on debating the issue. So just what can we do about this? Which approach is the right one – and why? Confused? I know I am, and I'm someone who knows which online spaces are actually out there, and what the harms are that children face in them.

## Do We Ban Children from Devices, or Delay Access?

In light of all the issues, it's understandable why there's talk among adults, including health and education professionals and lots of parents, of delaying access to smartphones or banning kids from using them. This is akin to telling a child, 'That area of the park is out of bounds until you are X years old,' when they can still see the area in the distance, and other children and adults will still talk about it. In fact, the icons for these sorts of areas will be visible on other devices such as smart TVs, tablets and devices used by older siblings, cousins, pupils and parents, who may often visit these areas of the park and then effectively broadcast about the events taking place there. For example, they may play videos on their phones that children can hear, and ask to see what the other person is watching, only to be told they can't.

Also, if your child lives in two homes or in a blended family, they might have opportunities to access that park without your knowledge, in which case you may need to discuss rules with the other heads of the household about devices and the internet (more on this on p. 114).

Remember, there may be far fewer safeguards in place once children are either out of sight of home or with peers who have freer access to online spaces. There are different ways 'in', as well as other children who can effectively get them a free pass by using a different entrance.

And that's not even taking into account the sheer number of these spaces dotted all around the park, some of which people who suggest delays and bans don't know about, as they're focusing on access points on just one device – smartphones – not the entirety of the internet.

The reality is that, if one area is banned, children will often make their way to another that they haven't been told is banned, such as gaming environments, and which the adults responsible for them may know little about; for example, those forums not listed as social media. And of course, where the children go, the bad actors may already be waiting.

> ### *Are Dumbphones the Answer?*
>
> You might be considering giving your child a dumbphone, which is a basic mobile phone that doesn't have all the functionality of a smartphone. In which case, you should be aware that dumbphones can reduce the frequency with which some harms are encountered in some instances, but not all.
>
> Before the iPhone was created in 2007, there was very little research into how many children owned dumbphones (or, later, flip phones). Instead, much of the research into children's internet use looked at what they got up to on computers or laptops, and didn't take into account material that could be shared from one phone to another via Bluetooth. We also lacked robust data about tech use among children as they transitioned from dumb to flip to smartphones and what this meant for their development, or the harms they encountered on these devices. So when claims are made that 'the iPhone destroyed a generation'[4]

we do not have the comparative base on which to substantiate them. Since 2020, we've become more tuned in to the issue of children's use of tech, but the fact remains that we simply don't have a wealth of data from which to draw accurate conclusions. (You can listen to the episode 'The Anxious Generation' on the podcast *If Books Could Kill* for a critique of Haidt's arguments or read my previous books *Managing Your Gaming and Social Media Habits* and *Online Harms and Cybertrauma*, which explain how we cannot rely solely on the findings of self-harm as an accurate measurement of how smartphones have caused issues.)

Access to the internet comes in many forms besides apps. I describe later how my own kids accessed extremely disturbing material via a URL shared in text messages. Also, many of these phones can't be used to track your child's location to ensure their safety in the same way that a smartphone can, so we need to consider what is most important to us as parents.

---

While bans can slow down a child gaining entry to the internet, the evidence surrounding age-restricted products and activities such as alcohol, vapes and sex under the age of sixteen (the age of consent in the UK) suggests that they might work, but often young people find a work around, such as using family members to provide alcohol/e-cigs.[5] Instead, bans and restrictions often give rise to a sense of rebellion in the very children they're meant to protect, which may lead them to find other ways to go exploring online without our knowledge. The secrecy of rebellion could put them at higher risk, while the shame felt, should anything distressing occur, is a reason for them not to tell us about what they've been up to in the first place. All in all, we may be inadvertently doing more harm than good by directing their rebellion to a space of secrecy and shame. And as we've seen, the perpetrators of crimes against children bank on these things.

In addition to this, if we impose age limits, such as banning smartphones or social media until the age of sixteen, children will have little practical experience of navigating online spaces safely before they are allowed to access them. We also need to take into consideration that children are given these devices for educational purposes and/or to carry out homework assignments, both in schools and colleges and at home. For example, what skills would a sixteen-year-old who'd never been on social media be likely to have, compared to one who was taught about social media from the age of thirteen, say, supported in using these spaces, and who learned about things like about fake news, grooming, bullying and managing terms and conditions, targeted adverts and adult content? And how might a sixteen-year-old with autism and learning difficulties manage when suddenly let loose on the internet?

So what about delaying access to the online world? Should we take this approach rather than a ban? In short, absolutely yes; however, this should be on a case-by-case basis, tailored to your child and subject to individual considerations such as the specific website(s), platform or game under consideration, the character and maturity of your child *and* whether this would be practically feasible within your household – or households if your child lives with more than one family. This is complicated for sure, and I cannot say that delaying is the full and true answer. This is part of an age-and-stage approach to child development, supported by the findings of psychology and taking into account a child's cognitive, compassion and empathic abilities, moral understanding and reasoning about right and wrong, their understanding of themselves as an individual in the world, any learning and/or mental-health difficulties or disabilities, and their maturity.

As you know your child best, you are best placed to assess whether they are old enough or mature enough to play video games that are rated U, 4, 7, 12, 15 and so on, or to watch certain

TV shows. It's up to you to decide which platforms on social media you think they can access and what they can manage in terms of content, people and communication.

In short, banning children from accessing smartphones isn't a win-win situation. And I suspect this is one reason why you are reading this book: because your intuition has whispered this truth to you. However, it is entirely up to you whether you want to ban, delay or supervise your child's use of and access to technology – and the evidence you need is in your children and how this works for you as a family. Remember that you can always change your mind if you feel that things aren't working out; after all, we have to make decisions, navigate situations and renegotiate everything we do as adults, so we can certainly do this with our children and technology as well.

### *A Note on Children with Social, Emotional or Education Needs, Neurodiversity and/or Trauma*

In over twenty-five years of working with families and children in this group, I have found they are simultaneously the ones with the most vulnerabilities in the online world and the ones who can best use the online space to help them manage their needs (emotional regulation) and find support and communities. They sometimes tell me it is their lifeline. It is often the space where they can be their true selves without the judgements that so often come with real-world interactions, which can highlight their needs very quickly. For example, a child with social-skills issues, such as difficulty making eye contact in the real world, which causes them distressing feelings or even anxiety, often compounding the issue, can meet peers and play games online without this being a part of their interaction, thus removing awkwardness or (as they tell me) knowing they are being 'stared at'. In the online space, being accepted immediately allows them to develop their social skills in many other ways and to feel accepted for who they are.

The campaigns that discuss banning devices or social media rarely seem to address this cohort of children, who use this online medium as a way to manage their needs, symptoms or life in general. Many children I work with are young carers, living with parents who are neglectful, abusive or absent through work perhaps, and are dependent upon the online world to connect with other trusted adults and supportive spaces, such as counselling, which they access on devices because they cannot leave their homes to attend appointments in person. Children are often talked about as one complete cohort – as one group who are all the same. To ban these children from technology could be perceived as tantamount to telling them that they must only access support in the real world and that it's the only way we can progress and develop as human beings. This is punitive, undermining and disrespectful to the human-development map, which is known to be a complex set of behaviours and personalities. It is discriminatory and judgemental. This group of children need education and encouragement in learning how to navigate spaces online. Technology and devices should not be taken away without due consideration as to whether that could result in a child ending their life because they do not have this outlet or a way to find support for their needs. And yes, that sounds like a shock-and-awe outcome, but it is an accurate assessment of the seriousness of the threat to the wellbeing of this group of children.

## Adam's Story

Twelve-year-old Adam was banned by his mum from using his smartphone, console and PC in his bedroom because he had been engaging in conversations online that were racist and homophobic. Adam's mum was doing what she thought was best by taking the tech away. However, Adam pleaded with his older brother to use *his* device at bedtime, so he could sign in to Snap and 'keep his streak up'.

Unbeknown to his mum, Adam started using other platforms and creating new accounts that he could sign in to on other devices at his friends' homes, too. He told me he was able to do this on a Mac at school, because it didn't have the locks that the PCs in the IT class did (the Mac and PCs were in different locations making this easier to do).

Adam's activities were eventually discovered, at which point the school safeguarding staff suggested to his mum that she turn off the Wi-Fi at home so that no one could access the internet at night, which would hopefully resolve the issue. They also recommended that his brother be reprimanded for allowing Adam to use his tech. Adam was to be allowed to watch his TV in his bedroom and that was it.

However, Adam had a smart TV, and when he went to bed he used the connection to sign into the neighbours' Wi-Fi, as their child, his friend, had given him the password to do so. Once again, Adam was able to access his accounts. He was able to meet his friends online and organise with them to meet up in the real world. His mum was exasperated and felt she was out of options, out of her depth and out of her mind with worry.

Giving Adam a flip phone (with access to nothing other than 3G, as they were at the time) to prevent him accessing 'the dangers online' would have been moot in this scenario, given that he was so resourceful and would still have been able to text his friends and arrange to meet up and continue his conversations with them.

As Adam was 'at risk', meaning that he could potentially fall in with the crowd of racists he was talking to, I had to work with lots of children's services (both statutory and voluntary) to help them understand the internet and how he could access it, as well as understand Adam's own vulnerabilities and what this might mean for his subsequent behaviours.

Working with him in the therapy room meant I could explain why we adults were making the choices we were and how we could help prevent him becoming entangled in racist groups. I also acted as his voice in meetings with authorities such as the school, social care and other children's services, which meant that Adam also had a say in his online activities, which we discussed together in a balanced and logical manner.

He was allowed access to his accounts and friends online, but only once parental monitoring software had been installed. His mum and staff at his school also started to make regular check-ins on his activities, and he attended some sessions with the local police and youth offending service. Alongside the safety aspects that were put in place, the fact that Adam felt heard by the adults in his life resulted in him feeling included and communicated with, which was empowering and allowed him to progress through his therapy and remain safe online.

## Know What You Are Trying to Control

The internet is a space in which we can wander about, go shopping, visit people we know, play, socialise, do our work and homework, spy on people in their homes (when they post images of it) and at work, if we so wish (using company IT systems no less), 'follow' celebrities (whether TV, media or pop personalities or influencers) or just people we 'know' from the real world who we've happened upon online. We can book holidays, browse information, search for directions, buy tickets, listen to conversations that are deep and meaningful or superficial and provocative, or we can watch plays, performances and other forms of entertainment.

In this space, we can spend time alone or with others. We can numb out, become bored or use it because we *are* bored, seek romantic relationships, and observe lots of humans and bots. And while we're there, we can be subjected to all forms of human behaviour, including violence, abuse, hate and division, and we can compare ourselves to everyone who's there now, was there in the past and will be there in the future. We're constantly surrounded by the novel and the new, by the ever-changing model of human beings.

But if you've never been to this park yourself, how can you really know what – or who – is there, or what you or your children might be exposed to along the way? How can we protect kids from the dangers in the city park if we aren't well-versed in them ourselves? The approach in this book, this mode of thinking and this way of being with our children is already how we raise them in the real world; however, I would like to suggest that the digital park is now very much a part of our children's real world too. So, in simple terms we need to become savvy about the city park ourselves, which means that we need to become familiar and comfortable with it rather than listen to the chatter on the streets about it. We need to turn up, lean in and learn – and that requires both curiosity and patience in order to learn the what, who and how of technology spaces. As I've been saying to parents since 1998, when I was installing computers and showing them the internet, 'Have a go, you won't break it!'

Go online, go into the digital city park and play with the apps, platforms and spaces, so you can see them for yourself. Inform yourself about any that your child wants to use before they're given a free pass to roam in these areas. Then, and only then, will you be better placed to assess any risks or dangers for yourself, which should make you more confident about deciding how much time you're happy for your child to spend there.

Now, I know that new spaces keep popping up, and, of course, the friends your child meets online won't necessarily be who you will meet in these places — you can't know everyone and every nook and cranny of the online park — so I would strongly advise you to keep up to date with important digital parenting and online safety messages by signing up to lots of newsletters from online safety companies and your internet service provider or phone-contract provider. You will find many of these listed at the back of the book (see p. 347). While you may initially feel overwhelmed at the idea of receiving more newsletters, you will soon get the hang of noticing the key updates and the things to look out for in them, and you can always pop over to my website for my Level Up club to get a direct Q&A with me on a monthly basis, too. Now, I work in this space, and even I won't have heard of *all* the platforms (it's impossible for anyone to be that knowledgeable), but I do my homework, and, having spent over thirty years using this technology, I can assess quickly what things are and the dangers they can present.

Educating yourself about online spaces means you can make better-informed judgements and choices about your child's interaction with them. It can also be fun to explore these areas *with* them by getting them to show you around, while also remembering they'll likely only show you the good spots, which are those where you might not see any behaviours or content that seems like something you need to worry about. (See also Resources, p. 347, for relevant links and support.)

## Can We Manage Tech with Tech?

For all that we might blame the shortcomings of the tech industry for failing to protect our kids, internet service providers, phone companies and providers of routers, devices and other computing equipment often do provide us with ways to protect ourselves online through applications like cybersecurity software. There are lots of types of parental controls, and you can use as many layers and services as you want or need. Parental controls are an extremely useful tool to have in your arsenal and can really help you to feel like you have some control (no pun intended). We'll talk about these a bit more in Part 2, but here is an overview:

Most often, the first layer can be supplied by your internet service provider, as this is how the internet gets into your house. If you use a computer, you might already have your own anti-virus software, firewalls, security and password protection and the now common VPN services (virtual proxy network). You'll need a browser application to access the internet, and on mobile devices you need 3G/4G/5G or Wi-Fi wherever you go to access your favourite spaces online. You can begin by heading to your service provider's website and typing 'parental controls' into the search bar, or by scrolling down the menus on the website's home page to find where this advice is located. Then read how to apply their set of parental controls to anything in your home that can connect to the internet. You can sometimes set up different accounts for you and your children, apply controls to the internet router or set up parental controls on specific devices. If you have trouble understanding the available advice, do contact their customer-support team, as they will hopefully be able to take you through it step by step.

Next, head to the Resources on p. 347 and choose one of the e-safety or online safety websites to take you through further steps and other ways to protect your devices in your home, including how to use the software that's in-built but not set up by default, to add on further layers of protection. For example, internetmatters.org.uk or getsafeonline.org.uk, to name a couple, provide accessible guides for UK residents and will show you how to set parental controls on each item you have, such as an iPhone, Xbox or computer. Companies like these also provide you with ways to stop, block or set time limits on specific websites, applications or platforms, which are referred to as parental controls. Some services put them on as default in some way, and some do not. If you've used satellite TV in the past, you may remember that you could set a PIN to be able to view certain channels. And now you can do almost the same thing with mobile devices, tablets, computers, consoles and TVs themselves. Many manufacturers of devices now provide means to 'lock down' specific apps or spaces or limit 'screen time'.

Also consider investing in a firewall and anti-virus software. Good cybersecurity software is an extra expense, I know, but it could protect you from losing your entire bank balance or savings and keep your child from accessing malicious sites – and that's priceless.

---

### Tech in Schools

Should we ban tech in schools or allow it? While I was writing this book, there were a number of live petitions circulating online from campaigners and some education professionals to ban phones outright on school premises, and even outside of school as well, which resulted in a couple of documentaries being made on the subject. The guidance from the Department of Education provided some examples of how to do this but ultimately suggested that that educational establishments needed to make the decision themselves as it wasn't a legal matter. And let me tell you what my young clients have been saying to me in therapy since this came to be – things like, 'They ain't taking my phone, fam,' and, 'As long as it's in my pocket/blazer/bag they just let us have it,' and, 'We're supposed to hand it in, but I'm not!'

Personally, I believe that the use of personal devices in educational settings can sometimes be disruptive, in the same way that someone tapping on a keyboard or with a pen or using a fidget spinner can be. But this is not a given, and nuanced conversations need to take place based on why children are requesting to have devices in their possession. So let's think about when and where they can be helpful – or not.

Some children may, to give one example, be young carers at home and have been given a phone so they can contact their parent should an emergency arise. This is the same logic as is applied to children being given phones so a parent can 'see' where they are or contact them for safety reasons. And some children have a phone because it makes them feel safe, confident and/or grown up, which goes back to the 4Ss of feeling respected enough to hold this responsibility. This can also help children feel they belong to their peer group.

To add to the complexity of the situation, the smart-watches worn by some children can be a lifeline if they have medical needs or disabilities. However, these devices can also access many of the spaces that a smartphone can, as well as 'hotspot' to other devices. So if we ban the phones, should we ban the watches, too? But I wonder if removing the smartwatch from such children might constitute medical neglect?

To arrive at clarity in all these instances requires some excellent direction from education departments or the government and this hasn't occurred to date.

All said, decisions about what we want to happen with personal devices in educational settings must be considered in more detail. For example, what happens with them on school transport? Or are we just talking about banning devices once past the school gates – and if so, what happens if something occurs just outside or just inside the gates? Moreover, other types of technology are essential to lessons, but this, again, means possibly accessing the internet. Should these be 'locked down' in some way? And can schools afford – or even find – IT staff with the right training to

> work with the many different systems, while ensuring the necessary safeguarding?
>
> Let's have more conversations before making big decisions, please!

## Screen Time – How Long is Too Long?

Another big issue is that of screen time – and, of course, what we mean by this. For argument's sake, let's say that we're referring only to the time spent using social media or gaming.

Given that we find ourselves in an online space that's like the city park, where all sorts of characters – good and bad – hang out, alongside your child's real school and sports-club friends, how long should your child spend there socialising?

Whatever the age of your child, this will likely be more nuanced than just allowing them to spend a set amount of time online, as you should also take into account what your child is actually doing there and the risks or harms in the specific environment they're in (see Chapter 6 for more on this). For example, the potential risk of your child spending an hour on solo Minecraft, say in the living room (where you can monitor them) with no contacts or online function, will be very different to them spending an hour on Snapchat (called Snap by kids) in their bedroom by themselves.

You'll also need to make choices that suit how you spend time together as a family and what this means for you all. How do you want to define quality family time? What rules might you want to introduce at home? And what happens at your home versus those of other family members? And if you define quality time as being when no one is looking at a hand-held screen, should this extend to the TV screen, when no one is talking to anyone else?

If you want to go to bed at 9pm, you'll definitely need your child to be off any devices by then. And you may want to have rules around things such as the time that family members start to wind down in the evening, or the use of screens during holidays and term time, to ensure everyone gets enough sleep.

Ultimately, the length of time you let your child use their device is a decision you'll need to come to with your child, and it will involve *who else you know will be in that park*, or who could be there – and what your child needs to know about these people, too. For very young children, you may also want to think about the potential effects that staring at a screen, instead of engaging with the real world, can have on little eyes and developing minds, and what the research suggests about this in relation to the development of language, social skills, reading ability and physical developmental progress. (For more on this, see Chapters 4 and 7.)

Our children are naturally curious about the world and as part of this they're willing, as we've discussed, to take risks and to find ways to tackle what they perceive to be challenges such as getting on to a site that's 'banned'. If I could invite you into my therapy office, you would see loads of examples of kids who've managed to find a way round any obstacles set in their path when it comes to accessing online content. (I'll be sharing one or two of them in this book.) Some of them leave me speechless at their ingenuity.

If you want to prevent your child from venturing alone into online spaces where dangers may lurk, and for them to learn how to navigate the internet safely instead, remember to go there with them; I will continue to talk you through how to do that in the course of this book, especially focusing on their formative years of using technology.

There is also, as we've seen, a place for parental controls and setting boundaries around tech, when used appropriately and in collaboration with children, and I will be describing how to do this, too.

'Collaboration', however, brings us back to the idea of connection and how, if we want to keep our kids safe, communication must be an integral part of that process. As the adults in their lives, we've got to keep talking to our children about how and why we're trying to protect them. This is not about soft parenting or having to explain everything and thereby burdening children with too much or inappropriate information. It's about communicating with them in a way that allows them to trust us to make the right decisions with them and on their behalf.

## Summary

- There are no easy answers to the question of whether or not to ban anything to do with tech, as the issues are very complex, nuanced and constantly evolving.
- Keeping kids safe online is a multifaceted societal issue that involves all of us, and we can't rely on governments or the big-tech companies to resolve it.
- It's important to be aware that children can be very resourceful when circumnavigating any rules we try to put in place around tech use, and they can sometimes be at greater risk if they feel they can't talk to us about the rules they've broken.
- Instead of outright bans, do consider delaying access to the internet in a way that is tailored to your child, taking into account the nature of any spaces they wish to visit.
- Spend time online yourself, visiting the sorts of spaces your child might want to frequent, so that you are familiar with them before giving your child a free pass to explore them.
- Sign up to online safety newsletters so that you are informed of emerging risks.
- Learn about parental controls and how to use them appropriately with your family.

# CHAPTER 3

# Addiction or Attachment?

I'm often asked by concerned parents whether they ought to be worried about the amount of time their child spends online – they want to know whether there's a correct age or time limit and if hanging out in online forums or gaming will destroy their child's attention span, rot or melt their brains and their ability to communicate, or even damage their IQ. All of which we look at in this book. But when it comes down to it, what most of them want to know is if their child is at risk of becoming 'addicted' to technology.

Are they right to be worried? In this chapter, we're going to look at what addiction is (and what it is not), how platforms encourage children to engage with them and what most children are really looking for when they go online: connection.

## Communicating Effectively

I'd like to take a moment here to describe a video that is often shared by campaigners for no screens for children. It begins with a mother telling her son to come off the computer. When he says, 'Just give me a minute,' her demands grow louder, until she's screaming at the boy as he tries to say, 'I'm just finishing this bit.' The boy is now dysregulated (meaning he's experiencing powerful feelings such as frustration and a sense of being ignored) and trying desperately to make her hear him – both because she's screaming at him and because she doesn't seem able or willing to spare the time to *really listen to* him. The battle results in her turning off the computer, thereby ending his session abruptly (a bit like kicking down a Lego tower before its completed), at which point the boy explodes and starts to throw things and hit out.

The message delivered here by several campaigners is: 'He's addicted! Look at his behaviour – he's just like a drug addict!' Yet when you understand child development and relational, conversational connection, it's obvious that this isn't the case. Rather, this is clearly a child who cannot communicate effectively (verbally or otherwise) with his mum, and vice versa. And this isn't just about an exchange of words; it's also about needs (see p. 80). Mother and son don't 'get' each other now, because when they're calm and collected (which we therapists call 'regulated') they likely haven't had conversations about things like the role of boundaries for technology use, what gaming is and how it works, or what – and who – is important to this boy online or any other aspect of his interactions with technology. The boy feels misunderstood, as his mum does by him, and neither of them is attuned to the other. The conversation between them is effectively a case of 'fear me or I will rage out' and both display this dysregulated behaviour.

Moreover, this situation isn't actually about addiction, as you will see. This is a quite simply an example of relational and communication difficulties. It is a missed moment of 'needs-based' parenting (see p. 81) and relationship. It's heartbreaking to watch, because the inevitable route of this behaviour is an escalation of outrage on both sides. Violence is a highly likely outcome, too – again, on both sides – and this life 'script' (which is how Eric Berne, founder of Transactional Analysis, describes the unconscious pathways that form when we're young) will be passed down the family line, so that when the boy becomes an adult himself he'll hand it on to his own children in turn. It is a life script I hear in therapy week after week after week.

## Why the Focus on 'Addiction'?

The focus on addiction in relation to tech use is down to several factors, one being that people often use the word 'addiction' when what they actually mean is, 'I like doing this thing [a behaviour] a lot.' (So, for example, they'll say, 'I'm addicted to watching my favourite soap opera.') Or they might use it pejoratively to mean 'I don't like it when you do that thing a lot' – but what they say is, 'You're addicted to playing on your computer, rather than spending time with me.' It really refers to how someone perceives a behaviour, either when they do it themselves, or when they see another person doing it. When used outside of clinical settings (where a diagnosis of addiction involves observed behaviour), an addiction narrative often springs from a victim mindset that suggests somebody cannot help but 'do' the said behaviour. However, this is different from actually being a victim or having biological markers that can be accurately measured and which would confirm the presence of a clinical addiction. Rather, it's a framing of how people think. To explain the terminology and how it can be a frame of reference and language use, let's dig a little deeper.

Psychopathological terminology derived from clinical settings – or what's called 'therapy speak' – is now commonplace on social media and in everyday conversations, to the extent that authors such as Abigail Shrier suggest its overuse has created a generation of overprotected children. The problem lies in how this sort of terminology is often used today to refer to something other than a serious mental-health condition.

When determining the presence of a mental-health condition for interventions and insurance purposes – such as addiction, a predetermined set of symptoms needs to have been present for a specific amount of time in accordance with the guidelines set out in diagnostic criteria manuals such as the *Diagnostic and Statistical*

*Manual of Mental Disorders* (DSM-V). Said clinical settings would also apply the term 'addiction' to activities such as gambling, drug and substance abuse (or dependency or misuse). However, the term isn't and has never been used in an official clinical capacity to describe behaviours in relation to sex, pornography, shopping, gaming, exercise, eating or the construct we know today as 'the internet' or social media. Nevertheless, these are now mistakenly considered to be clinical issues by many members of the public, not least because terms such as 'sex addiction', 'shopping addiction' and 'internet addiction' regularly appear in TV shows, books and online. To complicate matters further, these terms are occasionally used by clinicians themselves when speaking with their clients. Some health professionals also make free with addiction terminology to sell books and/or courses or offer treatment. (This often means that the emerging authority on whatever new 'addiction' is in the spotlight will also be the clinical provider of the solution for it.)

So why do we now use the word 'addiction' in relation to digital and online spaces? The main reason is because the mainstream media use it (a lot), some academics and anti-technology campaigners talk about this 'affliction' and it appears on many high profile and popular podcasts, when people describe either their own or others' use of technology. We've also invented new words – such as doomscrolling – to describe something that relates to our devices (like checking the news, scrolling or even picking them up). None of this means it's a clinical addiction (as you will soon see), but we use these words to try to communicate to people what we're struggling with when we don't have other language to help us describe it.

Of course, a loaded term such as 'addiction' can also mean that we, the observers and judges of a particular type of behaviour, can then apportion blame to the nature of the activity itself and thereby absolve ourselves of responsibility. We can even send the person we think is addicted to 'get treatment'. This then allows us to say or show that the problem lies with the addicted person, not us; it's the 'addict' who must be lacking self-discipline or willpower (which brings in blame and shame – see p. 42). This approach often also really means, 'I want someone else to fix the behaviour as I feel powerless.' It's a common feeling for many parents when their children won't do what they want them to and they feel they've lost any power over the situation. And it sucks because they don't know what to do next.

Using addiction terminology can help us feel like 'it's not our fault' when children won't get off the phone or a game when we say they should, or when they won't talk to us but prefer to stare at their screen. Instead, we can tell ourselves, 'Surely they can't help it – technology must be designed to get them hooked, just like alcohol or cigarettes. So it's not my parenting or anything about me that needs to change.' Parenting can be difficult, and we can find it hard to think that we should adapt or change our approach to meet our children or their needs. Because, well, we're busy and we're good parents (all of which is true), and, of course, we might tell ourselves, 'When I was their age I didn't get to sit around all day, doing that,' which might be true, too. But if we were to take a step back, we might just realise that perhaps our own inner teenager is having a strop and is a little bit jealous of our child. The fact is that what may look like technology, social media or gaming addiction on the surface – especially to us, when we don't necessarily have any formal training in mental health, and addiction terminology is the only language we have at our disposal – is rarely something that leads to a formal pathological addiction diagnosis, for reasons that we'll discover.

Furthermore, the phrase 'problematic use' is increasingly being used to encompass behaviours involving digital technology that become, well, problematic for a family or situation. In recent years, a political and academic argument has also been taking place about 'gaming disorder' (note, not 'gaming addiction'), a term that has now been added to one of the two main diagnostic manuals, along with a list of very specific and long-term symptoms.[1] The term has since been bandied about on social media as though it has been entered into the manual as an 'addiction', when that simply isn't the case. This is why the terminology can be so pervasive and has inserted itself into the parenting space, where many of us become frustrated at our children's behaviours.

The activity of children (or adults, for that matter) who use devices or who game for long periods, and/or who aren't behaving in the ways that parents, teachers or other adults might prefer around technology, has created this confusion in the first place, as have the many accounts on social media and news outlets that use the word 'addiction'. And of course it's become a term used by young people and children themselves to refer to activities they like. In reality, this sort of usage isn't referring to a clinical mental-health disorder but a moment in time, when it's often used to point out to a child by a parent or professional that they're neglecting other areas of their life (usually like their family, friends, playing outside, sports or homework, for example); and, while this is well intended, it isn't always be helpful.

What is important for our purposes now is to acknowledge that many parents do struggle with the 'get-off-the-screen' battle and feel powerless in relation to their kids' behaviour online, which is why I've created various social media videos explaining about different types of games and where the natural stopping points are in them, to make it easier for you to ask your child to stop playing a game calmly and easily. It's also why I've written an entire book about understanding the habits behind technology use (*Managing Your Gaming and Social Media Habits*) and what to do to change this when it's problematic, which I will summarise in a moment to help you understand the 'needs behind the behaviour'. As you'll see, the real issue is often not about the amount of time that a child spends online but who and what they are engaging with in a relational way while they're there; it's about what clinicians call attachment, and those very relationships we have 'out here' in the real world as well as 'in there' online. This is not about an addiction; it is about the innate human desire for connection to others.

## So, What is The Issue?

You wouldn't expect time spent speaking to a friend on the phone, playing football or chatting over coffee to a group of colleagues to be seen as an addiction – you would see it as *time spent socialising*. But time spent on games or using a phone can be misinterpreted by others, because as observers we can't always see what the appeal is, or why someone would do that thing for so long or, most importantly, *who* they are interacting with online for that long. Parents will say to me things like, 'Billy won't get off the game in time for tea', or, 'He wants to play with his gaming friends instead of spending with us or his siblings,' and misconstrue this as being a psychological and/or mental-health problem. Or a mum might complain, 'She's always on the phone and stays up late because she's "addicted" to it and won't go anywhere without it!'

Yet, as I've explained, the diagnostic manuals used by mental-health professionals like me don't use the word 'addiction' in relation to activities such as sports, hobbies (in general), social media or gaming. While the expression 'gaming addiction' pops up in the media, diagnostically we might only refer to someone's 'gaming disorder' if they've had a problem with this activity (as defined by whether it's been interfering in their everyday life, such as not going to school or a job) *for over a year*. It's a complex situation, but an issue such as an addiction to substances (which we would call a biological addiction), mostly concerns a medical diagnosis, rather than just a behavioural issue, and it relates to specific biological markers in areas of the brain that produce a neurotransmitter called dopamine (which I'll cover in depth soon), which can be measured. However, there is rarely a baseline with which to compare it – that is, we don't usually know a person's dopamine levels before the issue started. There is no blood test, to test for addiction, and many people will never be given a brain scan to find these biological markers. A clinician will often use a questionnaire and self-assessments to determine whether a behaviour constitutes an addiction according to the definitions in the manuals. Substance-dependent addictions can be treated with chemical drugs in many or most cases (which is kind of ironic, in that one chemical is being substituted for another), and I know from working with people who use alcohol or cigarettes how physically uncomfortable the process of withdrawal can be, yet it's sometimes the only way these individuals can stop using a substance. Then again, I've worked with many people who, in their own words, 'just stop', which is the antithesis of the addiction model and the reason why so many people think addiction is a matter of willpower, too.

Another layer of complexity concerns the psychology of desire, want, obsessive thoughts, compulsions and impulsivity towards the behaviour labelled as an addiction. This relates to our thoughts and not just (or) our biology, and it's led to what's called the psychological craving model, which goes hand in hand with the biological model. It's why treatments today often address thoughts, cravings or obsessing about the addiction and, again, this can often result in people finding themselves being offered interventions that can include medication.

Now, I'm sure that, even if we were to say our child or teen was addicted to their smartphone, the vast majority of us wouldn't want them to be treated with psychotropic or medical pharmacology drugs. Medical addiction is a robust and very different issue to what we might describe as a technology-based *behaviour*. So let's try not to confuse the two and instead find another way to help us understand this behaviour. (To that end, I'm going to be introducing you to a needs-based approach to being human, often called attachment theory, a little later in this chapter.)

Ah, I hear some readers cry, I've seen that this can be described as a behavioural addiction, then – isn't that it? Well, not entirely, although that's a respectable counterargument that I and other researchers often hear in this area. To explain what I mean, it would probably be useful to describe the difference between a medical model and the 'behavioural and psychological addiction' models, and what I professionally define as an observable behaviour driven by a (psychological attachment, emotional or developmental) *need*. So let's address this.

To define a behavioural addiction, I'd like us to step out of the dark fug of a teenager's bedroom and into the clinical brightness of a laboratory. In the 1970s, scientists carried out a series of experiments involving rats and a water solution laced with morphine.[2] The rats were initially caged in isolated conditions and had to press levers to access the solution. Many repeatedly pressed the levers for the infused water to the point of overdosing and sometimes dying, leading to the conclusion that they were either addicted to the morphine (which would have been a medical 'substance' addiction) or perhaps to the pressing of the lever that delivered the morphine-laced water (which would have been a behavioural addiction). Hmm. Which was it and why?

Some would say that it's the substance we ingest, such as heroin or alcohol, that causes us to become 'addicted', while others would say it's the related behaviour that's the addiction – say, winding down with a drink after work. There are also those who'd say it's the feelings relating to *wanting to* taste the substance that causes addiction. Scientists have never agreed on whether addiction takes place because of biological, psychological or behaviour-based reasons, or even the social setting. However, what all their approaches do consider is the production of dopamine, a hormone that facilities motivation and which we'll be considering in more detail shortly.

In a famous experiment known as the Rat Park, which took place in the late 1970s, the rats were divided into two groups.[3] Each group had access to two water sources: one was uncontaminated, while the other contained heroin (in the name of science, eh). The first group were kept alone in traditional laboratory cages with no company or toys, while the second group were housed in a more comfortable environment, with other rats for company and things to occupy them, like ladders to climb and toys to play with. This second group of rats didn't even go near the heroin water; however, the first group drank it to excess, leading to the conclusion that this was because they were bored and lacked social stimulation (note the use of the word 'social' here).

Just to add another layer to the various approaches to addiction, when the rats had been surrounded by other rats, another factor – the 'social' processes – was taken into consideration, leading to what is now called a bio-psycho-social model of addiction. This ought to have resulted in an amalgamation of all the existing approaches and disciplines, meaning we would consider all the factors in each case of potential addiction, yet people can still seek treatment based on only one discipline of thinking (the parts), which doesn't always address all of the issue (the whole). Most importantly, what is missing from this model is an understanding of the innate wanting to belong, to be safe, seen, soothed and secure in a relationship.

With respect to how you might see this played out on or with technology; a child may keep picking up their device to see if their friends responded to something they said or posted. The more important that friend is to them, the more they are driven to see if they have an answer from them. Or perhaps the child keeps going back to a game level that they are failing to pass, and on the surface you see them arrive home from school and rush to the console to try and beat the boss once more. On the surface, both of these observed behaviours look like the rats drinking the heroin water, but the emotional and psychological states underneath this are driven by a desire for belonging and connection to friends. They may want to be the best at a game so they can share this with their friends or discuss hints and tips with them, so this is also about connection and relational belonging.

Today, the various diagnostic discourses in the field of mental health tend to be more biased towards one of these approaches than the others. For example, substance dependency is viewed as being mainly because of biology, while behavioural issues are reasoned to be mainly the result of psychological distress. So it would seem that addiction is both robustly understood and maybe not understood at all, and that we only have a limited vocabulary with which to describe our behaviours. It's a nuanced and multifaceted topic, and all aspects of being human must be considered in order to understand and work with it to change the behaviour. (Interestingly, we never seem to use the word addicted for 'positive' habits and behaviours.)

But how does all this apply to human activity around digital technology?

## *Is It All About Dopamine?*

Dopamine is a bit of a celebrity nowadays. I have heard this molecule (the 'molecule of more', as one book calls it) discussed increasingly over the last few years in popular podcasts; and you've likely come across the phrase 'dopamine hit' yourself. So, very briefly, I'd like to explain the faulty pop-science take on dopamine, as used in everyday general conversations and by influencers, and even by some of those who study the brain (neuroscientists), whereby they reduce us to a single neurotransmitter that they say controls every aspect of our behaviour. But first off, let's not forgot we're very complicated beings and, as explained in Chapter 4 later (on neuroplasticity and the way our brains can change), we're able to make decisions in our lives that are not under the sole control of this molecule.

Once upon a time, scientists discovered an area of the brain that is now known as the reward system. (I have listed some book titles in the Resources section on p. 347, should you be interested in reading more.) What they found in experiments was that, when people were rewarded, the area of their brains where the neurotransmitter dopamine was present lit up. Neurotransmitters are what's known as mediators, as they are basically 'helpers' in the functioning of the body (also, not all neurotransmitters live in the brain, which can be confusing). While the idea that our brains release dopamine at the reward point of a behaviour has gained traction in popular discussions, it turns out that we actually get more dopamine released in the pursuit of a behaviour than at the end. So with that awareness, let's look at why this molecule is being associated with the pings and dings of technology use, and why we have been told by some documentaries and podcasts that we get a 'hit of dopamine when we get a notification', which is how big-tech companies get us to stay 'hooked on' or 'addicted to' their platforms. And I also want to show you how those 'hits' are more about relational needs and rewards.

We're all driven by needs, which include – you guessed it – the things we *need* in order to feel we are safe, seen, soothed and secure. In terms of understanding humans, these are the things we need the most. It's why the late psychologist Abraham Maslow and cognitive scientist Scott Barry Kaufman have both devoted a large proportion of their careers to teaching us we have these emotional needs before other psychological ones. You might have come across Maslow's hierarchy of needs (see p. 80), in which the 4Ss, as described earlier, form a fundamental layer.[4] And you may have noticed that habits involving technology, at a surface level, are often described as needs by children themselves (and probably most of us grown ups too); for example, 'I just need to do this' or, 'I just need to send a text'. Are these the same kind of *need* as the 4Ss, though? Well, sort of, because the drive to send that text or look at that new 'Snap' (video or text), for example, is a relational activity that can feel like an urgent 'need', especially if we've been taught 'not to be rude' and to respond to someone when they ask a question. And during the completion of that task, we will no doubt get a little hit of dopamine, by the way.

Attachment, which is the relational bond we form with someone (in real life), entails expressing our needs and, hopefully, those needs being met in the return part of the conversation; and it takes place in real time, in the here and now.

When you see a person looking into a device, tapping away, they are, in essence, 'talking', as well as reading the message, imagining the voice, settings, facial cues and more. They might also be responding to a message or post that was sent or made earlier that day, and which they can now see on the screen and feel compelled to answer – because this is how conversations take place. Now, the confusing bit when it comes to applying the language of addiction to the use of a device is often about the following: we pick up a phone to do something *with* it and *through* it – not because we're addicted to it, but because we have an end goal in mind that will satisfy our *need to connect*. In some cases, it might help us to complete a task, like banking for example – although talking about a banking addiction sounds a tad ridiculous, doesn't it? A device is both a tool *and* a medium. The tool is for the task in hand (opening apps, clicking on keys, using things like calculators), and it's also a *medium of social communication*, which is how we connect *through the screen* (like a portal) to the 'other person', who we imagine or can see on screen.*

This is why it's so complicated to measure accurately what is really going on at the level of someone holding a device in their hand, and whether the amount of time they spend staring at the screen is indicative of anything other than their eyes being focused on it, as we can't see into their brain to determine the cognitive processes taking place, or any behavioural/psychological/

---

* Our brain does this is a very complex imaginary manner and, if you are interested in learning more about it, do seek out the work of John Vervaeke.

relational ones, for that matter. Even if we measured, say, oxygen use or the areas that light up in the brain with an fMRI machine (or other devices like PET/CT/EEG scans), it would be incredibly difficult to say if someone is addicted because:

a) the molecule of dopamine is used for more than just rewards of 'likes' – it's used in need-seeking behaviours, too, such as finding food and mates, and motivation, such as goal setting.
b) dopamine can be present before we even pick up the phone – *in anticipation of* who we are going to speak to or what we are going to send or post online, for example (and we actually get bigger releases of dopamine in pursuit behaviours).
c) we don't say that we are 'addicted' to conversations, relationships or people in the real world, yet we seem to use this word to describe online activities.
d) people rarely use their devices only to socialise – they will use them simultaneously for tasks like banking and spreadsheets, or go on other apps or platforms like the news – so it's hard to measure this in isolation, when something else is or can be happening in the same timeframe.

All of this means we cannot measure robustly what is happening here and assign the addiction label to it. But perhaps we ought to try to understand which of our bio-psycho-social 'needs' could be met using technology, and how.

### *The Need for Connection*

If you were to ask a young person why they are on the phone or a game, they'll often say that they're engaging with someone directly, or with something (e.g. gaming or films), so that they can then *engage with someone about it later*. This is a socialising behaviour and in research or therapy we call this a relational process of 'attachment' (or, as I call it in this context, 'e-ttachment').

If that's the case, why do we use our devices? Mostly, I would argue that it's because it feels really, really good to have connections with people (or sometimes even an AI chatbot) for a relational purpose. It's innate in all of us. If you ask 'why?' and then listen carefully to the answers, like I do in my clinic, it might surprise you to discover that there really is no behaviour when using technology that isn't underpinned by this relational process, other than perhaps the use of spreadsheets, calculators and admin-type programs (but these too are often about performance and, in turn, getting praise – say, from your boss, or even from yourself).

So when Bobby won't get off the game, for example, what are those behaviours and the ensuing arguments really about? Young people and primary-school children both in and out of therapy tell me that the internet or gaming are places where they can just 'be' or hang out with their friends. And for younger children, the desire to use gaming technology can be about having fun (much like playing with the Lego or dolls) or simply doing whatever Mum or Dad do by copying them and using their own versions of technology, like the telephone, which is how small children learn. Some older children have told me that they like hanging out with friends online, who may be geographically farther away, so that it's not possible to go outside and play with them. Which brings us back to attachment, peer relationships and belonging – and, of course, need-seeking behaviours. In 2024, a report for Ofcom by the agency Revealing Reality[5] highlighted such processes in statements like: 'Those children who were gaming were often doing so as a way of interacting with their friends.' When discussing Snapchat, they noted: 'In addition to using it for one-to-one messaging, several of the children were in group chats, for example with friends from school, people from their area, or friends from their extracurricular interests.' Similarly, a 2023 report by Cybersurvey[6] highlighted that 49 per cent of boys and 50 per cent of girls said 'yes' in response to the statement 'Social media helps me feel closer to my friends.' (A point to note is that often these sorts of studies tend to separate boys and girls by default and don't consider other gender identities, which may or may not influence results.)

## Let's Try Looking at Things in a Different Way

Perhaps you're still not convinced? After all, if it's a question of thinking and feelings then surely that's still about a psychological addiction? Let's look at some of the common 'effects' of so-called digital addiction that are regularly cited online, and allow me to pick these apart for you:

### *A Preoccupation with Being Online*

There's the argument that one symptom of internet addiction concerns a preoccupation with being online. Let's imagine a scenario in which a teenager is talking online to her friends, but she then leaves a group chat to go and eat dinner, during which she thinks about the next time she can use her device to rejoin the conversation. Now, would that teen be preoccupied in an addiction sense, would you say, or in the sense of being concerned with group cohesion and belonging?

### *Lying or Hiding the Extent or Nature of Internet Use*

This approach is mostly taken from substance-misuse literature and interventions, where we can evidentially 'measure' whether someone has ingested a substance, which would, of course, reveal a lie through the resulting data (e.g. a blood test). However, lying is a cognitive process that requires us to think about doing a behaviour and then intentionally 'fibbing' to deceive another person. Keeping that in mind, let's consider the following statements: 'I can't and didn't accurately track my time staring at the screen, so I estimate that it's more, or less, than X.' Or, 'I don't want to be shamed by you, so I say it's less than it is.' Or, 'I hear that others have lower time scores than me, so I lie to fit in.' Or even, 'I hear others spend more time online, so I triumphantly say I spend less.' And lastly, 'I'm completely unaware of my time online, because I'm in flow', (a state of consciousness where you aren't in touch with time). Are these deliberate lies or mistruths? And if they are deliberate lies, what was I 'doing' on the screen to lie about? And what if our screen-time trackers measure the opening of the app but don't collect data about when we walk off to grab a cuppa or go for a comfort break (as I have on many occasions while writing this book): is the app then lying? Perhaps this is more about the inaccuracies of time, active and passive use of things online or what a person might be lying about, such as spending money or watching content that is unsuitable in some way?

### *Craving to Spend More Time Online*

I think this one speaks for itself. As humans, we crave relational connections in many ways and for many reasons. Cravings are fleeting and mostly feelings about wants and needs. It can be difficult to divide them into what's a genuine or authentic need and what's a passing liking of something. If you think your child is craving spending time online, try to have a conversation with them to find out what's really going on. What longing or fear might that craving really be about?

## *Secretive behaviour (regarding online use)*

Secretive behaviour is almost always linked to shame. If your child is being secretive about their online activity, perhaps they are simply curious about a particular topic or something they don't know but don't want to ask you. They can ask a search engine, and it will give an answer without the risk of humiliation. Furthermore, secrecy and privacy are normal parts of relational behaviour and most certainly part of growing up. But the privacy aspect is one that we parents and carers also need to keep our Spidey senses at the ready for. As we will see, there are instances where secretive behaviour can have sinister causes that will most likely have nothing to do with internet addiction and could be related to exploitation, which is covered later in the book (see p. 117).

## Game On

As we've seen, children and teens spend time online for a variety of reasons, one of which is simply being part of a community that makes them feel wanted. Some play games, so they can have a shared language with their peers when they go to school in the real world. For example, if you hear your child talk about 'being rushed', this isn't necessarily anything to do with you hurrying them out of the door, but could just be a reference to a mechanism in a game whereby players behave in a certain way.

When it comes to gaming in particular, another reason that children and teens can spend what seem like inordinate amounts of time in front of a screen is that they're aiming for mastery. In layman's terms, this is what you and I might call 'practice' if we were to talk about it in relation to activities like soccer, tennis, chess, backgammon or playing the clarinet. It's about achieving perfection, automaticity and expertise; in this case, being ranked as the best player.

'Practice makes perfect' is the meme (see page 198 for more on meme culture) – and so it does. However, playing for hours on video games is seen by some as a disorder or addiction. While, as we've discussed, your child is unlikely to have an addiction in the clinical sense, I agree that it's important to acknowledge the impact that this level of commitment to gaming can have on everyday functioning, such as a teenager not washing, eating properly or going to school in order to stay at home and play on computer games all day, which is certainly an issue. However, if we think for one quick moment about becoming the best in the world at, say, a game such as Fortnite, League of Legends or Rocket League, then those practice hours would need to be seriously high. But before leaping to diagnose a teen with a gaming addiction, I'd want to look into the range of reasons why they aren't going to school, which could be about avoiding conflict or bullying (so staying home playing games to escape the torment) or what gaming provides them with in terms of managing their emotions. It is also possible that they are playing online matches that pay out significant sums of money in different time zones.

There have been stories reported in the media in recent years of teens who have entered and won e-sports matches, winning millions. Would they be considered 'addicts'? This reminds me of a patient of mine called Eddy, whose story was not dissimilar . . .

### Eddy's Story

Eddy was an avid gamer who often shut himself away from his siblings in his bedroom. However, he could be 'heard for miles', according to his mum, and would often start 'rage quitting' (a term meaning being angered by something in a game and suddenly leaving) and throw his controller at the TV screen. He had broken three TVs and kicked a hole in the door of his bedroom. His mum had got angry with him and cut the plugs from his devices on more than one occasion. In the end, Eddy was brought to me for 'addiction', although I quickly found that there was another side to his 'need to play every day'.

Eddy was keen to play and make money from his skill. In fact, he had created a 'streaming' account where he could play his games and put them live online for other people to watch. His mum was unaware that he was getting 'subs' (subscriptions) to his channel, which meant that he was making money from them. When she discovered that he had earned hundreds of pounds she was both angry and proud. She wasn't sure that he was allowed to do this, and of course that decision needed to be taken by them as a family. But Eddy didn't spend long in my clinic for addiction, as it turned out his gaming was more about making money!

Often, the word 'addiction' is used by adults without any investigation into the 'why' behind an activity, as I have explained in this chapter. The frustration with getting teens in particular off 'the darned thing' often results in them being brought to my clinic to 'fix' what is thought to be a gaming addiction.

## The Nature of Needs – And How to Fulfil Them

We all have fundamental needs that must be met if we're to survive. Earlier, we mentioned twentieth-century American psychologist Abraham Maslow, who described these needs as forming a hierarchy, often portrayed as a pyramid.

If our basic needs for things like food and shelter (which sit at the bottom of the pyramid) are not met, we can die. Once we have the means to keep ourselves alive and safe, the next set of needs, according to Maslow's hierarchy, relates to love and belonging. We want to feel connected, to belong and to bond with someone else. And if instead we feel rejected, abandoned and alone, we will seek out those desires to belong elsewhere.

Forming attachment bonds is a crucial part of child development and a natural drive in primates, as confirmed in controversial experiments conducted on monkeys by American psychologist Harry Harlow in the 1950s.[7] In his studies, baby monkeys formed attachments to inanimate surrogate 'mothers'. The mother replicas were made of either wire or cloth (no food present), and, while the wire ones offered food, the baby monkeys formed much stronger attachments to the comforting cloth ones, overwhelmingly choosing to bond with them, irrespective of the offer of sustenance. As primates, we too have those same primitive drives, which means that children will naturally seek out these feelings too, although they may take varied approaches. If a child doesn't feel wanted, needed or seen, their drive to get those needs met by someone (or somewhere) else can be stronger than their desire to eat.

Unfortunately, knowledge about important things like attachment bonds does not drive e-safety or online safety policies. If you think about the kinds of risk involved online (more on this in Chapter 6), and keep in mind the sorts of needs-seeking behaviours we've looked at, you may be asking yourself what we can do to protect children from looking to fulfil their needs online. The answer is that we need to make sure we meet children's needs out here in the real world (you can watch my 2022 TEDx talk to see a way to do this from birth onwards) and this means that as a society we also need to create many more spheres of belonging for our children, which includes our homes, family, school and social spaces like sports clubs and youth clubs, so they don't always go looking to meet their needs 'in there' online. The Cybersurvey in 2023[8] highlighted that a lack of belonging can result in behaviours online that are riskier and which impact identity. This means learning to read and respond to our children's needs when they are little, and continuing to do so all the way through to their adulthood. We do this by communicating, hearing and resonating with them, while being empathic and compassionate. This is not 'soft' parenting (compassion can most certainly involve the word 'no'); this is child-centred and research-based (see all the books on parenting listed on pp. 347–9, as they are steeped in this), and it's how we can create a space for our children to trust in and communicate with us. We also need to be able to self-regulate, so as to effectively co-regulate our children – then they, in turn, can learn how to self-regulate themselves. (I'll be giving examples on how to do this and have included helpful books on the topic in the Resources, p. 347.)

I would also add that as a society we should be taking a broad-brush approach to e-safety and online safety that factors in need-seeking behaviours, which can then be adapted as required for each child. Safety lessons could include child development and social-communication strategies. And we should make sure those lessons engage with children in a meaningful way that includes them and enters into open dialogue with them, rather than treating e-safety as lecturing or 'don't-do-this' talks. (You'll find advice on engaging with children in this way in Chapter 12.) We should also create a process for professionals that reflects this approach in education settings, social care, policing and childcare, and any spaces children go to physically, like sports clubs, and wherever they can potentially access the online world on a mobile device. This is not just a job for parents, but for all of us, which means you will have to consider what e-safety measures and guidance schools and clubs have in place for your children when sending them there.

As individuals, families and communities, we can take a similar approach by talking about online risks to vulnerable children and teens in developmentally appropriate language they can understand. This means adapting it to their age and stage, using accurate and correct terms and avoiding tech speak or referring to body parts through euphemisms. We can invite them to be a part of the conversation in understanding risk, and then tailor what they can access online based on their responses to us.

> ### *A Note on Children with Social, Emotional or Educational Needs, Neurodiversity and/or Trauma*
>
> Sometimes, children with certain vulnerabilities, such as autism, may not even know when they *do* belong or *are* wanted, as they may not recognise the behaviours or words of others as being meaningful or displaying bonds of attachment and connection. They may not understand empathy in themselves, or in others. And they may not comprehend risk and consequences, so, rather than take calculated risks, they may gamble with enormous ones – like using sexually harmful language or inappropriate gestures and emoticons, or exploring sites that have warnings or age-gated content. Similarly, they may have obsessions and compulsions to be in certain spaces online, or to say or do certain things. They may repeat language they hear elsewhere in the hope that it represents the social 'norm'. They may seek out material that's inappropriate or falls into illegal areas as defined by the law or age-rated guidance. They may feel the need to share sensitive or private content about themselves and others. And they may become overly reliant on others in some online spaces.
>
> They may also use social media or gaming as a way to explore their identity, and for self-regulation or to enable themselves to cope with events. they may rely on the predictability of games because their own world, whether in their heads or in real life, is in chaos. Children (including younger ones) who can navigate the requisite interactions may buy and sell items online or in

games affecting them financially and, depending upon their age and social skills, they can be particularly at risk of exploitation. All these risks and behaviours can be traced back to a needs-seeking approach. This is why it's crucial to understand the needs driving the child or teen in question and what this means both at that moment and over time.

It's important to take an individualised approach to protecting children online and to understand that, just like children themselves, needs may vary. For a child with a 'spicy brain' (a term used to describe neurodivergence), for example, the needs they are seeking to meet may differ somewhat from those of a child who doesn't comprehend language, or one who is developmentally delayed and doesn't always understand the consequences of saying certain things in certain situations (or who lacks executive functions, as neuroscientists would say). It is possible to create an environment around the child that takes into account their particular vulnerability by using parental controls, keeping devices in view or perhaps sharing directly (casting) them to a TV, so as to monitor what is going on online. And we can also recognise the impact on children of any trauma, and in particular cybertrauma caused by certain online interactions, and the legacy this can leave on a child's body and brain.

Addiction literature often lists lots of 'symptoms' to look out for, and we've unfortunately come to apply the same sort of language to online usage as is used around hard drugs, alcohol and sex. But with your child's internet use, what we're really talking about, in many cases, is the joy someone feels when playing a game or using a platform to socialise, and their desire to connect with others. And as tempting as it may be to dismiss the friendships they form there, they can be just as valid as any made in real life.

Communication here, as ever, is key. If we can communicate well with our children in the real world, giving them our undivided attention to stop and listen, hear and really understand them, then we can have a positive impact on their future – and that is probably the biggest 'lesson' about relationships in this book. Whether they are similar to or entirely different from other children, the relationship your child has with you is the one of the most important factors in their online safety.

## Summary

- In a clinical setting, the word 'addiction' refers to a specific diagnosis. Today, we apply this word much more broadly to refer to those activities we enjoy and to other people's activities that may annoy or frustrate us, or that we can't understand.
- We might use addiction terminology to help us feel we're not to blame when we feel powerless in a situation.
- Children tend not to get addicted to devices, but they can become attached to them and attached to people through them.
- Attachment is the relational bond we form with someone when we express our needs and those needs are met by that person.
- We're all driven by needs, including the things we need in order to feel safe, seen, soothed and secure.
- Most kids use their devices to connect with others because it feels good.

CHAPTER 4

# The Effect of Tech on the Brain

In this chapter, we'll look at what we mean by brain development, from a child developmental perspective, and what changes take place; we'll look at how brains mature and the interpersonal skills we develop as we grow; and we will consider the attentional issues that are said to be on the increase in society and how this is linked to technology – if at all.

Besides worrying that their child will become addicted to life online, many parents fear that things like smartphones and apps are changing the way their child's brain works – that tech is creating attention issues (including ADHD – attention deficit hyperactivity disorder), driving a lack of empathy and ability to connect, causing language delays, or that it's increasing anxiety to levels never seen before in children. Perhaps the extent of that fear isn't surprising, as the mainstream media and online articles by often well-meaning yet ill-informed individuals can be guilty of scaremongering. Misinformation and stories like 'our attention span is now less than that of a goldfish' make for great clickbait online.

Concerns can also be fuelled by anecdotal conversations and articles saying that children who use technology have more distractions, and that devices themselves are a 'digital distraction' – like when we go to check our emails only to emerge three hours later, having got sidetracked by all sorts of online diversions. And a number of researchers,[1] including the Surgeon General in the US,[2] claim that loneliness is on the rise, with the finger sometimes being pointed at technology here, too, although there's no evidence to prove a direct cause-and-effect relationship.[3] (This is because we can't isolate loneliness as being caused by one thing other than not having a relational connection to others.)

Some parenting experts have written that there's a distinct lack of empathy in children nowadays because they use technology to bully each other (which does indeed happen), and claim that this is because there's no immediate feedback to show them the outcome of the bullying. And while this can often be very true, it isn't always the case; for example, in gaming environments people can be heard to be in distress, and they can send messages in real time asking for bullying behaviour to stop. Plus, a lack of empathy could be due to a particular child not being an empathic individual, or not even realising their behaviour has an impact, and the hurt they cause could be unintentional. In addition, bullying can take place both on and off technology, making it difficult to point to a specific causal link as a factor. So I'd like us to think a little more critically about articles that suggest X causes Y, and to consider human behaviour writ large instead.

I can understand parents' concerns, especially if they read that technology is causing all these problems. And while I'll be addressing these and other issues in more detail a bit later, let's double-click first on the general worry that tech is affecting our kids' grey matter.

## Tech and the Brain

To get us started, I'd like you to have a think about your own beautiful brain. Since the start of this book, I've been asking questions and sharing facts that have likely sparked moments of your own thinking. Perhaps you've even had to pause and put the book down, or reread a section or sentence, because your mind went off on a tangent or took a trip down memory lane.

What you might not have been aware of is that, while you have been reading, you've made new connections between the neurons in your brain (these are the little cells that pass information between each other). Now, although we haven't been measuring this scientifically, I can tell you that the discipline of neuroscience tells us that *anything we do has an impact on the brain*. In other words, your brain is literally changing because you're reading these words!

The brain's ability to change itself and make new neuronal pathways is called 'neuroplasticity'. It's worth paying attention to this word when it's used in the media and in literature about the negative effects of social media, technology and gaming, because, in all truth, *everything we do* creates neuroplastic changes – both positive and negative. But no one knows how for sure how technology affects neuroplasticity in isolation from anything else a person might be doing.

If we consider this sort of neurological response in the context of immersing ourselves in text, photos, videos and sound through a screen, it seems pretty clear that this is going to have an impact of some sort. But we cannot say exactly what this impact is, because the psychology and neuroscience suggest that, in terms of our individual responses, it's not as easy as saying that X equals Y or that X *causes* Y, as there are so many different factors involved.

Nevertheless, we can make generalised claims that certain topics will evoke certain feelings, and those emotions can create changes or associations in the brain that are quick to be remembered. Reading or watching a particular type of media will often evoke a common response in most people. This has been substantiated by experiments such as those in which people viewed varying types of content – for example, images of fields, animals fighting or faces of people showing varying emotions – and were then tested on things like their reaction speeds or their reactions to emotive words/images.[4,5] In a non-clinical setting, Christmas adverts are a prime example of something that stirs up a lot of feelings for many of us; certainly, in the case of advertising, the desired impact is for maximum penetration into our emotions. This is why Christmas adverts are often called 'tear-jerkers' – because they affect people so much emotionally. You might even have recalled a specific one as you read this; memory and the brain are fantastic, aren't they?

## *A Look At the Brain Science*

When it comes to concerns about the effects of technology on the development of children's brains, the area of the brain most often said to be impacted is the prefrontal cortex, located just behind the forehead. This area is described in neuroscience as being responsible for 'executive function', which includes (when it is mature, in adults) delayed gratification, decision-making, awareness of consequences, emotional regulation and attention (which we'll address shortly). It's said that in children and teens this area is still developing, which is why it's often mentioned in relation to risk-taking in children.

It's difficult to mark the exact point at which children begin to think like fully formed rational, regulated, emotionally resilient and forward-thinking human beings. (It's difficult to pinpoint when this happens with adults, to be honest!) But for now we can go with research cited by Dan Siegel in his book *Brainstorm* that says this change from child to adolescent to adult begins (and, I repeat, *begins*) at or around puberty, when the brain moves into the adolescence process.[6] But we do not have an exact starting (or end) point – there is no pistol fired to set us on our way, or a biological marker (yet) that shows the start of adolescence. And so we say 'approximately'.

It is safe to say, however, that the ability to use the executive-function area of the brain to regulate emotions, use language, remember to do homework or take their PE kit to school, get along with peers and take a considered approach to risk-taking goes a little haywire for kids for some years, until the brain has 'matured'. In terms of technology and a child's behaviours in online spaces, this means that things like risk-taking, critical thinking, understanding others and processing emotions, forming attachments and being driven by need-seeking behaviours to feel safe, seen, soothed and secure (the 4Ss – see p. 27) are all heightened or diminished and potentially unstable in some way during this critical period (as they also are in offline relationships, and in any experiences leading to online behaviours). The age and stage of an individual child's development, their temperament, what they're doing online and what other people or content they are interacting with (and how) will also be implicated. While this is very similar to how children have evolved into adults in the real world for a very long time, now we have the added complexities of the much faster and changing digital landscape in which they're growing up. (I have included some books on child-to-adult changes on pp. 347–9, should you want to read more about all this.)

Technology in all its forms will undoubtedly affect a child's development, and their development will, in turn, affect how they use and interact with technology, although exactly to what extent will depend on the individual, the content they engage with, how often they do so, how they perceive it and, most importantly, who helps them make sense of it in their lives and how. For example, viewing positive experiences online is more than likely going to be a pleasurable process that helps them develop feelings of kindness, empathy and compassion. Yet a child could engage with negative content and still develop those skills in response to perceiving pain in another person if an adult is on hand to guide them.

## Attention Issues

If, as we established in Chapter 3, kids aren't addicted to technology, then are they simply distracted by it? Has technology created changes in their brains that mean their attention span has been impacted in some way? It seems reasonable enough to suppose so, given that devices and games now make so many attention-grabbing noises and that children often use multiple devices or apps at the same time, or swap from one to the other in quick succession. All those pings and dings . . . it's enough to drive anyone to distraction, isn't it? In fact, it might seem only logical to us to deduce that they couldn't possibly be paying attention, because when we were in school we were taught that this meant not looking up from our books or not taking our eyes off the teacher at the front of the class.

Added to which, the constant refrain of teenagers in particular seems to be 'I didn't pay attention to . . .', 'I forgot . . .' They seem uninterested in us and can't wait to get back to their devices after dinner. Or they're constantly picking up their phones 'just' to check something. And, of course, we've all heard how social media platforms want to 'monetise' and 'keep our attention', which is why notifications from devices mean we can't get a moment's peace.

So does technology actually cause, create or exacerbate attentional issues, attentional overload and distraction – and do any of those terms adequately cover the issue?

Rising rates of attention disorders are becoming synonymous with excessive technology use, but this isn't a clear or robustly evidenced space, and that makes it difficult for us to really understand or for me to give you advice on this issue, other than by highlighting the following considerations.

Let's address the attention(al) hypothesis, which claims that the 'volume of media' being consumed leads to a lack of attention (usually in classrooms, or to parents' requests, I might add). 'Attentional deficit' is a term used to describe a pathological psychiatric disorder that is known in full as attention deficit and hyperactivity disorder (ADHD). However, in everyday conversation, very much like the word 'addiction', this is now associated with a wide range of behaviours, and the phrase has come to refer (in the online world) to virtually anyone who struggles to pay attention for any length of time (by which I certainly don't wish to belittle the experiences of those seeking a diagnosis or having major difficulties in this area). The diagnoses of attention deficit disorder (ADD) and ADHD have received a lot of attention (pardon the pun) in the 2020s so far, with newer language emerging, such as neurodiversity (which is a less formal way to describe many of the mental-health diagnoses that diverge from the neurotypical and include autism, ADD, tics and some cognitive issues and traits like obsessive compulsions and social difficulties). Many more adults today are receiving a diagnosis later in life, too. Thus, talk of neurodiversity, attentional traits, ADD and ADHD has become very commonplace on social media platforms, with individuals self-diagnosing these conditions based on a quick 'symptom check' found on there (some of which are designed by companies with no formal training).

But is it true that social media or gaming have caused an epidemic *lack of attention*? What if I suggested – and this is not a finger-pointing exercise – that children have learned to become more gregarious in their everyday behaviours in order to be noticed by their parents and carers because, over the last twenty-five years or so, parents have become more distracted by their own technology use? Perhaps children simply want their parents' or teachers' attention, time and recognition, and so have developed ways to secure them? And how do we separate attention-needing behaviours – which can look like them shouting at adults, hitting their siblings and running around when they are asked to sit still – from what we would call attentional difficulties? (And, yes, the behaviours I've just mentioned are often about attention-needing or need-seeking.) How is technology contributing (or not) to the changes in what has been called the attention economy of human beings, especially children?

I'd like to think about what the word 'attention' really means by turning first to the father of American psychology, William James, who said: 'Attention is the deliberate focusing on an item at the discretion of ignoring everything else.'[7]

So now let's consider how you are doing with your attentional processes to see if we can understand how this works. At this point, I'd imagine that your neuroplastic brain (see p. 89) is doing exactly what I'd expect it to. Either it's reading the words on these pages and *not paying attention to* the sounds around you, wherever you are (although, now that I've mentioned this, you might just become aware of these noises). Or perhaps you've stopped reading and gone off on a tangent about something else completely (this is exactly what brains do in meditation practice, and it can be enlightening to know that many of us do it). Perhaps you had a sudden idea and stopped reading for a moment; or you had an insight about children being so focused on gaming/their smartphones/their computers that when you shouted to them numerous times it was to no avail; but now you can see they were 'paying attention' – only not to you. Which, in turn, means they *are* paying attention, and this is sustained and focused, which is exactly the point William James makes in his academic argument. Thus, technology can indeed create conditions for focused attention, dependent upon the task in hand on the screen.

While some research shows technology to be a factor in the reported rise in attentional issues, most of the evidence is anecdotal and comes from stories and articles that appear on social media, in which individuals say they 'gave up their phone for X time' and they now concentrate better and feel less anxiety (and there aren't any six-month or one-year follow-ups for these examples in many cases yet).

Conversely, I can't, at the time of writing, find much research in favour of technology being studied with respect to *improving* attention, but, as the saying goes, 'an absence of evidence is not evidence of absence', and maybe we just haven't looked into it enough yet.

So for our purposes here, I would argue that if your child is engrossed in an activity online, keeps swapping games or devices, or is forgetful or has memory lapses and/or struggles in school, this doesn't automatically indicate that they have an attentional diagnosis that is a mental-health disorder.

In short, helping children concentrate often means making the task in hand fun, and setting a goal that they're interested in and that's important to them. We should acknowledge that different levels of difficulty can have an impact on this ability, and that boredom is a necessary part of our collection of feelings; sometimes we reach for technology when we are bored or come off it for the same reason, and this may signify, not an attentional issue, but one of relational misconnection somewhere. And memory lapses are also part of the human condition (in case I forgot to say that already!).

## Does Technology Impact Language Acquisition?

Anecdotally, it's been proposed over the past few years by teachers, parenting influencers and some academics and psychologists online that a delay in language acquisition is on the rise in under-fives because of technology, and that their reading and writing skills are affected, too. According to some arguments, it could be conjectured that the more time a child under five spends not directly talking to their parents, carers and other humans, but instead investigating life through a screen without looking up at the world in order to communicate with it and make associative connections in their brains, the less successful they will be in learning how to speak, read and write.

But just how do we learn to speak, and what's involved? According to Noam Chomsky, a globally respected expert in linguistics, we're born with the facility to acquire language. In terms of the biology involved, our innate ability to learn language, such as how we put sentences together, is linked to an area of the brain called the language-acquisition device. Language acquisition is influenced by maturing brain-development processes as well as the external environment, which is why children with disabilities or impacts on or to the brain during stages of development are expected to have less capacity for it. This can include children who've experienced trauma in the womb, and those who develop conditions such as foetal alcohol spectrum disorder (FASD), who often don't do as well as others in relation to language acquisition and subsequent academic outcomes as they grow older.

Research in child development also tells us that children's language acquisition is subject to the differing amounts of input from those who are around them and talk to and engage with them. Some findings suggest that children of around three years of age will have a vocabulary level that reflects a parent's level of education (meaning that parents with higher academic qualifications will have children who with higher vocabulary scores), while some research claims the level increases in children of parents with higher incomes. Still other research suggests that those who, say, receive more home parenting have higher scores.[8] What's more, a child's vocabulary is also believed to increase with the amount of one-to-one time they spend with adults, per se, with some research suggesting that the oldest children in the family often have the highest level of vocabulary compared to their siblings.

Nevertheless, it's not known *exactly* how language acquisition or an ability for language occurs because lots of factors are involved and it takes place out of a laboratory, over time, usually at home and in schools, so it's difficult to monitor it scientifically through experiments or research, or to predict exact outcomes. For example, sometimes children from low-interactive, low socioeconomic backgrounds do go on to have expansive vocabularies.

One thing we do know is that, if children are to learn and speak a language, they must be exposed to it, engage with it and be corrected whenever they muddle up their sentences. After all, we want our children to explain to us what they need and what troubles them as they continue to grow.* What's much less clear, however, is whether screens are changing the process, as is sometimes claimed – and, if so, how?

At the risk of sounding somewhat repetitive, we cannot say anything for sure about the isolated impact of technology on this (or virtually any other) aspect of a child's development, although there is some data to suggest that the presence or use of technology can interfere in the process of one-to-one interactions with children in general [9] and this may have an effect on vocabulary acquisition. (That said, it's worth also noting that many children have been able to develop language skills when living with hearing- or speech-impaired parents. So language development in young children is clearly very complex.) But we currently lack the long-term evidence to say with confidence that tech is having a detrimental impact on language acquisition. And to make the situation even more complicated, technology is developing at a faster rate than it takes a lot of research to complete, with most studies lasting from one to three years, by which time the digital

---

\* To include them in our world, we need to show young children how words and sentences are formed. Many parents and carers do this without any formal training by 'narrating' about their day; for example, they might say, 'Mummy is just going into the kitchen,' or 'Daddy is going to work now, and he'll see you later when it's dark outside.' We read stories to our children and use silly voices so they can hear intonation and humour, and learn about the structure of language before they go to school so they can socialise with other children there and make friends. Through stories, they learn about sharing, danger and heroes and heroines; they learn about metaphors, connecting and describing words. They also learn to read themselves, and the ABCs and 123s of speaking that will help them to be successful in life. And if we speak more than one language, our children may even become bilingual or little polyglots (which is a great word)!

landscape has changed yet again. When we consider that only twenty years ago these smart devices of ours didn't even exist, we have to move fast to keep up with today's advances and find any cause-and-effect relationship between tech and its impact.

One finding that is of interest (but still not 'provable', I might add) is that children who are read to by their parents on a regular basis seem to have improved vocabulary skills, while those who read to themselves later in life can similarly increase these skills. That said, blaming parents for not reading to children is not ok, any more than it's ok to blame them for choosing to use devices with small children.

Children with hearing issues or with varied learning difficulties, and the way they may use technology to *assist* them with language or to communicate, are another important consideration. Given the rise of social, emotional and mental-health difficulties (SEMH) and special educational needs (SEN) issues (as indicated by long waiting lists for diagnoses, children registered in education as needing support and claims for disability-related payments in the UK, such as DLA or PIP), can we really blame tech exclusively for impaired literacy and language skills while ignoring the positive role it plays?[10]

I think that, when looking at the suggested rising rates of language delays being cited, we can defer to the bio-psycho-social model of human beings introduced earlier (see p. 70), which would suggest that language delays are part of the spectrum of child development. According to the UK government website, 'in the most deprived areas of England the percentage of children achieving the expected level of development in all 5 domains and the specific domains of communication, fine motor skills, problem solving and personal social skills is consistently below the [national] average'.[11] This suggests that much more is involved here than simply technology's impact (which is not even mentioned as a causal factor). Moreover, articles like one that appeared in the *Daily Telegraph* in 2022 have cited the Royal College of

Speech and Language Therapists suggesting the overall delay (in language) was attributable to the lockdown period, with no mention of technology in the research or article as being *a* cause, never mind *the* cause.[12]

To conclude this discussion of the complex question of language acquisition and tech, I found the following summary in a 2023 meta-analysis methodology study (meta-analyses are a good way to assess the overall research landscape) on children and the relationship between speech delay and smart media:

> Studies have highlighted an association between excessive screen usage and speech delays in young children. However, proving a direct cause-and-effect association is complex due to various influencing factors like parenting methods, socioeconomic status, and the overall communication environment. A prominent theory suggests that excessive screen exposure could replace crucial face-to-face interactions between parents/caregivers and children, negatively impacting language development.[13]

In addition, the meta-analysis also showed that introducing electronic devices at a later stage of development (over the age of two) was found to 'positively affect a child's language development', while 'educational apps and shared media engagement with parents correlated with stronger language skills'.

All of which points to the fact that it's complicated, as I've said, and that language-acquisition delays could be caused by several factors and not just technology.

## *The Importance of Thinking for Ourselves*

Given all the conjecture about the effects of tech on young children, it's more important than ever for us to start reading beyond the headlines. With that in mind, I'd like to look next at some research conducted in Australia in 2024 proposing that it's the amount and frequency of speaking by a parent to their child that matters.[14] The research also suggests that the number of words spoken is important to measure, rather than the quality of the parent's language skills or the relationship of conversing patterns (such as how long they last). That being the case – and here I am being a little provocative, while also posing a serious question: surely when *parents* are on devices and not speaking to their child (and/or the child is also on a device), this might be considered detrimental in terms of the child's language acquisition? But is this a fair assumption? Moreover, in suggesting that it is, do I seem like I'm blaming parents? I hope not, because I'm aware that we all need to use our devices for many reasons and sometimes we'll do so in front of our children – but this doesn't make us bad parents. If we did so repeatedly at the expense of engaging with our child, that might be a different matter, but it still wouldn't necessarily equate to being bad parents. However, my point here is that we should be aware of our technology use in front of our children when they want to engage with us.

But back to the study (one often cited by online influencers). Researchers gave a group of mums (no fathers were included in the study) recording devices to be worn like T-shirts and used to record all the chatter taking place between them and their children:

> *Findings of this study support the notion of technoference for Australian families, whereby young children's exposure to screen time is interfering with opportunities to talk and interact in their home environment. This finding has implications for interventions and supports aimed at promoting a language-rich home environment, with families needing support in understanding the potential association of screen time with opportunities for children and adults to talk and interact in their home environment.*[15]

I'm not interested in allocating blame, but I do wonder *why* the mums in this study were not talking to their children. I'd like to know the answers to questions such as these:

- Were the mums busy working? Were they concentrating on a task, or reading?
- Did they lack confidence in baby talk and 'motherese' (the simplified and repetitive language often used by mothers to speak their babies)?
- Maybe they just didn't like to talk at all?
- Were the mums neurodivergent or did they have low levels of language skills?
- Did they have negative self-beliefs about their ability as mums, or were they scared or worried about the responsibility that having children brings?
- Were they aware that they were being 'tested' somehow and therefore embarrassed, nervous, worried or self-conscious?
- Were any other thoughts playing on their minds?

So can we really take at face value the findings from headlines only, as shared by influencers or media who make claims about a study without providing the research? It's important that we think critically when we're presented with these sorts of claims, so that we can sift the facts from the theory and the theory from the fiction. This sort of critical thinking is a life skill we'll be looking at in more detail in Chapter 8, as it will help both you and your child navigate online spaces more safely.

## Other Developmental Milestones

Let's take a look at some other developmental milestones now and how tech may or may not affect them.

## Fine motor skills and body posture

As we've seen, observing an infant's fine motor skills forms part of a child-development assessment in the UK and involves those movements we learn when small in order to use our opposable thumbs, wrists and fingers for small and close-up actions. These are the skills of pinching, pulling and holding, among others. Babies develop by learning to grasp and hold smaller and smaller objects; in Chapter 7, we will discuss the effects that technology is having (or not) on these movements, such as children being able to type, swipe and move a mouse or cursor on devices.

It's also worth noting that the ways in which we sit or lean over our technology can impact how our bodies grow, especially when little ones are holding tablets or smartphones, which may weigh quite a bit. This is also true of VR and other head-worn technology. This can put strain on the body and in particular the spine, so we need to think about the movements (or lack thereof) in our children's postures when using technology like this. They need to be able to move about and exercise to develop a healthy posture and for their organs to work optimally. If they are moving when using head-worn technology, we need to be mindful about the potential effects on the body of wearing heavy equipment for prolonged periods. Here again we don't have the full data yet on all this, but these are things we need to think about.

## Hearing

Some robust findings over many years have found a causal link between loud noises, or loud music, earphones and deafness or hearing impairments, so an association between using technology in this way and hearing issues is not going to come as a surprise.

There is emerging research about the impact of closely worn, in-the-ear headphones such as the ear bud, which can emit radio waves and potentially affect the body with radiation or EMF.

This is contested due to the type of non-ionising radiation it produces, which has not yet been shown to cause damage to cells, and because there is a lack of long-term evidence, but it is still of interest to many.[16] Noise-cancelling headphones that silence outside noises are similarly raising questions about what our brains do with this absolute silence effect when making sense of the world; that is, when we are getting 'surround sound' from the device but not the corporeal world our bodies are in. It is not yet understood how this affects our brains.

## *Eyesight*

As far as the development of the eye in children is concerned – including its shape and function – what's known as the 'stabilisation of the prescription' does not occur until they reach their teens. This means that we need to think about the impact a screen might have on the eyes of growing children. Technically, it's the glare of the light that the screen emits and the distance between our children and the screen that we need to consider most.

Findings about the effects of blue light (a specific wavelength) associated with screens have been sensationalised for many reasons that have mostly turned out to be untrue, given the way our eyes work, as they don't filter out just one wavelength alone. However, screen glare looks blue – hence the hype around it (you will see more about this later in the book). It turns out that brightness matters more than the wavelength and, of course, the length of time spent facing this bright light. To help children develop healthy eyesight, we should encourage them to enjoy more natural light outside (which includes outside of classrooms, too) and to use a range of relaxed (divergent) far-away focusing, as well as doing close-up work, such as writing in books and using technology. Eyes develop slowly and issues that arise in childhood can become difficult to mitigate later in life, as you will see in Chapter 7.

## *Empathy and learning*

Worried parents often tell me they have concerns about their child not being kind or caring to others, especially when they hear older children playing online or see what they've said in messages or group chats. They worry that technology might be playing a role in this. An experiment comes to mind that suggests this isn't altogether true.

In the experiment, which took place in Israel in 2019, infants aged from five to nine months were asked to watch a 'story' about a circle and two shapes (a rectangle and square) on a TV[17,18]. (Note the use of a screen here!) The shapes interacted with each other on screen. In particular, the circle appeared to 'block' the rectangle from climbing a slope.

After watching this film, the children were given some shapes on a tray. Can you guess which shape they picked up? Yes – the 'bullied' rectangle! The researchers theorised that the children perceived the rectangle as being hurt or distressed and so picked it up, thus demonstrating empathy.

You may have seen your own small child display a range of emotions when watching an animation on a screen, or you may have come across videos on platforms like YouTube of children displaying specific emotions while watching cartoons or TV. In these cases the young child is connecting with the character or person on the screen and they are embodying their learned empathy and compassion you model and use with them, and applying this to understand the characters story. Technology isn't getting in the way of this process as children of this age seem to see past the screen and connect *with* the character.

My personal favourite is a clip from 2015 of a two-year-old girl who is crying while watching the film *The Good Dinosaur*.[19] She explains she's upset because the dinosaur is sad because he fell into the water. Even more extraordinarily, she goes on to reason that now he wants his mama, and she tells the character to 'Say

Mama!' to call her to him – implying that she understands both the story *and* what the dinosaur himself needs to feel better. Empathy is a skill of connection and cognitive compassion about what is needed to help – and this little girl demonstrated all of this when watching a cartoon character, thus showing that the development of empathy had clearly taken place with her parents and other family members in the real world in her infancy.

Everything we do affects our brains, for better or worse. However, as things stand, no one knows for sure how technology impacts our grey matter in isolation from anything else we may be doing. This degree of uncertainty may seem unsettling when it concerns the effects of tech on children, but there is still an important step that we can take to help limit the potential for harm: we can keep talking to our kids about what they're interacting with on screens and invite them to think about this and how it relates to the real world. For example, in the video clip I just mentioned of the little girl watching the dinosaur movie, her mum is sitting next to her and asking her about her reactions to the story: she's encouraging her daughter to verbalise her emotions and express her empathy, which will also help to develop her language skills. Context and communication are key; our children's brains are like amazing sponges, so let's make sure we're there to help them soak up all that's good and nourishing, both in there, online, and out here, in their activities and relationships in the real world.

## Summary

- The impact of technology on a child's brain will depend on the content the child engages with, how often they do so and how they perceive it. Most importantly, it also depends on who helps them make sense of it, and how.
- Rather than inevitably leading to problems with paying

attention, engaging with tech such as online games could help a child focus in ways that are beneficial.
- The research on technology's impact on language is still inconclusive, and our best course of action as parents is to carry on reading to our children and talking to them as much as possible.
- Wearing heavy head-worn devices could potentially affect a developing child's posture. They need be able to move about and exercise to develop a healthy posture and for their organs to work optimally.
- We know that loud noises can adversely affect hearing, but the current research is limited as to how technology such as noise-cancelling devices affects children.
- Staring for too long at bright screens can be detrimental. To counteract the effects of this, ensure your child spends time outdoors in natural light, where they can focus on objects in the distance.

## CHAPTER 5

# Love, Respect and Belonging – The Importance of Connection and Communication

Connection and communication have already come up numerous times in the book so far, but in this chapter we're going to really hone in on these ideas, and see how crucial they are when it comes to being in relationship with our children and tackling some of the more challenging aspects of tech use.

While I would always recommend doing research into the types of cybersecurity and parental controls that will work best for you and your child or children (see pp. 349–51), the most important tool you have at your disposal is your relationship with them. And although it might seem counterintuitive at first, you should show an interest in their life online so as to keep the lines of communication open between you and stay connected to them.

To this end, I recommend the CPR approach.

## The CPR Approach to Parenting

We will talk about contracts, agreements and boundaries in detail in Part 2, and the idea that, when you create them, you should ideally make them relevant to a particular time period (say, before/during/after holiday periods, when they turn a specific age or before getting a particular item of technology or game). But what this means is that you will need to adapt and renegotiate your contracts and agreements from time to time, based on any changes taking place. This calls for good communication and is one area where what I call CPR parenting becomes helpful:

- *Consistency*: this is about showing up consistently with the same attitude to parenting, which should, ideally, be child-focused; and it means being willing to listen to them and their opinions (although you don't have to agree with them).
- *Persistence*: this means sticking to that approach no matter what setting you find yourself in. Thinking ahead, you might sometimes feel like you're being judged by other parents for doing things differently to them, which can be difficult to cope with. But this approach is really important for building trust with your children. They need to know they can trust you to be predictable wherever you are, and whoever you're with, as this helps them feel like they matter, whatever the circumstances (and it's why teens, in particular, will push back at you, just to check).
- *Resistance*: this means not giving in to the 'pleeeaaasses' if you've made a rule that's in their best interest. You should explain the reasoning behind it, because there's nothing more difficult or frustrating for a child than a parent who says, 'Because I said so' without giving an explanation. This is not soft parenting and perhaps if they are dysregulated you can come back to this approach later, but do remember to communicate boundaries in this way.

Claire's story, below, demonstrates how CPR can form part of respectful and effective communication to achieve a balance that suits all family members.

> ### Claire's Story
>
> Thirteen-year-old Claire was given a smartphone 'contract' by her parents when she got her new phone for Christmas. She signed this diligently because she was keen to 'get to where [her] mates were' online.
>
> In the contract, her dad stipulated that the phone wasn't to be used at the dinner table, which proved a little difficult during the Christmas period while Claire was still learning the rules of spending time online with friends and teaching herself her new boundaries.
>
> Then, when she returned to school after the holidays and we took up our therapy sessions in January, Claire started to get upset that her older sibling and dad were both using *their* phones at the table at dinnertime. She felt it was unfair as they hadn't had to sign a 'contract', and she was trying to understand why Dad would say one thing and do another.
>
> In discussion with the family, we decided that Claire should be given a family contract that meant certain tech rules applied to all the family members and that she could hold her parents and siblings accountable (which she did on several occasions). This also helped all the family to share tech-free times together. However, there were some boundaries about Claire's use specifically, which she could abide by in the knowledge that there was fairness in the family. This resulted in much more harmony around the use of technology in the home.

## How to Approach Parental Controls with Your Child

Parental controls will often be a first line of defence in keeping your child safe when you're not available (for more on these see pp. 193–263). However, while you can use them to support your child's digital journey and learning and to ensure their safety, they shouldn't be used as digital 'can'ts' to simply block or restrict their access to the internet. Which, of course, they ultimately will do, *but*, if they are put in place without prior conversations with children or teens, from their perspective they can feel like a challenge, a punishment or a sign that you don't trust them.

Once again, it's important to keep engaging in conversations with kids about the world online, which includes discussions about the use of parental controls. This can help us adults get beyond that knee-jerk 'because I said so' and find out what's really going on in a situation from our child's perspective. It's a bit like saying, 'Drive safely' to an adult when they are about to set off on a journey. What we're saying in that instance is: 'I trust *your* driving, but maybe not other people's.'

So when you're thinking about installing and using controls, I would suggest that you say something to your child along these lines (adapting your language according to their age and stage, so they can fully understand what you're telling them):

> I trust you to try to navigate online spaces safely. However, there are people online who won't have your best interests at heart, so these controls are to prevent others from accessing you and your data or tricking you in any way. Some people online are cybercriminals or cyberbullies, and there might be content that's inappropriate for you to see, so this will help us to lower the risk of that happening.
>
> As we use the internet together and we learn, then maybe some of these controls can be changed to match your skills and because you're growing up. They won't always be in place but, for now, sometimes I can't be there to protect you, so this will be like an electronic version of me [the adult] keeping you safe.

I'll be returning again and again in this book to the issue of trust around the choices we make in order to protect our children. An intrusive parenting style can lead to a lack of trust, and then rebellion, giving perpetrators of crimes against children ways to exploit them. That's why my mantra is:

*Check* In *With, and Not* On, *Your Child.*

Checking in with someone is a bit like someone saying to you, 'Hey, how are you?' And then they really listen to your answer and give you their time. It can feel like they truly care about you – and you know this, because they just didn't ask in passing how your day was. It's a bit like the difference between stopping for a proper chat or going for a coffee versus just shouting, 'Hi' to someone when you see them in the street. It feels really good to be heard (like being safe, seen, soothed and secure – those 4Ss again).

Conversely, 'checking on' can feel like someone is trying to catch you out, as if they think you're untrustworthy. It's a bit like them creeping up on you and asking, 'What are you doing?!!!' (Yes, with three exclamation marks!). It's like a game of 'gotcha' and you might feel they're out to get you. This does not feel good.

When you check in with your child, you're trying to let them know you care, and not trying to trick them or catch them out – because children who experience the latter learn to be secretive so that they won't get caught. You really want to encourage an open dialogue with them, no matter their age. (I'll talk more about how to do this in Part 2, and you'll also find some useful books in the Resources, pp. 347–9.)

I know that getting the balance is tricky and at times fraught, when our natural desire to protect our kids risks turning into overprotection – which is a difficult enough aspect of parenting to begin with, without having to take digital technology into consideration. When it comes to keeping our kids safe, perhaps we can start thinking of ourselves in terms of being their guardians and gatekeepers. This means that, instead of imposing inflexible rules on them, we talk to them about the reasons for putting in place age-appropriate controls and boundaries, and we're prepared to revisit these as and when circumstances allow.

## *TV PINs, Channels, Streaming Sites and Apps*

As well as your children's own devices, do think about any shared spaces in your home that have a smart TV in them, so that, if necessary, you can restrict your child's access to channels that might show inappropriate material.

In days gone by, when satellite TV was the latest thing, there were locked TV channels and some that only began broadcasting after a set time, like 7 or 9pm. However, watersheds are pretty much a thing of the past now that we have access to live TV, recorded programmes and the ever-increasing numbers of streaming apps available on the TV in the living room. That's why I'd suggest that access to channels like Prime, Netflix, Disney, YouTube and other apps like Spotify should be locked by a PIN and that your children should *have their own accounts* for these, which you can set up and control.

Lock all the channels that you don't want your child to access and keep your PIN private when using the remote control. Remember that little eagle eyes will soon discover where you're placing your fingers on the control buttons. Also, keep an eye out for anyone watching an inappropriate show or channel when little ones are around, as they do take notice of what's on the TV.

You can block access to platforms like X (formerly known as Twitter) or other social media accounts in your home using parental software on routers, your internet provider and on specific devices and apps. However, posts on X and other sites can be still shared on other websites, search engines and in messenger apps. You can buy phones and devices that prevent access

## LOVE, RESPECT AND BELONGING

to this material and associated apps, but be aware that children will be able to access the material on other devices and in other homes, so you may need to have conversations with other parents and households about *their* use of parental controls, gaming and accessing online content. Unsupervised access and lacking parental controls on systems at other houses, sadly, is one of the most cited reasons in my clinic for children seeing inappropriate content (for example, at their grandparents' or friends' homes), so it's well worth thinking about how you can protect your child when they are with other people by talking to the adults in those spaces. And have more conversations with your child about this issue and what they can do, too.

Here's an example of the sort of approach to take with other parents/family members:

> I wanted to ask you about your technology rules for when Emily comes round to yours on X day/time. At home [insert your rules here – maybe: we don't allow devices in the bedroom or access past 9pm, to enable her to have a great sleep for her brain health, and we have restrictions about the kind of content she is allowed to engage with]. Can I ask what your rules are, please, so we can make decisions together about technology and access to it, in her best interests and to keep her safe online?

The reply will enable you to decide about your child visiting their homes. I deliberately use the word 'content' to open up dialogue, as each family will view content within their own frame of reference. And you have a right to say no to your child going to the home in question if you feel the rules there would expose them to harm (in the same way that you would protect a child from a home where there are weapons, drugs or sexual content). You are the parent; you decide.

We live in an age where parents can – and need to – protect children at other locations where access is available to technology. We must now make this a feature of our everyday conversations, for the welfare of our children and any others we may be looking after. And, of course, we must include our children in our decision-making, too. For example, if you're happy for your child to visit another household, you might have a conversation with them along the following lines:

> I spoke to your friend's parents about technology use in their home and I've decided that to keep you safe [insert whatever safety measures are now being put in place]. Because of this you can go, but we should have a conversation about how you can tell me if these rules change or are broken in any way, or if you feel at all uncomfortable. Perhaps we could have a phrase or emoticon on a text/message so you can let me know you are uncomfortable and would like to be picked up?

On the other hand, if after speaking to the other party you are unhappy about the tech rules that are in place, you might have this sort of conversation with your child:

> I spoke to your friend's parents about technology use in their home and I've decided that to keep you safe on this occasion you will not be going. This isn't because I want to spoil your fun, or I don't trust you, but because their house has different technology rules that might put you at risk of seeing something that we don't agree about. This is a decision by the grown-ups and because I love you and want to keep you safe.

This may be met with a dysregulated response by your child – so in comes the CPR parenting!

## Additional Software and Devices

There are other safety solutions on the market that you can buy, including phones or systems that can enable you to see your child's messages, gaming chats and where they navigate online. However, if these devices and systems aren't explained to children or they are used in a way that's inappropriate for their age and stage, my experience is that they can be viewed by them as a form of 'spying' that shows a lack of trust. As it happens, these systems are part of what are often referred to as monitoring software, called spyware apps by young people (the meaning has evolved from the initial definition of the term 'spyware' in cybersecurity).

Some of these systems can also help you keep track of your child's device and, therefore (you hope), where they are, through geolocation services. Again, these can sometimes be used like spying software and children may or may not feel reassured by them. They may also feel they get no privacy because of them. While knowing where your child is at all times of the day may reassure *you*, it might be perceived very differently by your child, depending on their age. (I've worked with adults who've spied on their partners using this kind of software, so it's an issue for many grown-ups, too. We can also experience what I call 'blue-tick distress', when apps show others when we're online, which can feel intrusive to some people.)[1] Is it a good thing that today we can always know where our children are? Perhaps, like me, you grew up at a time when you could wander off to play and when you got home your parents would greet you with the words, 'Where have you *been*?' It's almost inconceivable today that our parents genuinely didn't know where we were, when, thanks to technology, we can know our children's every move (unless they're using a dumbphone that doesn't track their location).

You must make your own decisions around the use of these types of devices and software with your family. If you do use them, I'd strongly encourage you to include your child in the decision-making, implementation and reasoning behind your choices at some point in the process. Children and teens don't like being presented with these sorts of measures as a foregone conclusion, whereas, if they feel included in the thinking or in a conversation about them, this can help them to feel seen and part of your world – and you will still get to use the devices and software in question if this is how you want to parent in a world of technology.

I have included in the Resources (see p. 347) information about safety and online safety organisations you can visit for information about guidelines for you and your family. This will help you to keep up to date with emerging risks and known issues, and it'll also support you in realising you're not alone in this parenting world.

### *A Note on Children with Social, Emotional or Educational Needs, Neurodiversity and/or Trauma*

Children with these difficulties or labels often have a riskier profile in terms of keeping themselves safe online, and the use of parental controls, monitoring software and daily conversations about life online is often more of a necessity when parenting them than an option. Vigilance over their activities is a priority, both through your own watchful gaze and through the protection that software can provide when you're not around, not least because children and teens with these difficulties or issues may be at higher risk of criminal behaviours because of either what they do or what's done to them in the online and gaming worlds.

Having a discussion with your child will require adapting your language to meet them in a way that empowers them to be safe online if you aren't watching every keystroke or listening to every conversation they have. For example, if you wish to have a conversation with them about the types of dangerous individuals known by cybersecurity or online safety professionals as 'bad actors online', you may want to substitute this phrase with something like 'bad people', 'tricky people', 'liars', 'cheaters or criminals who might disguise themselves as friends' or 'hackers'. (As I mentioned earlier, 'hacker' can mean a cheater, as well as someone breaking into computers or profiles.) Ask your child how they would spot one of these people and help them to understand that it can be very difficult for lots of us to do so. Ask them how they find out about the rules of the games (they might be called 'terms of play') and why people might say things or behave in the way they do online. Then explain why you think that monitoring software can help them stay safe.

Again, as in the examples of conversations given earlier, explaining that your actions and concerns are about others online and not necessarily about your child's ability to stay safe can help them to feel you trust them. This, in turn, creates a space for communication between you and increases the likelihood that they will trust you with their experiences and the issues they face.

Many children in my clinic tell me they're good at spotting online cheaters, liars and criminals when in practice they are not. If your child is particularly vulnerable, you may want to radically restrict their access to certain platforms or content. To do this, use the parental controls available from your internet service provider and follow the safety advice that is available online. Helplines and websites for this are listed on p. 349.

## Exploitation, Consent and Sexual Material Online

I'm aware that this section may make for uncomfortable reading, especially if your faith or beliefs go against any of the talking points that I'm going to be suggesting. But remember, this book is just a guide, and you absolutely do not have to go along with everything that I suggest.

I know talking to your child about this subject might be uncomfortable or awkward, so this section is here to provide you with an approach which says to your child, 'If I, the parent, can talk about this, then you, the child, can talk to me about it too'. This models to your child that you are open to talking about sex and other content that your child may happen upon, so they can see, feel and know that you can handle what they bring to you. We have to demonstrate our openness and this section can help you do just that.

What follows is a generic conversation about an everyday movie that you can tailor to suit yourself and your child when initiating conversations about pornography. Some of it is more likely to apply to teens but not necessarily exclusively so. You can also adapt the questions to any movie or actor, and to discussions on how we get agreements from people in the real world to be filmed in places like streets or parks, such as YouTube interviews or citizen journalism by people with smartphones.

Always follow your child's level of comfort; *don't keep going with the questions if it's clear that they are unhappy or not engaging with you*. You can stop this discussion at any point and resume it another time.

- I'm wondering, how long do you think it takes to make a James Bond movie? What do you think is involved in it? [This is a question about the production, actors, locations and so on . . .]
- I'm wondering, what do you think about the 'romance scenes'? Do you think actors are happy to do them? Do you reckon they would get completely naked for more money? [And/or, if appropriate for your child's age and

stage:] Is it necessary for scenes to depict them naked or having sex? Do people want to watch that, really?
- So what are your thoughts on people filming themselves being naked, kissing or having sex? [Again, adapt this to suit your child's age and stage and level of comfort.]
- [Only continue if your child is engaging and comfortable:] What about uploading it for others to watch? Or maybe being filmed for others to watch? Do you think they get paid or are acting for free? Do they even know about being filmed?

Go slow with these questions; you don't have to ask them all in one go. Your child may well ask why you're 'being all weird' or 'obsessed' about sex. This is a common deflection, meaning 'I'm uncomfortable'. And you can reflect that you notice their discomfort and stop for today. This gives you a further conversation for another time (if you wish) about how some people in pornography scenes can feel uncomfortable, too; also, whether they think it's ok to carry on with sexual activity when they feel this way.

Only if conversation is flowing, additional questions can include:

- Do you think that the people in these videos will: regret it /are ashamed of their bodies/diet/take drugs/would tell their family/could be (or were) blackmailed/agreed to this/or were hurt?
- Do you think most people your age (or older or younger) watch these kinds of videos and why? What do you think the impact is on them?

By asking these questions, you're having a conversation about children in general and keeping it about your child's opinions, not your own, to avoid them feeling judged or shamed. When you can comfortably discuss this sort of topic with them, you can encourage further conversations, such as: 'I know young people of your age can sometimes send these videos to each other, or even watch them alone, and I thought we could talk about the legal side of this.' (In the UK it is illegal to view or share porn under the age of 18.) Or you could ask whether, if they saw something they thought was wrong or illegal in these videos, they would tell you or another trusted adult. Being a tech-smart parent in this context means understanding that we may not always be the ones our teens want to talk to and that there may be another relative or family friend who they would feel less embarrassed speaking to.

## Respectful Relationships Online and in the Real World

I have heard it claimed (online, in the mainstream media, at conferences and in conversation) that children and teens are changing how they relate to each other (both in their friendships and romantically) because of technology. The argument is that they have little contact with the real world, due to either looking at screens all the time or because of ear buds blocking out the passing conversations around them.

There are also claims that children today (teens in particular) have little empathy for each other (see Chapter 4 for more on this) and that they can fall out over the slightest thing. This can be because of a 'funny' post that isn't so funny, or racism or sexism, or even the fact that they can be silenced or silence each other with their ability to block and mute. This can go even further, with whole groups of people silencing or 'cancelling' each other.

Cancel culture and other such extremes are often fuelled by misleading information, which is why teaching children and teens about critical thinking becomes a high priority for us as their parents and guardians who want to protect them. Violence and the weaponisation of words have become synonymous with the narratives of the far left and far right and, in my view, the violence that feeds these sorts of extremes is in dire need of quenching with compassion and tolerance.

We can breathe a little sigh of relief here because *we* can most certainly have age-appropriate conversations with our children and teens about kindness, and about not blackmailing or coercing people; we can have conversations about patience, compassion and empathy, and what it's like to listen to someone and to be listened to – and we can demonstrate this by doing it ourselves *with* them. We can teach them the importance of showing respect for both themselves and others by showing them respect, too. Because if we show respect to our children, they will invariably learn what respect feels like; they will begin to develop trust in us, and it's often then that they will come and speak to us about things that bother them (though not always). When they can really see how respect and compassion are done, this will hopefully translate into the real world, as well as online. If this is what we're aiming for, we stand a chance of achieving it if we behave with them as we want them to behave with others – and with us.

### Cassie's Story

Cassie was seventeen and had been questioning their gender when they arrived at my clinic. They came to me for overwhelming anxiety, which they said was because of 'the stuff' they were 'interacting with' online. They had been sent images and news articles in messages from their online group of friends, and they constantly used chat-forum-type social media spaces to share information about surgery to enhance their 'queerness'.

In doing this, Cassie found that they were becoming increasingly confused about their gender, because the more they used these apps the more they were being sent radical opinions and views about the rhetoric of 'not being queer enough'. They told

> me they didn't know if they believed they were queer or if they needed to use another label to determine who they were.
>
> Cassie would often end up in tears because they were now seeing hateful posts about their queer friends from others who 'didn't believe in queers' and they were frightened to say anything online to defend the queer friends in case they received the 'onslaught of the mob'. Cassie didn't have any adults with whom to speak about this issue as they thought 'everyone hates queers', telling me, 'My dad is one of them.'
>
> Cassie and I worked on using social media in an intentional fashion to reset the algorithms (we'll talk more about these in Chapter 6); we discussed the options to report, block and mute specific accounts and to report incidents when their friends were being attacked online.
>
> This topic was sensitive but I wondered whether, if Cassie's father had been a tech-smart parent, he could have helped them see this was about conflicting information, cyberbullying and hate speech, as well as about the issue of gender.

With a more tech-smart, open-door approach to discussions, our children will be more likely to come to us with complicated problems such as Cassie's – problems they need us, as the adults in their lives, to think about with them and to support them with.

## Understanding Attachment

Love, belonging and respect are born out of a child's 'good-enough' attachment in infancy with their primary caregiver, as the pioneering psychoanalyst Donald Winnicott would say. Another prominent psychoanalyst, John Bowlby, proposed that there are good things that should happen in our early development, like our needs being met in a timely and sufficient manner; and then there are those things that shouldn't happen, such as abuse and neglect. I would add that another thing that shouldn't occur is the disrespect of a child's feelings by the adults around them, as their feelings matter to them.

The good-enough attachment begins in infancy and is reinforced throughout a child's life, meaning that as parents we can keep adding to it at each age and stage of their development, with what I have heard called 'sprinkles and glimmers of gold', through our warm, empathic and child-focused parenting behaviours. We can apologise for our behaviours when these are out of sync or dysregulated, and we can mop up shame wherever we can. This, in practice, doesn't mean we are 'soft' or excessively liberal parents caving in to our child's every request or whim; but it's also not wielding the hard, iron rod of power-based parenting seen in authoritarian approaches. We have authority and compassion and we make the effort to connect with our child's experience, because they aren't yet an adult with the full range of emotional-regulation tools at their disposal. Until, one day, they are.

Years of research and many books (see Resources, p. 347) about childhood, parenting and relationships have highlighted that if we, or our children, don't feel part of a decision-making process and feel powerless instead, this can block trust. This is why communicating effectively with your child is so important: your child has to know that when you make a decision about them (and about their tech use, for the purposes of this book) it's because you're acting in their best interest. Through approachable and compassionate tech-smart parenting and age-appropriate conversations, you can give them a great start to being online (and in real life) with people, while staying as safe as can be. This, in turn, will foster a deep connection, mutual respect and the best possible relationship with them.

And to strengthen that relationship you can begin by modelling the behaviours you want your child to adopt, including communicating with others lovingly and respectfully. The CPR parenting approach can be a great help with this, opening the way for difficult conversations about topics such as sexuality and respectful interactions with others that will help to protect your child while reassuring them that they have been heard and respected, too, so that they will be less likely to rebel in ways that may put them at risk.

## Summary

- To open the way to healthy communication with your child, adopt the CPR parenting approach: consistency, persistence, resistance.
- Involve your child in the decision-making and reasoning behind the use of age-appropriate parental controls.
- Encourage open dialogue with your child to make sure that they feel heard, valued and understood.
- With a tech-smart, open-door approach to discussions, your child will be more likely to come to you with complicated problems, rather than resorting to secretive behaviours that could make them more vulnerable.
- If parenting a child with vulnerabilities, parental controls are more likely to be a necessity than an option, but do still talk to them about your reasons for using them.

CHAPTER 6

# What Are the Risks That Children Face Online?

Some of you reading this may be millennial and Gen Z parents with direct experience of the sorts of issues that children can potentially face in, on and through technology, because you experienced versions of these yourself when you were younger. There will be those of you who watched early internet 360P videos, and who know of certain chat forums and memes and what it's like to be online with creeps and weirdos – yet it's only in the last couple of years that people have started to say technology 'ruins childhood'. Perhaps this is because adults were previously unaware of what happened online, so kids back then were left to explore the digital park without any of the safeguards that can be used today. And it may be true that technology did adversely affect children to some degree, because an entire generation of technology users (which could include your own parents) went fast and hard on using it without ever questioning what, why, how or where problems might arise or what harms their kids may have faced – until events such as the Covid-19 lockdowns highlighted the problems in ways that could no longer be ignored.

Today, we're much more aware of the risks and know that people can behave in shocking ways online, yet the onus to sort out these problems is often placed on concerned young parents or those who are catching up as older parents and grandparents, albeit with precious little support or guidance on how to do this. Amidst all the conflicting arguments and advice, it can be difficult to know what steps to take; for example, when the dialogue in the mainstream media says that you mustn't give children technology before the ages of, say, ten, twelve, fourteen or sixteen, you'll likely feel obliged to 'follow the rules' – because you think that *surely* the political and global experts are offering these recommendations based on hard evidence, when that isn't always the case. Similarly, the blanket advice is often to keep children away from smartphones and social media (yet for some reason not the internet and gaming spaces), rather than telling you how to raise your child in a world that is already a faster, AI-driven space. As we'll see, smartphone use is only one of a whole set of things you need to consider – which is why I'm here to help you understand the real situation online and how to navigate the potential risks safely with your child.

And of course, as we know, there are dangers out there. When children and teens access online spaces they enter a global community, where they can encounter all sorts of people and material; some of this will educate and entertain them, but some may be deeply upsetting or even traumatic. As a long-term clinician in this area, I really want to emphasise here that this is the biggest concern I have about our children's welfare, and to separate it from the general debate about the impact of technology and screens on mental health. This issue is about safeguarding – keeping our children safe from predators and material that isn't suitable for them. Because like the dangers that we warn our children about in the real world (remember the city park?), sometimes things can go tragically wrong. This is why it's important to understand what the real risks are, so that we can speak to our children about them in age-appropriate and informed ways – and they can be confident that we really do know what we're talking about.

WHAT ARE THE RISKS THAT CHILDREN FACE ONLINE?

## Just Who is Your Child Communicating With Online?

By its very nature, the internet is a space of interaction and connection. And the major and most worrying problem around safeguarding kids online concerns the individuals they can encounter there and what they share with them. While kids may 'meet' some individuals who will want to befriend and support them, others may wish them harm. We can't necessarily see the criminals online, so we tend to lean into the TV and film stereotypes of such people (perhaps wearing hoodies, while hanging out in basements). However, to follow a glib meme, anyone can be a dog on the internet (who would know?), and now, with the additional challenge of AI programs that allow for fake identities through face and voice manipulation, this means that anyone *can* literally be anyone else in digital mediums.

Children won't always tell us if they've been contacted by anyone or shared intimate images with them (whether their peers, adults or even bots), so exact statistics aren't available. However, the figures that have been gathered by services and websites who deal with issues such as child sexual abuse suggest this is a key area of concern. In the US in 2024, the National Center for Missing & Exploited Children (NCMEC) and law-enforcement agencies estimated that the numbers of reported intimate images of children and child abuse peaked at around 100 million (a figure that seems impossible to compute, I know).

If we wish to keep kids safe online, a priority has to be to protect them from coercion by bad actors, who could be grown adults (including people we may know), older children or even children of a similar age, or individuals pretending to be any of these who might be using programs or AI to change their identity.

When bad actors contact children of any age, they often ask

them to take and send, record or forward images of their bodies (which can begin as innocent images of them in clothes, or of body parts like feet), or they ask them to turn their cameras on while they take screengrabs of them, which means the child isn't even aware that they've shared an image.

In a world of AI that can manipulate imagery, including completely innocent photographs, *we* need to keep this in mind whenever we share images or video of our children online, too. Even images of fully clothed children can be used in nefarious ways, using AI that 'undresses' them. Bad actors are only interested in getting these kinds of images, then finding ways to get more of them, usually through a form of blackmail called sextortion. The case study below will help you to understand this issue and think about the sorts of conversations you should have as part of your tech-smart parenting.

### *Evie's Story*

During one of our sessions together, fourteen-year-old Evie mentioned that her hands were 'cute'. She showed me pictures of her hands and her friends to show me the 'non-cute' and 'manly' ones. I asked about taking hand pictures and what this meant for her. Evie went on to explain that she had also taken pictures of her feet, shoulders and knees and sent them to other children her age.

When I enquired further, Evie added that she'd also sold pictures of her feet to a 'randomer' (an unknown person) for £50. We discussed this and whether Evie was aware of the intention behind a requirement for these pictures (yes, people want images of feet). She told me she was happy to send images that weren't intimate and to be paid for them, as the 'kids in school do it like on the OnlyFans website'.

> Luckily, on this occasion the images of her feet were not used to blackmail Evie for more intimate ones with threats to share them with others, but I've worked with children in the last decade who have been sextorted (see Kendra's story, p. 249). Evie and I talked about why it wasn't a good idea to share images of herself – especially not with strangers – as even a photo of something as seemingly innocuous as her feet could potentially give someone a means to hurt her by blackmailing her.

Once images have been sent, they are stored, shared or 'collected' by bad actors for several purposes, including sexual gratification and monetary gain (blackmail/selling and trading the images). This can also lead to them asking for more images and often for more explicit ones, as a relationship builds between them and the child or teen. They may also share the child's details with other bad actors, or blackmail them for money or to recruit more children (where the first children contacted invite their friends to also send images). Sextortion has been a growing issue in recent years and one that has tragically resulted in children's deaths, with an increasing number of boys becoming suicidal because of it. Again, I'd like to emphasise that *while this is a real concern, it's a potential and not a guaranteed outcome.*

So yes, disturbingly, people like this do exist; and no, they are not always men, even though research in Australia in 2023 (that looked at UK/US/AUS) shows that most perpetrators of this sort of crime are white males (and often in well-paid jobs and with families of their own).[1] They may even be people you know, like and trust in real life. I've come to call these individuals the ogres in the screen because of how they operate and the fact that we often don't know who they are, until (or unless) they are caught. Below is a story I use in training to explain about these ogres – you can adapt and use it with your children in an age-appropriate way.

### *Beware the Ogre in the Screen*

Stories like this one often impart important information about characters we ought to be aware of – such as the big, bad wolf, the witches and the ogres. Are you sitting comfortably? Then let's begin . . .

Once upon a time, a very tired and busy woman wanted just a few minutes' peace so she could sort out her household bills. As she was counting up her beans, she let her youngest son, a curious little boy called Oscar, play quietly in his room. While he was there, his attention was caught by a strange picture on the wall. He gazed into it. It was a magical mirror.

When he looked into the mirror, Oscar realised he could see marvellous things – a whole other world. There were lots of smiling people and wondrous sights. Then, out of the blue, a friendly voice spoke. The owner of the voice said his name was Victor and invited Oscar to play a game. Oscar liked games and he liked the sound of Victor, so he did as he was asked. And Victor promised him gold.

But the rules started to change, becoming stranger and stranger. Victor became more demanding and more threatening. He told Oscar not to say anything to anyone about the game or the worst would happen. Oscar was frightened. He didn't know what to do. Just then, his mother came into the room, screamed and turned the mirror to face the wall. For Oscar had been talking to an ogre. And ogres can hurt children.

In the real world, there are ogres online similar to Victor. They are the bad actors – people who might want sexual images of children and who will entice them and promise magical rewards for 'small favours' collected in secret. And these ogres are in the spaces you trust. They're there in those small screens. Those places inside the screen where your children do their schoolwork. The place where they should be safe – your home, their bedroom, the bathroom.

These ogres are real and, yes, I know this is scary. Some will tell you what the ogres look like and how to spot them. But they can change their appearance. They can even be other children. And ogres lie. They say they're friends, but they're not. They're anything but.

So you and your child need to help each other detect the ogres in real life. You must chat about them and discuss how to stay safe from them. These monsters hide in plain sight in screens and they really hate parents talking to their children about safety, trust, digital citizenship (socialising online), e-safety and what or who a friend online really is. But, most of all, they hate that they can only entice your child if they are unsupervised – so they bank on you being too busy to notice.

If you speak to your child and don't allow unsupervised access to devices with cameras in the bedrooms and bathrooms, there is less chance that an ogre will ever ensnare them. (For an example of how to discuss this with a younger child, see my story about Freya in Chapter 8.)

---

It can be so frightening to think about how what we do in all innocence online can be misused and abused by bad actors (ogres), and how this has become more prevalent in the last few years. But – and you might want to take a moment to prepare for what I'm going to say next – we must be aware, too, that there may be some bad actors on the internet and social media who we already know or consider to be friends. Sadly, we may never really, truly know anyone's true intentions, so the advice I offer is to keep what is on your phone to yourself and your family.

Be aware that, if you upload images to sites that you trust (like social media, where you have a list of friends and family), these images can be copied by the people who can see them. It can be worrying to think that, in these spaces, offenders against children may often be known to you such as members of the family or your friends. This can be a horrific thing to come to terms with, but these individuals can often come across as genuine and likeable, and have gone to considerable effort to befriend you and your child, or they could be someone who you added to your friends list many years ago but have never interacted with online since. Sometimes, they may even be a family member.

This is why we need to think carefully about where we place our trust in posting our children's images online within our circle of friends and family.[2] One failsafe suggestion is, if you have any doubts at all, don't post images of your child that can be screen-grabbed or copied. Instead, keep them in a file or on a device that you can show to people in person when they visit your house.

Another piece of advice is to ask your child before you post their images in family chats or on social media, and talk to them about them posting their own images. Be aware that you may not notice signs of bad actors online or even know them; however, trust your gut in those instances where you feel you might not want that social media friend down the street seeing an image of your child. Talk to your child about what to do if you find an image has been used for nefarious purposes, and see p. 248 for information on what you can do if so.

## Violence Online

Scary, violent and distressing material has been around on screen for quite some time. In fact, it's been part of our Western culture since at least the 1950s, when it started to be broadcast on the TV news or in documentaries. This type of material used to be broadcast after a watershed on TV to prevent younger children from seeing it, but the situation has changed since then. While images of violence still feature in newspapers, magazines and TV shows, documentaries and films in the cinema and on video, and we have regulatory systems in place for most of these media, in the online world we lack this sort of regulation globally. We've put in protections for children in some of these spaces, but not all.

Parents and researchers have been saying for a long time that we don't want children to see any form of violence until they're old enough to cope with it. This is why there are film and video classifications in place. The problem is that those classifications don't exist on many online platforms. This means that children can be readily exposed to violence on streaming services, YouTube and anywhere else that videos can be shared, like social media.

If safeguards like parental controls (see Chapter 9) aren't in place, children can see the equivalent of an 18-rated movie at the drop of a hat, as digital platforms don't prevent this in the way that terrestrial TV used to do with watersheds, or the cinema does with age-gated screenings. In fact, sometimes the children's versions of platforms, like YouTube Kids, allow cartoon violence or violence in other forms to slip through their filters, appearing further on in some videos (for example, a video might play in its original format – seeming at first to be a normal episode of *Peppa Pig*, say – but then change to different content later on). Once reported, it can be removed, but the viewing has already taken place at this point. Children can also be exposed to it by viewing the content on other children's devices, outside of the family home, or on other accounts or devices owned by adults. (I'll be discussing this in more detail later on, too.) I've worked with a number of parents who've been devastated to discover that their child has viewed violence online, especially if it's featured death or severe injury. Children can be profoundly affected by this sort of content, and experience cybertrauma, even if they say they aren't bothered by it.

Sadly, there was a major sharing of material (mostly on X) during October 2023 that I will call 'war gore', showing the massacre that took place in Israel, and images of this continue to emerge on some platforms. I've worked with children who've seen this material and I've encountered it myself. Images of the conflict in Ukraine have also surfaced online, shared on social media platforms that children use. Statutory services like Prevent exist in the UK because content relating to radicalisation and terrorist material also exists online, as well as sites that show torture, and these can overlap with war-gore areas, too. Parents naturally want to protect their children from seeing this sort of material, which is all too readily available and accessible online.

Sadly, there's not enough global regulation to prevent our children seeing this content (just yet). Moreover, we don't know the full extent of it, as there are so many hidden spaces where it can be shared, such as through Snapchat and accounts on end-to-end-encrypted (E2EE) systems such as WhatsApp, Telegram and other message apps, where content is concealed from anyone other than the users viewing it. This means that researchers, regulators and often even law-enforcement agencies cannot see this material, unless it's shown to them directly (or through recorded images like screengrabs). We know it happens, but we don't know to what degree.

Which is where *you* come in. Given the likelihood that children *will see* school fights, riots, murder scenes, shootings, massacres and/or war footage online either on social media or on news channels (which can also be shared on social media), we need to consider both the before and after of exposure to this world of pain and hurt. We need to have those important conversations with our children; we need a space where children can tell us the things they see; and, on a larger scale, we need a system that allows them to report it to the big-tech channels and for the big tech to actively do something about it (and to let children know clearly what they've done when they have done it). We also need to know which channels have this material and what their 'community standards' are and how children can understand these 'rules', and where they can seek help. For example, I have seen content of this nature shared on X (formally known as Twitter) and, although X states that its platform is 'primarily not for children' and has safeguarding rules and policies in place for minors, in my experience, despite those rules, children can access violent, graphic, gory and sexual content.

## *How to Approach Violence Online*

We live in turbulent times, and it can feel hugely upsetting that we can't protect our children from exposure to all the violence that's out there. However, we can show them that we are aware, that we care and that we're there to protect them and shield them from fear, harm and distress wherever possible. It's also worth mentioning that even when you think they're not listening to you (when you're chatting in the real world), chances are that they will be.

For example, if you mention in conversation the name of a social media platform or an event taking place (perhaps a viral video of the 'world cup fight'), that may pique your child's interest such that they head off to search for or access it. Children I work with who are as young as seven or eight do exactly this: they hear something their parents say or something that's mentioned on the radio and then go and search for it online. Sadly, one child searched for images of the abuse of a cat by a footballer, as the incident had been mentioned on a children's TV programme (*Newsround*), which resulted in them seeing a video of a cat being kicked.

Another example of this was the 'Momo Challenge', in which it was reported to parents by letter, email and social media posts that children were being harassed online to perform scary tasks and see a frightening face. The parents reported the hoax to other parents (via phone calls, chatting in the playground and in Facebook groups) and it sparked a global panic, leading to even larger numbers of children engaging with the trend online: the more they heard about it, the more they sought out the content, and shared anything relating to it. It's a bit like algorithms – in fact, I called this effect the human algorithm in a blog about this topic. We must be aware of what we say and do around children when it comes to online issues, and make sure that we're properly informed about them in the first place (in case they are myths, like the Momo Challenge). Kids are always listening!

This can feel like a double-edged sword: while I'm advising you to talk to your children about online issues, I'm also saying you should be careful about which issues you bring up for discussion. This is about the skill of communicating information in an age- and stage-appropriate way. So you might ask a younger child, 'I wonder what you think about people sharing stories online that have people getting hurt in them, and what you might do if you saw or heard about one?' This sort of approach is generic enough to address violence without telling them it relates to a video of a particular event. You can then have conversations with them about violent online content and explain that they'll likely see differences of opinion about this, and that some people might even see it as funny. This can also act as a starting point for discussing 'why people argue online'. You might say, for example, 'Why do you think some people are mean to others on social media? And why online and not in person?' Or, 'What do you think about clips that people share of upsetting material, like war or violence? Why would they do that? Who else can see and what might other people do or say?'

Explain the platform(s) to your child and talk about it. As many of the books listed on pp. 347–9 suggest, open dialogue with your child helps them develop trust in you, critical thinking (see p. 217) and the ability to bring problems to you. I'd also suggest that this tech-smart approach is helpful (and hopeful) in the long run because of the connection that you and your child build through using technology *together*.

## We All Make Mistakes: My Story

The truth is that what we don't know or understand, we can't protect against. And I'm no different, which is why I want to share a story from my own children's online lives when they were still very young. Now bear in mind I'm a tech-savvy parent, and my kids had already been introduced to the use of computers, email, message apps and critical thinking about the social networks that they used at the time, the games they played. We spoke about people online and the utter rubbish that existed there, and we visited websites together to discuss their content. And, as part of my work, I watched the evolution of the main social networks and had a job in schools as a sex and relationships educator. I worked with nine- to eighteen-year-olds and discussed with them how they used the internet.

All the same, I was unwittingly out of the loop about what my own children were up to until after the event, which still returns to haunt them all these years later. And, I repeat: I was the tech-savvy parent.

The fact is that my children witnessed some very disturbing material (involving a graphic murder) when they were around eleven and twelve years old. They viewed it on flip phones, no less, with peers also accessing it through a direct URL that had been shared with them in text messages and MSN message apps, taking them straight to a certain website.

I later discovered that the same website was visited by kids at numerous social clubs outside of school as well as in it, and I can also tell you that this video was witnessed by an enormous number of children in several secondary schools in the county where I was teaching, who used it as a 'character-building-' and 'coming-of-age-' type ritual in order to belong to their peer group. Years 7 to 11 shared what they had seen in the lessons where we discussed it, with responses like 'it was sick', 'I vomited', 'I can't get the video out of my head' and 'I couldn't stop looking'. Very few of them said, 'I won't watch it'.

Was I upset that my children had seen this? Yes, I was devastated that they'd been exposed to this material as a 'laugh' or a rite of passage through which to become one of the gang. But as I look back, I can see that no matter what I did as a parent in my own home, and on my own or my kids' devices, I could never have hoped to stop the use of technology *in other people's houses*, as I trusted the parents and made assumptions about their knowledge without discussing it with them. And this is the first 'ping' of a penny-drop moment that I hope you'll have, too. Let my failing be your saving grace.

Just as we don't generally have conversations with other parents and family members about their household technology rules, or what protection is in place, we tend to make assumptions that schools protect their own devices through the IT team. (Today, most schools in England are being trained in filtering and monitoring software by a great company called South West Grid for Learning, who really understand how tech is used in schools and can help professionals keep children safer online too.)

Was I aware that this material was being shared by children – I repeat: children – in the school yard and via messaging apps? No, not until after it had occurred. So how did I know about this? Because my children discussed it with me and we talked about the material, about the nature of human beings, about life and death, and why other children might show this material and the function of doing so.

And I continue to this day to have conversations about this material with adults, most of whom are now aged around thirty, who saw it as children, and tell me the websites are still in existence. So please be aware the internet is a place of historic videos as well as newer emerging ones and websites still exist with older graphic material too.

Did we fail that generation of children? Yes, I believe we did, given the number of adults I speak to who can still recall the video in a heartbeat, and those who've seen similar content that, they tell me, is 'burned into' their minds. At the time, no one really knew how to stop it or was educated about these harms. When the first generation of internet children began exploring social media spaces, the platforms didn't stop them watching or sharing this material either. Those who saw these violent videos have shared with me that they didn't understand why they watched it (other than that they were kids), but watch they did, and now they wished they hadn't because they feel scarred by it. More importantly, according to them, the adults who were around at the time, including their parents, teachers and professionals, did nothing to help them; they didn't know about it, so how could they have prevented it? As one of them told me, 'The e-safety teachings at the time tended to be more about not sharing your date of birth and address online, not the chat forums and spaces where we were exposed to the internet as it was and still is.'

## *Knowledge is Power*

The feeling I had back then is a heavy load to bear and I don't want you to experience this. It takes quite a bit of self-compassion to forgive yourself for not knowing, or for not being quite tech-smart enough to have been 'ahead of the game'. And today, alongside images of war and violence, sexual harms, misinformation, terrorism, hurtful and hateful language and polarised opinions and rage, we have all the issues that are arising with AI, too. Fortunately, though, we're now in a place of *knowing* more, enabling us to *do* more to protect children from this kind of content. And so we *must do more* – and that is why you are reading this book. Because, if we know, we can prevent and help.

In my case, as you know, I was well versed in online safety and cybersecurity. *At home.* But sadly, that's where it ended. I could not control other people, but I could have had direct conversations with them to help protect my children. Even then, I could never have fully controlled the world outside my front door or changed the fact that my kids might happen upon something that would cause them distress. On one occasion, I was walking to school with them (when they were around six years old), and we witnessed a road-traffic collision. I was unable to prevent them seeing this, and, yes, someone was hurt, and in that moment my children learned all at once about first aid, care and compassion, ambulances and the loud noise they make and swear words (in all their glory and from passengers, myself and others arriving on the scene).

Now, I'm not saying the ubiquitous, numerous and prolific violent, graphic and sexual images and videos are the same as witnessing a crash. I am just illustrating the fact that preventing your child from seeing challenging events is impossible and that they are almost guaranteed to view disturbing things at some point in the real world or online.

So we've established that we cannot protect our children from all worrying material, but not all of them will experience a major trauma response to it, provided they have a person with whom to process it and to talk to when they need to. That's why we have to open the way for them to come to us with their issues. However, if your child remains unwilling to talk to you about it, there is absolutely no shame in getting expert help, such as the support of a qualified therapist. We need all the help we can get today, as both the online and offline worlds can be so unpredictable.

Speak to other parents, family and relatives about this issue as delicately as you can, but in an informed and confident way; the intention isn't to frighten other parents, but to help them prepare their children for technology use and protect them in the process. You could create your own Facebook, WhatsApp or Snapchat group for other parents, friends and family, or you could join existing groups online to speak to other parents; and you can show or send information about online safety issues and worrying material to family members. (You can even show and share my social media videos – see p. 347 – which cover more topics than I could fit into these pages; or join my Level Up club to ask questions directly once a month for more detailed answers.) The more we're all aware of this issue, the more we can begin to think about what children have access to and how we approach our parenting in this space.

---

### Take Five

Processing the idea of violent material online and the exposure to this of a child of any age is troubling, yes. Outraged, disappointed, bereft and even speechless are all common reactions to this issue. This is why I'd suggest taking a pause here. Take a break, grab a brew, take a walk, phone a friend or whatever works for you. And breathe.

---

## Exposure to Pornography

Sadly, most of my clients who've been exposed to pornography, and/or impacted by what they've seen, have been children and teens with vulnerabilities such as emotional, social and learning difficulties, neurodiversity or trauma. Children with vulnerabilities may have experienced some form of trauma through viewing this material, as well as events in real life.

Over the last fifteen years or so, I've found that youngsters can encounter many different types of pornography (as I will discuss shortly), and they'll often have conflicting emotions and thoughts about what they've seen, the nature of which can vary considerably. In general conversation with people about this topic, and in clinical and educational settings where I'm supporting a child, the adults often automatically assume that any children who've viewed pornographic material have encountered it via porn sites, or that they've been watching the 'worst' kind of pornographic material. Pornography is often portrayed by mainstream media as being violent, misogynistic and abusive (which I hear echoed in the academic domains). These terms are also used in discourse by those with particular values or faiths and religions that are against pornography in all its forms, or people who don't understand what pornography is overall, or how it sits in the discipline of sexology and how it is an overarching term used to describe many things (not just the types of videos described here). All this hugely impacts how willing youngsters are to talk about what they've seen – especially if they think adults will view it as being something shameful, horrid, nasty or wrong. If they think other people will take a moralistic and value-based stance towards them because of it, they can become steeped in shame and confusion and, in many instances, they won't tell anyone. Alternatively, children with social communication issues might talk about what they've see in places like the classroom without understanding the impact this can have on others present.

Some children may be curious about this sort of content and, after viewing it for the first time, they may return to see more of it because they feel excited by it, confused or wary, or they just want to understand it. Some may never seek it out again, and some may look for it via search engines (or AI apps), using sexual language they hear others use in gaming environments, for example, and they may then be exposed to sites that host many different types of porn. Moreover, they may not realise that some of it is illegal or that watching it under the age of eighteen is illegal, too. Pornography is a minefield of consensual and non-consensual recordings, and may contain images of people under eighteen who could be mistaken for older (hence the term in the industry, 'barely legal'). Sadly, very young children being sexually abused can also appear on these sites. There are, as yet, no safeguards to protect against what children may happen upon on a porn site, or to prevent them from viewing this sort of material once they've gained access to it.

They can also be tricked into opening direct messages that show them pornography; they can find people talking about sex, a lot, on social media; they can see highly sexual content on Netflix, Prime and YouTube and they can be subjected to language that is pornographic in gaming. Let me tell you, it can be very disconcerting to hear a five- or six-year-old talk about what they've seen (they don't usually call it porn until they are around ten years old in most of the cases I deal with). Or to hear a fifteen-year-old struggling to explain that what they've seen does not involve the issues they've been told about in their sex-ed lessons, such as violent acts, but is somehow more appealing – because it shows a couple in their own home, say, engaging in foreplay. They may not understand that this is still pornography.

This confusion also applies to young people who've accessed cartoon types of porn, gay or lesbian porn, disability porn and other genres that aren't discussed in their school lessons (assuming these lessons have even been allowed in their education settings). When we teach about only one type of porn (which is curated and professional) and omit the rest of the large and varied space of pornography, we can do a disservice to the children and teens who access it via a plethora of ways and means, and who then discover a vast range of different types of material. There are so many approaches to and outcomes of pornography that we cannot use one simple term to describe them all.

We most certainly need to have informed conversations about accessing this sort of material, which requires us to understand what the range of material is, how, where and when it is accessed and by whom (what cohorts and ages of children and other factors such as neurodiversity, trauma and disabilities that academics have not yet studied). This may even require us to begin naming and talking about the different types. The field of sexual-behaviour studies has more to offer adults in these discussions (due to the nature of the content and the age threshold of eighteen to access it legally), but perhaps we can adapt this approach to children's education in an age- and stage-appropriate manner.

Having worked with lots of children and teens, my primary concern is that this content can sometimes be very shocking, frightening and, at times, traumatic for them to see (as well as enjoyable, but I'm not getting into this in detail here), and we need to understand how this might influence their beliefs and behaviour about sexual activity and what they might find a turn-on, exciting and more when they become sexually active themselves.

The field of sexology (the scientific study of sexual behaviour) rarely focuses on the age group of emerging sexual adolescents – it's an 'adult' area of study, as mentioned – so a lot remains to be researched if we're to be fully informed about the impact of pornography on developing adolescents. This is further complicated by the fact that porn and sexual behaviour are difficult to measure. From what children and young people have told me in my clinic, it certainly has a huge impact on those who've been abused.

Unfortunately, by focusing exclusively on pornography we tend to forget about the other kinds of sexual content, such as semi-naked adults, kissing, foreplay and simulated sex that's rife on TV and in the high street (for example, in shops selling sex toys and lingerie). There is also what I call the 'not-illegal-not-porn' porn – material that is full of sexual insinuation or about sex but not illegal – that children can be exposed to online by qualified, and many unqualified, sex educators, who talk about sex and foreplay, demonstrate sexual acts with props and use sexual language (such as teens and adults who share social media posts about things like the 'perfect blow job').

The effect of all this online content on a child's emerging sexuality, sexual preferences and sexual behaviour hasn't yet been studied to a robust large degree because of the ethics involved in asking children aged under fourteen about this subject directly. However, in the last few years research carried out in the space of online-safety disciplines has asked adults about their memory of porn viewing as children (memory issues can be a factor here), and, in research carried out by the UK children's commissioner (2013–23),[3,4,5] children over fourteen years of age were asked about accessing porn online. This research showed it was common to see porn around 11 years of age. Some citations and discussions online suggest it can be as early as 8, and I have worked with children as young as five who have viewed porn. This means that we currently find ourselves in a time when there is a considerable amount of confusion and both moralistic and real concerns about children and sexual content online, and we are unable ethically to ask younger children about the subject.

Viewing pornography is absolutely not suitable for young children, while allowing them to view sexual content involving adults online (or on TV) can become cloudy in its definition; it's a parental choice and a difficult area to assess, when we consider the existence of things like TV shows about animals mating and adults in the real world (such as parents) surrounding them expressing affection and kissing.

We should also acknowledge that children under the age of thirteen, or with the sorts of vulnerabilities mentioned earlier, may be impacted by sexual content in ways that are traumatic (although this isn't a given). We must consider the impact on a child of seeing sexual activity in others in the real world or online, especially if family values are not in alignment with same-sex relationships, for example. It's a personal decision that you must take;

however, the fact remains that sexual content *is* available online, and you will need to decide what you are happy for your child to view and be impacted by.

The situation is perhaps less clear when it comes to teenagers closer to the ages of sixteen or seventeen, for example, and whether they will be adversely affected by viewing some types of sexual content. (I would argue that it won't be appropriate for some teens, especially those with vulnerabilities, and would strongly urge you to use parental controls to limit their access to 18+ content – see p. 262.) Signs that this may have already happened include the sort of nervous-system dysregulations we'll cover later (see p. 215), changes in mood, avoidance of technology or friends, and anything else that seems to have changed in your child. Dialogue could help you assess this, but, given that many teens aren't always in the most conversational of moods with their parents, this could be tricky. So this is one instance where someone like me, a therapist/sex-ed professional, can be of help. Teens often don't talk to their parents about sex before engaging in it, so we must do more, both as a nation and globally, to make this conversation less uncomfortable for them. This means *we* may need to get comfortable with being uncomfortable first, to make this an everyday rather than a taboo topic.

## Child Sexual Abuse

It is important to highlight the fact that children and teens can be exposed to sexual content online that may include images and videos of minors and very young children. This may occur on porn sites or other online areas that they have access to.

Some research is under way at the moment globally into how children – particularly those with vulnerabilities – can be affected by this material and then seek it out more. While there aren't yet any clear conclusions, in my view we must do our very best to prevent children and teens ever viewing this sort of content. As discussed, using parental controls and having conversations about these issues is our best defence in lowering the likelihood of this ever occurring (for more on this, see pp. 117–120).

Many adult offenders say they were exposed to material of this kind before the age of eighteen, so we can make tangential links and conjecture that it does indeed influence sexual behaviour in adulthood. Moreover, some studies are beginning to show a correlation between learning and social vulnerabilities and the crime of viewing this material.

It's important to remember that this sort of content is illegal (it represents a crime scene in which a child is being abused), as is the viewing of it. If your child or teen is exposed to it accidentally, you should not take screenshots or record the material, and you must report it to the police in your area as soon as possible, which in England you can do by dialling 101. And please note that this is not the same offence as seeking it out purposefully, so please don't feel too anxious about reporting it. You can also find helplines in the Resources, p. 347.

---

### Take Five

This subject can often create a level of discomfort, so this self-care break is intended to be a way for you to think about your own nervous system.

If you have the space (and are not driving and listening to this on audio), I'm going to invite you to stand up. Next, reach up, stretching your arms as high as they can go, and breathe in. As you breathe out again, flop forwards, like a rag doll, and sigh. Slowly bring yourself back up to standing and notice your breathing. Pay attention to where you notice it the most, and how deep or shallow it is. To finish, take a physiological sigh, as described on p. 295.

> ### *Maisy's Story*
>
> Maisy was eleven and had been subjected to a terrible start in her early life, which, sadly, included sexual abuse. She often talked about the videos she'd watched online, which included pornography and horror movies. Maisy was interested in seeing if the experiences of the people in the films matched her early life, because she was trying to understand what had happened to her.
>
> Maisy wasn't a pornography addict or sexually deviant – she was simply trying to make sense of her world. She was a confused and traumatised little girl, who had been able to view this material because of her living arrangements at the time, where access to this sort of content wasn't restricted because the people she lived with didn't even know it could be accessed.
>
> Looking beyond the viewing of pornographic material, it's clear that Maisy needed a tech-smart parent or carer who could reduce the likelihood of her accessing to this material. It was also important that she had adult support, such as the help of a psychotherapist to help her understand her past abuse and what she was attempting to reconcile herself to through her online behaviours.

## The Impact of Trauma

Some children – although not all – who witness graphic scenes of sex and violence may experience cybertrauma. Now, as I'm a therapist specialising in this area, trauma is pretty much my main frame of reference, so, yes, I tend to see it everywhere when it comes to content online. While I appreciate that not everything that is seen or interacted with online results in trauma for children, some of the symptoms of trauma don't appear immediately, so we need to keep a watchful eye on our children when they use technology, to which end it can be helpful to understand what trauma is (and is not), so that we are able to notice if it manifests in them.

It is a huge area and many great books exist to help you understand it in depth (see Resources, p. 347), but for simplicity's sake we could describe childhood trauma (including instances of cybertrauma) as relating to what is called a significant event (such as abuse, neglect, viewing violence) that happens to a child at some point between their conception and adulthood. Obviously, trauma can affect adults, as can cybertrauma, but my focus for the purposes of this book is on children right from after they've left the womb up to the age of eighteen. This traumatic event can leave a lasting legacy on the body and brain in many ways, including impacting how the body communicates with the brain and vice versa. In response to trauma the brain can become chaotic and loud, sending information to the body to move to safety, which can manifest in some children as high energy, running around or low-level jiggly-wiggly movements (such as tapping, bouncing of legs and restlessness); or it can fall quiet and instead send 'stay-still' signals to the body, which can look like lethargy, zoning out or dissociation. Ultimately, childhood trauma can affect how children seek to meet their needs both in real life and online. When it comes to technology, this cohort of children are at more risk of, for example, being exploited and shamed and engaging in behaviours that they may not think through.

## Algorithms

Simply put, algorithms are computer programs that calculate an outcome. Other descriptions of them include pesky, manipulative, individualised and targeted marketing, feed-filling foes that entice us into expressing rage and polarised views, and/or engaging in competitions to be the loudest voice online by sharing content – only to be served more of the same to cement our cognitive bias. Algorithms are designed to maximise our engagement with online spaces. They pull us into the wormholes.

It's been suggested that eye-tracking calculations can and will be used by algorithms in the future (ahem, I was going to say if they're not doing so already, but that makes me sound like a conspiracy theorist) in order to measure how much we like or dislike the content that we interact with. Which is, to be fair, ingenious in terms of data collection in order to find trends and patterns.

Algorithms mean that certain issues can then be amplified at an exponential rate, depending upon how users interact with content, and calculations are made as to what's clicked on most often (or not) and looked at, or the time it takes a user to pause or scroll past. It notes what's shared and liked, what someone tries to avoid, doesn't want to see or does. This increases exponentially the chances of a teenager, for example, being harmed by issues such as body and health, extremism, suicide ideation or self-harming, which we will be looking at in Chapter 9. The harm can also be aimed at teens through advertising and by services and organisations that pay to be in their feed. At the time of writing, legislation such as the Online Safety Act (2023) in the UK is being pushed through and is intended to avoid preventable harm to under-eighteens from marketing techniques and algorithms that promote this kind of content, but I'm not entirely convinced that big tech won't develop ways round this. If you explain to teens that the tech giants are using their data to 'manipulate' them in this way, they are often perturbed by the idea. However, it's questionable whether they'd actually change their digital or online habits once they learn this.

In short, keep talking to your child and teen about the way they are marketed to, why the content they see is curated by the algorithms that use their data and activities to send them more of the same sort of content, which can lead them into what is called an echo chamber (in which there is a confirmation bias of their views), and how, if they want to reset this, they can – on some devices – uninstall and reinstall the app, or use it without having to sign into it (which you can do with apps like YouTube) to prevent algorithms 'learning' about them.

## Online Grooming

The word 'grooming' can sometimes confuse people when applied to online settings or abuse, so perhaps it would be clearer to say manipulated, coerced or exploited by others online. This can happen for several reasons, one of which is to get a child to send money, gifts or items from a game or in an app to other players (or bad actors). However, the word 'grooming' is also often used to mean exploited by offenders into sending intimate and sexual images or videos by camera.

Grooming can take place in gaming through chat-enabled functions (text or voice) or by being invited to download other apps that can send images, and also, of course, on social media. In these cases, sometimes the person doing the grooming might first share items, images or money with a child, who then returns the favour in the belief that they're sharing things with a friend. In games, these can be assets like characters, in-app currency, skins/outfits and accessories. These shared things (or the requests for them) can also include images of the child, dressed or undressed.

In today's world, it's therefore sensible for a child to say no to sharing any photos of themselves with other people on the internet, unless they or their parent or caregiver knows the other person in the real world and trusts them implicitly. (Even then, there is the potential for harm; to give one example, images can be changed by the undressing apps). On a practical level, you need to have conversations with your child. Talk to them about sharing anything with people online, such as photos, videos, money, items, skins, gifts and other in-app transferable things. Explain that it's absolutely ok for them to check out who someone is and to run this past you. This means talking to them in advance, and telling them they can show you their phone and you will check 'with' them to work out who someone is *together*.

## Issues Related to Grooming

You should be aware that sometimes children may be used to recruit other children into spaces where a groomer is lurking, so as to lure them into sharing images and videos of themselves. Often, there may be some form of monetary gain on offer, and it may also involve a contest of some sort in which children are pitted against each other and lied to about their importance so they'll do more illegal things for more money. Perpetrators of crimes against children who try to groom teens in this way may even persuade them to carry out business on their behalf, such as selling drugs or meeting people in real life to do things in person.

Another form of exploitation concerns money transfers and money mule-ing, which means holding illegal money for the criminal and then transferring most of it back to the criminal and getting to keep some. This is illegal and can involve substantial amounts of money. For kids, it's usually enough for them to buy something that their real-life friends will see as a 'gift' or 'earned' item (such as a designer handbag, trainers or a coat), as well as enabling them to buy things for their avatars and top up their own accounts. Those who do this are often insecure and trying to fit in somehow (remember the needs-based approach of understanding behaviour – see p. 80); or the cash rewards could be of benefit to them (or their family).

Keep an eye on banking, PayPal and other money transfer apps or gift cards that your child, particularly teens, suddenly starts asking about. There are ways for them to set up accounts where they can receive money, so be on the ball about this and talk about it with them.

## WHAT ARE THE RISKS THAT CHILDREN FACE ONLINE?

The problem of exploitation may well become exacerbated by AI in the future. Tragically, a fourteen-year-old boy took his own life in 2024 because he was 'tricked' by an AI chatbot into believing he was in a real relationship (through the emotive responses he received from the AI bot, and the exploitation of the e-ttachment he experienced), according to his mother, who took the chatbot's creators to court (at the time of writing, the case is still ongoing). AI chatbots also sit inside some games and social media apps, such as Snapchat, and they can now emulate empathy, curiosity, connection and attachment, which has escalated the risk they pose to young, vulnerable teens and children who find themselves playing with these apps. And when we think about the risks of artificial romantic relationships we can also think about the risks that teens make and take too, such as engaging in risky sexual behaviour. It's anyone's guess whether these bots will try to persuade them to share intimate images in the future – or how long it will be before the bots start sharing intimate images with them! (Which, of course, would not be real images, but they may be created by the AI programs.) Goodness only knows how they will evolve and in what ways they might further muddy what are already very murky waters.

Given we don't yet know enough about AI and the rate at which it will advance, it's best to be prepared. Again, we need to be parents who are open to having conversations about relationships and sex, which I know might make some of you feel uneasy or even queasy. But don't worry – I'll be sharing examples of how to do this, without sounding uncomfortable, weird or out of your depth, in Part 2, and there are also some pointers to further help in the Resources (see p. 347).

> ### *Take Five*
>
> Pick a song or a tune you like from your Spotify, iTunes or other music-based app (oh, the irony of me suggesting a tech-based intervention here), or grab a CD. Play the music as loud as you can handle, or as loud as you feel the neighbours will tolerate, depending on where you are reading this. Dance and sing along in any way you wish. And if dancing is not your thing, you can always shake your wrists, then your arms, and wobble or bounce your legs. Move your limbs until they feel somewhat tired. This will help to dissipate any energy that may have built up in your muscles while reading this chapter. Yes, this happens, and it's subtle – until it is brought to your attention.

## Cyberbullying

Cyberbullying is a complex phenomenon and has many derivative forms that I've written about extensively elsewhere (see Resources, p. 347). For our purposes, let's define it as bullying that takes place in online spaces. This can include making comments on posts, the sharing and resharing of posts and the adaptation of images or videos of a person. It can also include: 'flaming', which is the deliberate antagonism of a person or group online; constantly being on someone's posts (stalking or over-liking them); direct messages; 'kicking' from gaming or social media environments (being removed from a game or a WhatsApp group, for example); abusive language in gaming; spamming of party invites (when a person keeps sending invites to join them in a game, which can be annoying because of the non-stop pings or the flood of notifications over your own game); or the spamming of posts prompting notifications on a person's social media account, which

# WHAT ARE THE RISKS THAT CHILDREN FACE ONLINE?

can appear/sound on their phone if these notifications aren't turned off. If you've ever heard WhatsApp, Instant Messenger or Snapchat notifications repeatedly pinging, you'll know it can be irritating, for sure. And although silencing the phone is always an option and some manufacturers will allow you to put your phone in 'focus' or 'do-not-disturb' mode, this sort of spamming can be a form of bullying when it involves a pile-on by a number of people who 'spam' one child to cause annoyance.

Cyberbullying can take many forms, on many platforms and often by many people. It is harassment that can continue long after the school day, and it can be aimed at all of the places a child is online (such as their social media and gaming accounts). It can be relentless and hard to get away from. Children can become avoidant of certain pieces of technology or platforms, or try to handle the issue on their own. Like the conversations you have with your child about their friendships at school or sports clubs, taking an active interest in their online friends and friendships can help you keep your ears open to trouble and harassment. Alongside this, helping your child learn how to block, mute and report people can empower them to keep themselves safe online. Finally, if you always keep a space for your child to have open conversations, this will help pave the way for them to come to you if any problems arise, which might include seeing other children being cyberbullied.

And now, *breathe* . . . We've covered a lot of ground in this chapter, from the threat of bad actors manipulating innocent images and grooming children, to the risk of kids viewing violent and sexual content, to the manipulations of algorithms and the problem of cyberbullying. It's a lot for anyone to take in and it might feel overwhelming. Fortunately, there's also a great deal we can do to protect our kids. That's why I'll be offering you lots of practical advice in Part 2, up next, as we walk together through the ages and stages of digital parenting.

## Summary

- Keeping children safe from exposure to unsuitable material and predators is one of the most pressing issues around protecting them online.
- Safeguarding means being aware of the potential for harm, which is why we need to accept the ugly truth that offenders may often be known to the family.
- Bad actors can manipulate innocent images of children, so it's best not to upload family photos.
- Have age-appropriate discussions with your child about issues such as sex and violence online.
- Do consider using parental controls to limit access to 18+ content.
- Express an ongoing interest in your child's online activities and friendships, as this will create the space for them to come to you with problems like viewing inappropriate content or cyberbullying.

# PART 2

# Your Practical Guide to Keeping Kids Safe Online

In Part 1 we took a wide-angle look at many of the concerns and challenges you might come across in the online world. Here in Part 2 we are going to dive a little deeper into parenting around those issues with practical help and advice for you to work with. The first three chapters deal with age groups, but, as you know, our children are all different, and rigid groupings by age – or anything else – don't always apply, so treat these as a rough guide. Then we're going to look in a little more depth at some of the key tech-smart parenting principles, such as productive ways to set boundaries and how to create a strong and supportive connection with your child or teen through engaging them in conversation. (If you have an uncommunicative teen, don't worry; I'll be offering tips for that, too!) There's also a chapter on troubleshooting, with scenarios you can draw on if things do ever go wrong.

## CHAPTER 7

# The Early Years – Ages Zero to Five

Help! Should I be worried about giving my toddler a smart device? What's the right age to start letting them play with a device without it affecting their ability to learn language? What about eyesight? And if I do let my them play with a device, how can I get it back off them? Does looking at screens mean children won't learn empathy? Are there any particular issues I need to avoid?

The answers to these questions are in this chapter, and we'll also be looking at things like guidance about intentionally letting your little one play with a phone or tablet – without guilt. As always, it's important to think critically here and sort out the facts from the theory, so that you can decide what works best for your family.

Given the lack of long-term research, and the low numbers of studies that have taken place thus far, we can't say with certainty that technology *won't* cause developmental issues, or how we would measure these accurately, although I will say that it seems to be another area of blustery claims, as we'll see. However, I hope you'll realise that I am pro-parent. And also, on a reassuring note, that technology can help us manage tiny people and occupy them in a number of situations (more than giving them our car keys), so that we can get on with our jobs – whether as parents or working from home.

But let's start with whether we need to be worried about the impact of tech on small children acquiring motor skills (see also Chapter 4) and their ability to perform tasks.

## Hands-on in the Early Years

Over the last few years, I've watched videos of children aged between zero and five pinching at pictures in magazines or making swiping motions in their sleep. The accompanying captions often proclaim: 'Technology is ruining child development!' But while it's true that small babies probably can't understand the difference between paper and a tablet, is it really fair to say that their development is being ruined by tech? Perhaps they're simply seeing images of eyes, noses and mouths and touching them because that's what they've learned to do in the real world. Ask any parent with long hair, glasses or a moustache and they'll tell you just how much babies love to grab, pull, touch, pinch and stroke these things. In fact, at twelve months old or younger, can infants really tell that a face in a picture is different from real life? (Babies can't recognise themselves in mirrors until they are around eighteen months of age.) So are we really saying that pinching and swiping toddlers are the beginning of the end? Or rather, could this simply mean they're learning the skills they need in today's world?

In the UK, health visitors specialise in working with families and their children up to age five to improve and promote health and identify any needs or concerns. Their job includes checking that infants are reaching important developmental milestones. To do this, they test things like a child's hearing, sight and range of movement, including that pinching movement we can make thanks to the opposable thumbs gifted to us by evolution. These dextrous digits of ours enable us to pick up tiny objects like seeds and use certain tools. This is a motion we lucky humans have engaged in for millennia, and it is now hardwired in most infants. Pincer, pinching and other fine motor movements are indicative of child development in the right direction. Also, it was already observed that babies made these sorts of movements in their sleep long before the advent of technology.

Of course, where they can, babies will copy the movements of the adults around them to help them navigate the world. For example, if we were to imagine a group of cave dwellers who needed to swipe on a tree trunk or pinch a small flower to get food, would we expect an infant cave dweller to copy and become adept at these movements, too? Yes, I think we would. After all, it's ingrained in babies to survive.

Today, we have moved on a bit since the age of the Neanderthals, and now require those same skills – such as swiping, pinching, (double-) tapping and other fine motor movements – to use various gadgets like fridges, microwaves, TVs, keyboard and computer mice. That being the case, it seems reasonable to assume that children will learn these skills, too, by copying us. In fact, if they're to succeed as adults in a world of technology that calls for exactly these sorts of movements, it seems logical to expect them to do precisely that, and even to encourage them, just as we would teach them how to do something like catch a ball.

### *A Little Boy's Story*

When I was training as a child therapist, part of my course requirements entailed being able to understand the world of parenting and infancy and how we become the people we are in our families and society. To do this, I had to observe infant behaviour by effectively living like a piece of furniture with a family for an hour a week and watching their baby's growth and development, without interacting with them at all. This, without a doubt, was the most incredible aspect of my training, as it allowed me to see first-hand how all the theory worked in practice.

> From about 2010 to 2013, I observed a little boy who was growing up in a family where technology existed in the form of mobile devices and tablets, TVs and DVD players and, of course, toys. The little boy had two older sisters, who were already using technology and gaming before he was born.
>
> When he was about six to eight months old, I noticed that he wanted to be a part of his siblings' and parents' lives in all that they did. He wanted to get his hands on that TV remote and those devices, including a phone to chew when he was teething, and he wanted the associated pleasures of TV shows and music. He was already learning to swipe, tap and bash the devices to get what he wanted from them. While he wasn't yet talking, his motions were often accompanied by noises emulating chatter.
>
> My observed baby swiped, scratched, touched lovingly, pinched and hit the screens of devices he was in contact with, so his mum quite rightly began to teach him which movements to make when he wanted something. This applied both to technology and non-technology, such as not biting his sisters and not hitting or screaming when he wanted something, but trying instead to articulate his needs through words and actions. Would I say she was a bad parent for letting him use technology? Nope, not at all.
>
> I remember her showing him photographs on a tablet (rather than a physical album) as part of a shared experience in which they looked at the pictures together and talked about them, albeit on a screen. This is an example of the communication process in early childhood that is so needed between child and parent.

My own children were introduced to computers when they were around three years of age. They learned how to turn one on, how to use a mouse and how to play and have fun on it. However, they weren't left alone with it, as I'm pretty sure that at that age they'd have pressed all sorts of keys and probably deleted the entire operating system. It was only ever a shared experience. If they were small children now, in our age of smartphones and tablets, then I'm confident that it would be much the same situation, and I'd sit alongside them while they played with these devices.

> *TIP:* Chat with your infant, toddler or young child when you use technology, whether you're making a phone call, turning over the TV channel to find something to watch or sending a text. Involve commentary such as 'Mummy/ Daddy is pressing the mouse, clicking the button, swiping, closing, etc.' and activities such as those mentioned in the case study above.

## Babies and Touch Screens

Rather than worry that our kids might turn into blue-light goblins glued to their screens, don't we want them to learn how to navigate their environment, given this *is* their environment and technology isn't about to go away anytime soon? And why are we so surprised when an infant can't tell the difference between a picture in a magazine and one on a screen? To my mind, that sort of approach is what's called 'concrete thinking' and lacks the nuance needed to understand child development.

Babies learn through touch, manipulation, pinching and putting things in their mouths to see what something feels like and what it does when they touch it. Just ask a cat or dog what being near a toddler is like! Unfortunately, when it comes to babies and tech, this sort of basic and nuanced approach to understanding child development is often tossed aside in favour of fearmongering headlines.

The following case study illustrates how technology can be a helpful companion for infants and toddlers in times of stress, and a great way to manage your child's emotional capacity and skills. I marvelled when I witnessed this next moment; it was a great example of the positive use of technology with a child.

> ### *Flying High with 'Technology Together' Parenting*
>
> I was on a flight that had been delayed by several hours. It was way past midnight by the time we all boarded. A man took the seat next to me, while his wife was seated in the row behind us. With her were their three children, whose ages ranged from about one to six. The six-year-old was sitting quietly in her seat with a tablet, the middle child was already asleep and the infant was getting increasingly frustrated. She was clearly not happy with having to sit on Mum's lap – she wanted to stand up and move about.
>
> Before the plane started to bump down the runway, the infant's father took her and put her on his lap, next to me. Then he got out an iPad with a child-friendly case. He placed it in front of him and the little girl began to swipe on the screen and opened a game.
>
> I noticed that no matter what she swiped, the screen didn't leave the game, so kudos to this parent for setting up the controls to stay on the game. As she swiped, her dad talked to her about the shapes and colours she could see and had her naming these (albeit incorrectly most of the time). But here was a dad using technology to co-regulate with his tired and fidgety child. Bravo, Dad! (And I'm sure many of the other passengers were grateful for this too, so double bravo!)

*TIP:* Look for things on devices that spark conversations with your child, such as photographs and games. Talk to your toddler about what they can see on the screen or what they're watching and ask them about their thoughts and feelings. Also, consider looking at educational play-based games and activities, as the research suggests these can be helpful for language development.[1]

> ### *A Note on Children with Social, Emotional or Educational Needs, Neurodiversity and/or Trauma*
>
> Children tend not to be diagnosed formally with these sorts of vulnerabilities until they are about five or older. However, this doesn't mean that you can't make adjustments for your child's use of technology early on as you see fit. This may be a way that you can help them to stay calmer, like holding a 'blankie'. I've found in my clinic that younger children who have gone on to receive these diagnoses have often been avid users of technology and have engaged in behaviours with it that can look repetitive (for example, playing the same game, listening to the same music and making the same movements in the same order). It can be difficult to tell if your young child is not wanting to give up the device because they are overstimulated (in their nervous system, and not necessarily by technology), tired and cranky, or whether they have a neurodiverse presentation. This is why the advice that follows in this chapter can apply to all children, with or without diagnoses or vulnerabilities, and I hope it will offer you some help and comfort. A point to note is that neurodiverse children around this age often find solace and seem calmer when they get to play a repetitive noise or game. They may be using this as a way to manage their tics, stimming patterns (repetitive behaviours such as rocking, pacing or flapping their hands) or compulsions.

The following story is a little further along in the developmental years discussed elsewhere in this chapter, as it concerns a boy aged five. His parents were tech positive and told me he had been using technology since 'before he could walk'. They used controls and software on his devices to keep him safe and when he was a preschooler had spent many an hours talking to him while watching YouTube. (By the time I met him, his spelling and vocabulary were excellent.) They allowed him to develop the skills necessary to use apps with their supervision, and I was very impressed at his adaptation to the world he found himself in. As you will see, by the time he came to my clinic he was already skilled at using technology, too. In fact, I found myself wondering how the skillset of other children his age would compare with his and what this might mean for future generations of scientists, engineers, doctors and technology experts.

### *Marcus's Story*

Marcus was working with me for issues that had nothing to do with technology. He was absolutely fascinated by dinosaurs, dragons and many animals, and he talked to me and his mum about them using the various figures I have in a sand tray in my room.

Marcus wanted to show me a YouTube video of his favourite lizard, so we asked his mum if we could use her phone. He took it and, in under three seconds, he'd opened up the YouTube app and started typing in his search words. He must have done this search in the past; his auto-search terms brought up the video name right away.

Next, in under a second, he clicked the video title, flipped the phone to landscape mode and maximised the screen. He skipped to the part he wanted to show me and grinned. 'There, see it?'

I repeat, Marcus was only five years old. I was amazed and said so.

This was motor-movement learning, this was skill acquisition and this was a set of tech skills that will serve Marcus well in the future. This was automatic, learned knowledge that now sat in his motor cortex (located in the brain's frontal lobe, the area that controls muscle movement, balance and posture) – and it outskilled mine.

The incident also showed that Marcus could converse and that his language development exceeded that of the average five-year-old. We watched YouTube videos together and I saw that he could name the animals correctly, with excellent pronunciation, including the names of extinct dinosaurs and animals he hadn't seen previously. But what was more significant than anything else was that he was adapting to his environment, and, if we think about what learning is all about, this is it. I know I would be very confident hiring someone who was as skilled as this as an adult, let alone a child, in a world of technology that is ever-evolving. Learning is about so much more than just passing tests in school and YouTube often provides space to expand knowledge beyond this classroom approach. I do hope that we see the benefit of being able to learn in this way, and I am sure AI will do a grand job of making learning even more exciting!

So what can we learn from the dad on the plane and Marcus's story? Perhaps it's that not all technology use is bad for, or delays, language development, as has been proposed online? As suggested at the outset, there are many variables that can affect language acquisition and a child under the age of five could very likely even benefit from a 'shared' experience with an adult around the use of technology, rather than it being used as a passive babysitter for them, which I think is where the hullabaloo about delayed development stems from. So let's enjoy technology together, parent and child – although of course you must make your own decisions for your family about how much time this takes up, and how you will use technology together to enhance your child's development on your parenting journey. As part of this, I'd like us to look next at the amount of time small children spend staring at screens.

> *Take Five*
>
> Remember when the tiny person in your life was aiming for their first word, first walk and more, and how you marvelled at their progress and tenacity, and encouraged them to keep going? What joyful moments those were. Bask in the feeling of how wonderful your child is, and in your part in helping them to develop. Take a few minutes to reflect – perhaps unearth a photo of those times – and smile to yourself, knowing that you are always doing your best, and that, as you read this chapter, you see the many things that can affect development. And give yourself a break on the 'bad-parent' narrative, if that's what's been happening.

## Limit Time Staring at Screens?

Let's revisit those developmental milestones we tend to look for in babies and small children from birth to age five. I want to address the issue of children's eyesight and their use of screens first, as this receives quite a lot of attention on social media and in the mainstream headlines. Then I will expand some more on the sections around fine- and gross-motor movements, posture and physical development (including exercise and nutrition), return to the discussion on empathy from Chapter 4, and also consider attention and cognition in this age group.

Today, there's a growing consensus that the use of screens for prolonged periods can affect how our eyes work in terms of dryness and strain, for both adults and children. Moreover, reports suggest that short-sightedness (myopia) is on the increase, notably among children.[2] In the US, a Vison Council report found a rise in children wearing glasses, from 12 per cent in 2015 to 14.5 per cent in 2020.[3]

An *Atlantic* magazine article from 2022 titled 'The Myopia Generation' cited research from 2016 that suggested that by 2050 half the world will be short sighted and it infers the cause of this increase in short-sightedness to be – yes, you guessed it – screen time and usage.[4] I think it's important to read the original research if it is being cited or relied upon so I went back to the original study, which named many things that can affect myopia. The study said:

> *The projected increases in myopia and high myopia are widely considered to be driven by environmental factors (nurture), principally lifestyle changes resulting from a combination of decreased time outdoors and increased near work activities, among other factors.*

It went on to suggest factors including diet, high pressure education and light levels, as well as use of electronic devices.

As British physician and writer Ben Goldacre says repeatedly in his book *Bad Science*, 'it's complicated', and the effects of this complex interplay of many lifestyle changes is not clear-cut in the science findings; nutrition plays a major role but is often overlooked. This is compounded by the kinds of jobs we engage in on a day-to-day basis, and the fact we cannot isolate these for research. Close work, such as time devoted to writing and reading tasks on paper or magazine mediums, is difficult to distinguish entirely from the use of screens alone for similar tasks, and time spent on each of these varies for all of us.

As touched upon earlier often the demon that emerges from the screen-facing debate is the blue light emitted. This has increased the sales of 'blue blockers' (glasses with lenses designed to filter blue-light rays to help prevent them from entering the eyes) and lighting-level software on smartphones and PCs. However, when I looked into this I came across some interesting opinions, ideas and further questions to consider.*

In the absence of any robust research into a rise in eye-related conditions for infants and the under-fives that might be attributed to screen use, I asked opticians whether they've found that cases of myopia in children are on the increase and if they think (or know) that this could be ascribed to technology and staring at screens. They informed me that yes, myopia has increased to a degree among both children and adults, and conjectured that this is most likely due to near-sighted tasks being on the rise, such as reading, writing and practical learning, play or work-related tasks in schools and at home (as the research currently suggests). However, there are no clear causal links as yet, and it's not known to what extent the increase in myopia is correlated to screen use (or, I guess, how we could measure this accurately and remove those other factors). Like everything else in this area, we need more research to establish cause and effect. And although we do need to sort the myths from the facts, I'm not dismissing the way that screen use is causing more scrunched-up faces as we strain to see what's on our hand-held devices. So, even in the absence of data relating to any long-term effects, I would urge caution and ask that you do please take care of your eyes and those of developing children.

Given that the eye takes several years to develop full stability

---

* I'm very interested in this particular subject because when I worked in engineering in the military, my work was focused on optic technology, and my undergrad dissertation discussed eye-tracking machines. Our eyes continue to fascinate me, both in terms of their impact on our understanding of this world and in relation to technology. For example, the way we focus on screens means our eyes 'converge' in front of us, which can evoke certain states in the nervous system and create feelings of security and safeness, or, at the other extreme, cause us to be on high alert. It's still an area of study that needs more research.

and that problems with eyes and eyesight can be more likely to become permanent the lower the age at which they occur, it's likely to be in the best interest of children under five (and at any age, to be honest) to take frequent breaks from screens to relax their eyes. As younger ones may not recognise the need for this, parents and caregivers need to be their 'eye-development' patrol officers and do it for them – see Tip, below.

One very specific area in which screen time has been considered to be ok (somewhat) is when children are using an application like FaceTime to talk to loved ones. This was a prominent discussion in the lockdowns of 2020, when of course seeing people's faces in the real world was limited to the eyes only because of masks and distancing, which meant that infants and young children may not have been able to pick up on the subtle non-verbal cues of the face (an important part of our development in human communication and socialising). As such, video calls with Grandma or Grandpa were perceived as being acceptable, even if only for limited periods, because we effectively had no choice. Sadly – and this was a missed opportunity to get really great data – although we do have self-reported measures (which are likely to be biased, skewed and not accurate) we did not have research taking place at the time in homes where children were exposed to more screens, or time on screens. How much more time little ones spent on screens is anyone's guess. The research today is retrospective and trying to work out what has changed in child development since these lockdowns occurred, and whether this is all really because of screens or if it also has to do with the lack of socialising in groups and in society. No one really has the answer here.

*TIP:* Encourage your child to take regular breaks from screens and to look at something outside or at least 20 metres away (this encourages what we call divergent focus). To do this, you might find it helpful to take your little one outside to look at something 'over there'. Aim to do this for a few minutes for every twenty minutes of screen time (and, yes, I know that this time is going to interfere with their games).

It can also help our eyesight if we try to live according to the circadian (daily) rhythms of natural light, in harmony with the seasons of sunlight from dawn to dusk, and to use lower levels of lighting at night. Reducing screen time for devices held close to the face, such as phones, in the evening is a good way to slowly move into a sleep routine, while avoiding screens before bedtime is helpful, too.*

---

### Take Five

Given what's been said in this chapter about how continued and long exposure to screens with close-up work and poor lighting can contribute to worsening eye health (for all of us), take a short eye break. This time, I invite you to find a well-defined distant object (through a window or by going outside) and focus on it. Define the edges, the colour, the contours, and describe these to yourself in words. Take five minutes for yourself while looking at your chosen object, and think about the miracle that is your eyesight.

---

## Other Areas of Consideration for the Under-Fives

Very small children can, in my opinion, benefit from technology when it's used with them in responsible and interactive ways. But it's still important to make sure that this is part of a healthy and

---

* For a helpful article about eye heath and risks, see: 'Myopia management in clinical practice', Association of Optometrists website. Available at: www.aop.org.uk/advice-and-support/clinical/scope-of-practice/myopia-management-in-clinical-practice.

balanced lifestyle. That's why I'd like to look briefly at a couple of other important areas to consider when parenting the under-fives.

## Nutrition and Diet

Now, you might be wondering what on earth nutrition and diet have to do with tech and small children. And it's a fair point! The reason I'd like to put on my nutritionist's hat now and mention diet in this context is mainly because a healthy diet is highly related to good eyesight. Eye health can be impacted by the food we eat, or don't eat, and a healthy diet will support good eye health by detoxifying and preventing the 'build-up' that can occur at the back of the eye. Another issue (although this mainly relates to older children) is that many kids who sit in front of screens for extended periods of time can often be found snacking or grazing (and I'm not attacking anyone's parenting here!).

Eyes benefit from oily fish which contains omega 3 and cruciferous vegetables which contain a compound called sulforaphane (such as broccoli, cabbage, sprouts and dark, leafy greens). You really need to be getting vitamins A and D into this age group too for health eye development – which is found in eggs, spinach, carrots, mushrooms, red meat such as liver (but not too much per week) and fortified plant drinks – although how you do that in your food choices (and get the little one to eat them) is up to you.

## Vitamin D, Sunshine, Exercise, Physical Development, Posture and Motor Movement

Another helpful tip – both for eye health and for spending time away from screens for an active body and mind – is to get young children outside when possible for a boost of vitamin D and exercise. Of course, running around and playing are great ways to build stronger bones and healthy bodies and to improve posture and gait (how we move) as well. Again, how you do this with your child is up to you, but we all need sunlight (without staring directly at the sun, which is damaging to the eyes), and we cannot get this indoors. Movement and play help build physical development and gross motor skills (meaning large body movements such as climbing, running and walking), and can help with a child's finer movements, too (pinching daisies, for example) and being able to use their fingers and toes within the major movements. The use of other hands-on things besides devices helps strengthen tendons, ligaments and muscles, and this can help with posture and brain development too, in what's called bilateral stimulation. Moreover, obesity is on the rise globally, and a way to stave off excess body weight is to be active. Plus, little growing people have lots of energy, so helping them channel this into playful activities can help. And, of course, as mentioned earlier, their eyes will benefit from longer-range focus when outside.

## Attention and Cognition in the Under-Fives

Child-development and early-years practitioners pay close attention to this area when visiting families in the early days after a child is born, and it's one that health professionals continue to observe as a child progresses through to nursery and on to school. One of the issues is that we now know lots of children can present with learning difficulties that may not be picked up until they are, perhaps, over the age of five. That's why we need to be especially aware that their skills of attention, reasoning, thinking and all the 'higher-brain' processes are still being formed at this tender age, alongside language acquisition and emotional intelligence.

When it comes to tech, as I've said, this age group benefits most from spending time in the co-created use of technology – that is, you use it together with your child – and that they learn to develop their skills of paying attention *with* you by doing things together. Children in this age group learn mostly through play, so technology can be a great tool here and you can even play educational games with them. Limiting time on any activity, with or without technology, is going to help them develop their ability to maintain focus (and happily, help is at hand on p. 179 for when it's time for them to come off a device and hand it back to you). But don't expect a five-year-old or younger to be a patient student, because many things are occurring in terms of their brain development, which means that their attention can turn elsewhere at the drop of a hat.

## Just a Moment to Yourself . . .

While it's worth realising that learning how to interact with screens is an important life skill in today's world, it's also true that for many parents they can be a way to keep the peace and occupy their children while they get on with other stuff. The use of TV has been a staple of parenting and family life for many years (since the late 1950s) and, importantly, it isn't the 'wrong way' to parent. Phone and tablet screens are just a newer kind of entertainer. The world we now live in is high in stimuli, so a good old-fashioned rattle is unlikely to be a baby's first choice when they realise the shiny, flashing lights of that thing *we're* holding is the other option. And it works both ways – because it also means that, if the parents hand over the shiny, flashing thing to the small person, Mum or Dad can grab a moment to eat a warm meal, which can be a rare treat when you're looking after a little one. In the past, when we wanted to distract our children while we made a cup of tea, programmes like *Teletubbies* or *Blue Peter* saved the day. And content rumbling away on a TV screen in the background is much easier to manage and supervise, in practical terms, than it is on a small device, as TVs often sit up on a unit where you can keep an eye on them, whereas devices can be held close by a young child (with screens out of your sight). Locked systems and parental controls can therefore be a lifeline when it comes to preventing accidental viewing of content that is inappropriate for children under five.

> *TIP:* Babies often want the specific thing *you* have, because they make an association with it, in much the same way they might want to play with your car keys or your food. A big hint here is to have something your baby will want to hold that isn't your phone; for example, you could carry around a special blanket, a spare set of shiny keys or a baby version of technology. And if you do give your baby your phone, ensure that they can't access any apps – so password-protect it, and move your apps to different screen pages just to be sure.

But what about when a tablet or phone is given to a toddler with apparently no thought at all? The intention with which technology is offered or used and whether it's as an automatic pacifier or a considered choice is important. Sometimes we'll give technology to our toddlers and young children to make our lives easier (not necessarily a bad thing), but, if it becomes an automatic habit, then I'd recommend really dialling back and thinking about what you are doing and why. It's a bit like the story of Goldilocks: the key is finding the approach that's just right for both you and your little one.

So do parents routinely make bad choices around letting small children play with gadgets, and have they become digital pacifiers? Before we start blaming and shaming the parents of small children, let's acknowledge that it's a tough job at times and sometimes we do give out sweets, treats and, in this case, devices for our own sanity. And to be honest, if handing over a device can help a parent to stay regulated – i.e. calm and emotionally in control – it is a tool in their arsenal that will help them to co-regulate with their child, so that everyone in the situation is able to keep calm.

Yet some parenting 'experts' have taken a demonising approach, suggesting online (ironically) that any use of a device is 'bad parenting', which, again, shows a complete lack of understanding of every family's individual circumstances.

You and I know you're doing the best you can. The fact that you are here, reading this book, is proof of that. So go easy on yourself when the internet tells you that you are a sh*t parent for giving your infant a tablet or smartphone. Because you know what? Sometimes it's the only thing you can do in the moment. If you have more than one child, it might be the only way you can get a warm cup of tea and time with *your other children*.

Most of us don't have a choice about tech being present, so, rather than not allowing infants anywhere near it, why don't we learn what it is, how to use it, how to allow it, how to manage it and how to harness it for appropriate learning and development? This might include learning how each device operates and how we can get into those sections with photos, go online and download apps ourselves – oh, and an example from my own learning curve here; find out how to change the text back into English if it has changed to another language. (This has happened to me more than once, so I know the pain of a locked device . . . *en Français*!) It's also worth considering taking some e-safety lessons or reading e-safety newsletters to learn how to use parental controls effectively and stay up to date with the ways in which technology is changing (see Resources, p. 347, for places to visit online). Learning how to harness technology and keep it in check in relation to your child is a lifetime project that will require you to keep having conversations with them, and with the adults in their educational settings and any places your child goes to, because each area will have access to technology in varying ways. But most importantly, keep doing what you're doing here, putting your child in the centre of your learning, just as you are doing by reading this book. It's such a positive and active thing to do. Bravo to you!

## *An Aside: On Getting Through the Night*

To focus on the parents of very small children for a moment, infants require round-the-clock care and new mums and dads in particular need ways to manage those interruptions in the middle of the night, which tend to be based on feeding their little ones (and will likely mean their sleep is going to be out of sync, which can impact their emotional-regulation skills).

Staying sane when your sleep is interrupted can be difficult (it's no coincidence that sleep deprivation is used as a torture method). So please don't judge parents and carers who use different methods, including technology, to help themselves stay alert when getting a baby back to sleep by means of either lulling, breastfeeding or giving night feeds with a bottle. These parents can come under particularly harsh attack; some people criticise nursing mothers for not maintaining eye contact with their baby while they feed. Admittedly, this is important for creating an emotional connection. Babies need to look at faces in real life so they can learn the language of emotional expressions and social interactions. However, sweeping judgements and criticism don't help anybody. Besides, if you've ever fed a baby in the night you'll know that they tend to be sleepy and keep their eyes closed, so there isn't much eye contact going on in most cases.

While I remember those night feeds as being peaceful, they could also be very boring. Sometimes infants fall asleep as they feed, only to semi-wake and continue suckling, which means the whole feed can take a long time. So what would you do, or did you do in those moments, at 3am, when your baby's eyes were closed? It's important to acknowledge that parents who fall asleep during night feeds could potentially hurt their child by dropping them or choking them with

> the bottle, for example. That's why I'm all in favour of
> supporting parents to remain alert during the night feed until
> it's finished and for them to choose how best to achieve that,
> with or without tech. It's a matter of making considered
> personal choices according to the circumstances you find
> yourself in. However, please note that this short interlude has
> been about managing night feeds and is not an endorsement
> of regular technology use in front of infants and toddlers.
> Occasional or pragmatic use is the approach I'm advocating
> for here.

### *CPR in Action: Taking the Shiny Toy Back*

Ok, so you're the exhausted parent of a fractious pre-schooler. You're just treating yourself to a lukewarm cup of tea while little Daisy pastes sticky handprints all over your tablet. Time soon to put it away and rush to the school gates to pick up her older brother. But what's this? Daisy has other ideas. She doesn't want to give it back, not while she's having such fun. Her bottom lip forms a sulky pout, her nose scrunches. Daisy shakes her head: 'No.'

What are you going to do?

It's worth noting that, when you give your child something they like and feel secure with, such as a pacifier, blanket, teddy or a bright, shiny thing like your phone or tablet, which is enchanting their every moment with its pings, dings and dazzling colours, this level of pleasure is going to be difficult to stop suddenly, especially for a small child who can't tell the time, or indeed understand the concept of time at all.

First things first here. As we discussed in Chapter 3, no, they're not already addicted to the device. However, they are having fun, are engaged and like what they're doing. And when pleasurable things, such as sweets, toys and portable devices, are taken away from children, it can often result in a dysregulated response. Small children are less adept at emotionally regulating themselves than an older child, to whom we can explain a natural stopping point and who can comprehend (to a degree) when the 'end time' is approaching. So if you wish to encourage them to stop whatever they're doing on your device, you will need to be the timer, regulator and controller in this situation. To paraphrase Bruce Perry, the child trauma therapist who gave us the 3Rs model – '*r*egulate, *r*elate and *r*eason' – you must regulate (yourself first and then them), before relating to them about what's happening and, eventually, reasoning with them as the temperature cools and everyone begins to return to how things were before the event. This is not an easy process, by the way, and takes practice.

In real-world terms it means, rather than surprising your child by bringing things abruptly to an end and then expecting a calm response, preparing them in advance by saying something like this: 'I know you want to carry on playing and you're [name the emotion present, which is more than likely going to be 'frustrated']. I hear you and I don't like to stop having fun either, but it'll be time to stop soon.'[5] Keep repeating this before you take away the device, to help your child regulate themselves emotionally and come to terms with their imminent loss (and it can also help you to prepare to tackle any frustration that might be heading your way). This is where you need to be regulated, too. Then, as you calmly reclaim the device, keep on speaking to your child and repeating yourself to them. They may very likely fall out with you at this point, in the hope that you will change your mind, which means they will show that frustration in their behaviour. This is where CPR parenting comes in and you stay on target with your approach, being *consistent*, *persistent* and *resistant* in the face of their response.

Once you've reclaimed the device, you can explain more about the reasons why you had to end the play session ('We've got to pick up Jack/visit Grandma/go to school/go shopping', etc.).

However, the child must be in a place, space and time to hear this reasoning, or they'll likely react badly to it, and yell, 'I don't want to go see Grandma!' for example.

Trying the reasoning part with children before or during the taking-away stage doesn't work for any parent I know and they often end up losing it themselves, and shouting or snatching back the device. In these situations, the child learns some or all of the following: that they don't matter, that you don't care and that this is the way to get what you want from people. But by speaking to your child calmly and patiently, you're acting from a place of co-regulation and being a different sort of role model for them.

*TIP:* When preparing to take back treasure like digital devices from your child, think about how you felt (or feel) when the disco ended, the cake was all gone or you had to leave an enjoyable event. Pretend you are talking to an infant version of yourself, and you will see how soothing this can feel (hopefully). Keep going like a broken record: stick to the same words and the same tone to establish the ending of playtime. (You'll find some books to help with this in the Resources – see pp. 347–9.)

## Issues to Avoid for Under-Fives

When it comes to protecting your child, you're their first line of defence, and, as we've discussed, ideally you should be present with them when they use technology. Most of the issues for this age group tend to be from accidentally seeing things that can scare them, taking pictures with the camera that may be of intimate parts of their bodies, or other children taking pictures of them. It has been discovered that some children in this age group play on devices with cameras by themselves, perhaps in their bedrooms, and some have been encouraged by groomers to get undressed in front of the camera (or to engage in sexual behaviours when using services that are live, such as video platforms). So my advice here is: do not allow a child to be left alone with a device (or with other children who are using one) or to be in the proximity of one with a camera without adult supervision.

To prevent accidental viewings of material or accessing apps where they can interact with others means that, if you buy or give a small person a device, or let them use one, you should lock it to accessing things that aren't suitable for children. This means that your second line of protection consists of software interventions like filters, firewalls and parental controls (see box below), which will ensure that they cannot get into spaces and apps where images can traumatise or shock them. This can even include your photos, for example (because consenting, romantic and sexually active adults do sometimes take pictures of things that little people shouldn't see).

You should also ensure that the history in your internet browser, or apps like YouTube, don't allow them to use or see searches that adults might have been using. (I once worked with a child aged five who was able to access porn this way.) Make sure no adult sites or social media are accessible through 'click-and-open' apps installed on any device they use. If any of these apps are on your device, do lock them away on another screen page, or pop them into a folder and or subfolder (which some devices allow to password protect) all of which makes accessing them more difficult (what cybersecurity professionals call layered access).

Whatever action you choose to take, remember the goal here is to make access to images and/or other people difficult for your child and to prevent an accidental click-and-open process. (For more on this, see p. 183.)

> ### *Parental Controls for Under-Fives*
>
> There are so many apps and ways to install parental controls, and they are all subject to the internet provider, phone manufacturer, telecoms provider and software in question, so I cannot provide you with a comprehensive guide here. However, the general approach is fairly similar across all of them: the settings need to be at their highest and strictest protection level, with PINs where possible, and password-protected to restrict access to inappropriate material and to prevent accidental turning on/off or circumvent the controls. Also, ensure that devices, apps and games are not linked to credit cards without PINs or approval passwords known only to you (and be aware that little eyes can very quickly learn your finger movements for passwords and copy them, so always enter these out of their sight). Head to the Resources, pp. 347–51, for details of providers and e-safety advice centres that can guide you in the specific technology processes you will need.

While choices about the type of tech you give your children access to are up to you, I do hope this chapter has given you some ideas on which to base those choices for younger children.

The question remains about whether screens are 'bad' per se for children under the age of five, especially in relation to the topics we've covered so far, such as eyesight, fine-motor movements, language acquisition and changes in the brain (neuroplasticity – see Chapter 4). Speaking as a professional in this area, I would agree with the research I've cited suggesting that interacting with children verbally and non-verbally is the best way to create secure attachment bonds (see p. 122) and to improve their language and communication skills and understanding of the world. It's through our interactions with children in the real world that we can inform them about behaviours and feelings such as taking turns, sharing, empathy and, of course, how to let people know about the troubles they're facing or feeling. These skills can then feed into the behaviours they action through and on their devices, both now and as they grow up.

The fact is that their world now includes technology, which won't be going away any time soon. Helping them learn how to use it – mindfully and intentionally – and to adapt to a world in which it is their everyday experience is how you can empower them and help them to navigate online life safely, with good citizenship skills, too – just like in the real world, where you teach good manners, social norms and etiquette. So conversations about tech should begin early, and this age group is the best place to start.

## Summary

- Avoid taking away digital devices without preparing your toddler to stop playing with them.
- To protect their eyesight, limit the amount of time that very small children spend gazing at screens, and encourage them to go outside and look at things far away, too.
- Don't leave children in this age group unsupervised with technology wherever possible, and do put appropriate parental controls in place.
- You're the parent of your child; you get to decide what works best for you, your little one and your family.

## CHAPTER 8

# 'But All My Friends...' – Middle Childhood and Tweens: Ages Six to Twelve

Asking questions and being curious is a fundamental part of human nature, which is especially obvious in young children. While toddlers continually try their caregivers' patience by asking 'why?', children aged between six and twelve will often test what they're told as part of learning to navigate the world. Because it's now, in middle childhood, that their attention span and their ability to think critically increase and they start to become more independent. But what does this mean in terms of their relationship with digital devices and the world online?

In this chapter, we'll be looking at the ways in which children in this age group interact with technology, such as their increasing demands for all the latest add-ons or in-app purchases and what drives this. We'll be covering some of the thinking involved in the dos and don'ts around apps and gaming.

We'll also be considering some of the claims that are made in the media about children in this age group, concerning issues such as delayed gratification and whether we should be worried about the effects of dopamine, the feelgood hormone that's associated with rewards, and the ongoing debate about screen-time 'addiction' and the pre-adolescent brain (you can always return to Chapter 3 for more on these).

We will also be looking at the significant risk of accidental viewing and exposure to harm if certain apps and platforms and games are used, despite age ratings that appear appropriate for your child, such as games rated by UK age ratings called PEGI as; 4+, 7+ and 8+, not to mention those rated in film and cinema (BBFC) as suitable for ages 12, 12A, 15+, and 18+.

And we will look at ways to protect pre-adolescent children when they are online and why it's important for them to develop the skill of critical thinking. While we'll be revisiting issues touched on earlier, we'll be going more deeply into them, from a more practical perspective, with helpful age- and stage-relevant tips for you to use with your child.

## Middle Childhood: An Age of Both Innocence and Wisdom

I love working with children who fall under the broad umbrella of middle childhood. They often astound me with their existential wisdom, logic and verbal fluency; yet I'm equally amazed by just how diverse this age group can be. The rate at which different children develop between the ages of six and twelve can vary incredibly. Sometimes, I'll find myself working with a mature six-year-old who comes across more like a sixteen-year-old, while I've also known twelve-year-olds who behave and present more like children half their age. Despite the range of maturity within the middle-childhood grouping, however, I have found technology use is often similar for all the children within it, in the sense of the drives to use it and the desire for the social media that is used by their siblings, peers and people they play with online.

The most common form of technology use in this age group is gaming (with no disparity between the sexes, although this age group plays against as many strangers online as sixteen- to seventeen-year-olds) and gaming can be on a console or hand-held tablet.*

Chronological or biological age aren't what matters most when it comes to keeping your child safe online. Instead, the important thing is for you to assess to what degree you think your child *really* understands the world and the online park that is the internet. Some kids will say that they understand something just so their parents will leave them alone. Ascertaining this means repeatedly having conversations with them about keeping safe online and other issues related to the internet, so that you can be confident that they get what you're telling them. If they do, they should be able to explain it back to you – so you'll have to ask them to do just that. This is how you'll know if your child has really taken on board what you've told them.

## What Worries Parents of Children in This Age Group?

It's difficult to know what parents worry about in particular when it comes to their children's tech use because the questions asked in surveys are quite vague ('What bothers/worries you the most?').† We know from this that they are anxious about their children spending time online with the potential to come across content, contact and commercial risks that they won't know about; but mostly, I think, parents' fears originate in the fact that nobody has explained fully or sensibly to them what staring at screens can result in in terms of either benefits or harms. Instead, we've created a bogeyman, as though screen time is equivalent to consuming junk food, drugs or even cigarettes. It's a bit like the

---

\* See Ofcom, 'Children and Parents Media Use and Attitudes report' (2024).

† 49 per cent of parents of this age group are worried about screen time, according to Ofcom 2024.

situation in the 1970s, when parents told their kids that their eyes would go square from too much TV, or that they would become zombies from staring at screens.

A minority of parents do know that the correct minimum age is thirteen for most social media apps such as WhatsApp, Instant messaging (IM), Snapchat, Facebook, TikTok, Instagram, Discord, X, YouTube and so on.* However, some knowingly allow children on to the sites before this age, which is why we need to talk about the risks and benefits of these spaces to children under thirteen.

The benefits can include the positive aspects of connection, community, support, friendship, learning, reading, mastery of technology skills, growth and understanding of social norms, agency and autonomy, consideration of risk, independence, education, play, development of cognitive skills, motor skills, attention and attention to detail, technology progress, immersion in the nuances of life, emotional regulation, information processing and exposure to the languages, ideas, opinions and experiences of others in the world (metaphorically and globally). And for those who use exergames (gaming forms of exercise), there are also the benefits of movement, co-ordination, sharing, health benefits for their hearts and cardiovascular systems, and staving off disease through playful and motivated gaming. This is not a comprehensive list and some of these benefits could be subject to variables, such as age and stage, maturity and vulnerabilities.

The risks include exploitation, grooming, viewing harmful, illegal, inappropriate or scary images, texts and videos (leading to cybertrauma), exposure to adult material, bullying, artificial-intelligence risks, mis-/dis-/mal-information and isolation from others.

Parents tell me they worry about strangers contacting their children, sexual content and, particularly since 2023, interactions

---

\* 32 per cent know about age limits, according to Ofcom 2024.

with artificial intelligence (including robots and programs). They tell me they are worried about AI because they don't understand it and think it's dangerous, although mostly they can't explain why. In my parenting club sessions, I regularly hear parents say they're concerned they don't know how to stop AI or prevent their children from using it.

While many children in this age group are gamers, they're not all social media users, per se, as many do not possess the knowledge or skills to use those kinds of platforms in the way that older children do. However, it's worth being aware that they may have access to versions of social media linked to gaming, such as Discord, a form of group chat, which is commonly talked about in online gaming spaces. Many children aged between five and ten have told me that they have access to this social platform, while WhatsApp and TikTok are now being mentioned more frequently by them, too, with research in the UK stating that over 50 per cent of under-thirteens have lied about their age to access social media apps.* We can do our best to support them in navigating these spaces, and many children do receive online safety lessons in schools (but may not implement the strategies they are taught), but we may need to monitor them more closely through our own parental software and conversational check-ins, in ways that are tailored to their age, stage and individual understanding (especially for children with special educational needs or vulnerabilities), as I would say that most children in this age group won't be ready yet to access the internet without parental supervision.

### The Biggest Risk

Based on my own experience, I feel the biggest risk to kids aged between six and twelve is *unsupervised* access to the internet, which includes the use of gaming, social media (and other websites) and

---

\* Ofcom 2024.

chat forums for which they're underage from both the perspective of neuroscience and the chronological age ratings applied to these spaces, because this can expose them to unsuitable content and contact with bad actors.*

During the course of my clinical work, my research and over twenty-five years of speaking with parents (and being one myself), I've found that one of the most significant challenges parents face is the ever-growing pressure from their kids to let them be 'like everyone else' when it comes to using tech, especially now that the cost has reduced significantly and there's easier access to online gaming through the sort of hand-held devices carried around by children in this age group. The peer pressure on you and your child often results in the need to 'keep the peace' in some way – but at what cost?

The numbers of children aged between six and twelve who now have smartphones or go online – some 96 to 98 per cent of five- to eleven-year-olds, according to an Ofcom report from 2024[1] – triggered quite the debate in that year, with journalists and campaigners sharing stats from the UK and around the world to highlight the ubiquity of this issue (and as always this is a study that captures a small percentage of the 60+ million people in the UK). However, the last major study into this age group from the US was conducted by the research company Pew in 2020/21 (as they do not have an Ofcom in the country), so internationally and globally we (parents and society) are still playing catch-up to some extent with what is actually going on online.[2,3] Nevertheless, it's not such a recent development as you might think. In fact, I can recall an article published around 2015 by London-based Internet Matters, one of the leading e-safety organisations in the UK (for whom I write, as one of their experts), which reported that many ten-year-olds had smartphones. *Primary Times* also reported the

---

* This view is based in the consultancy work I do, my PhD research findings and the clients I have seen for over a decade.

average age of smartphone ownership in 2015 as being ten.[4] *Tech-Crunch* (a large US online newspaper) also showed this in 2016, so this has been consistent for some time.)[5] More recently, it's been suggested (online and in surveys) that the age at which some kids get their first smartphone is slightly lower, at around seven or eight, but we don't have a robust mechanism for measuring this, as it's only captured in those surveys that parents are willing to participate in; while many children start gaming on consoles at around the age of five or six using hand-held devices like Switches or static ones like Xboxes or PlayStations.

We don't know exactly or accurately what children can and do access via their smartphones, because there are spaces online that law-enforcement agencies, parents and non-criminals can't access in order to see what's going on there, as well as ways to hide online activities. And big-tech companies don't currently share the data with academics.

Based on my own experience, both professionally and as a parent, I want to emphasise my number-one takeaway for children in this age group, which is to minimise and prevent unsupervised access to the internet where possible. Ideally, you don't want your child – especially if they have vulnerabilities – to spend time alone on devices in places like the bedroom or bathroom. Instead, you want to be able to keep an eye on them, which means encouraging them to use their devices in the same area of the home that you are in.

Now, I know how hard it is to be surrounded by multiple devices buzzing away and the noise of children reacting to their games and the content they're watching. At times, with my own children I felt like I was in some sort of torture chamber with ongoing music, chatter and gaming talk, while I tried to decipher their language and what exactly my kids were interacting with as they used technology. My patience was tested with the bings, dings and pings, and early internet song memes getting stuck in my head on a loop (still!). But the thing is, if you can't see what your child is doing, you can't see what risks they're taking. You will either need to hear and see them yourself, or you will need help with this, either from another parent or with parental controls. (I'm not going to suggest older siblings do this for you, because they may just let their younger siblings into unsuitable areas or allow them to see content that you wouldn't — because that's often just how older siblings behave.)

But let's be realistic: while the best advice is to keep our children in sight and within earshot when they're on their devices, many families have more than one child. And sometimes each of those children has their own console or device. So while the idea of supervising a child's digital play looks great on paper, do you have the patience, ears or space (whether mental or physical) to herd all your children and all their devices together in one room, so that you can supervise them all at the same time? Especially if this means that, in doing so, you can't get to your own devices or TV or do your work without a cacophony of noise emanating from several devices, say, and a bunch of shrieking children?

Unless we suddenly develop super-human levels of attention and skills at multitasking, we might have to make choices about who can go on what device at what time and for how long, so that we can supervise what each child is doing and with whom. Given that children may also need to do their homework, revise for exams or share the use of a device for other activities if there is only one, it can be overwhelming trying to manage everyone at the same time, but I know you've got this, and to help you there are some handy tips and advice on setting boundaries in Chapter 10. And of course, parental controls are your staunch allies here, too.

## Parental Controls for Six- to Twelve-Year-Olds

*Consider* For this age group, the most effective way to think about parental controls is to consider what you don't want your child to be exposed to, with the caveat that you still need to supervise this process yourself, because content can still slip through the net. So use the controls as a second line of defence, while acting as the gatekeeper yourself. You will also need to revisit controls at times, as your child moves past the age of eight, towards ten and then towards twelve, and then perhaps once more as they transition into using social media spaces, as the next chapter discusses.

*Implement* Prevent unauthorised access to accounts on streaming and TV channels that have content that is rated 12+. Install PINs or passwords and ensure that access on tablets, TVs and computers all matches up (see Resources, pp. 349–51). Block access to social media apps other than, for example, YouTube Kids (bear in mind that this is aimed at children up to approximately age eight, so you may need to reconsider when they reach that age and ask for different videos). Use the blocking functions from your internet service provider, device manufacturer and contract provider where you can; you can always purchase parental-control software online or through companies specialising in digital technology. Ensure gaming spaces (parties/messages and in-app purchases) are set up so that they can interact only with other children they know in the real world, that you can approve friend and message requests and that all in-app purchases are protected by passwords and PINS. Ask your child not to use headphones or headsets when playing, so that you can listen in to the chatter in games when possible.

> *Monitor* Be aware of any new friends and new friend requests and keep an eye out for bullying, exploitation or buying 'stuff' online. Also monitor conversations that take place over games, new language that develops (such as 'gyatt' and 'skibidi', which were popular in 2024), and keep up to date through internet-safety newsletters from reputable sources (see Resources, p. 347).

Even when we put all the above in place, the issue is complicated when children may have access to devices belonging to their siblings or the family as a whole, along with streaming services and smart televisions. You may well also need to think about your child's access to devices outside of your home, such as in the playground or at after-school clubs. And what about if your child spends time at someone else's home, or indeed if you host sleepovers for their friends? Then you may need to talk to the parents and guardians of any friends your child spends time with or the people who run extracurricular activities, and ask about their approach to devices and digital safety.

As part of these conversations with other parents and guardians, and depending on your child's age, you will likely have to talk to these people about devices not being used out of sight, what sort of content can be accessed on your child's devices now the controls are in place and why they are there, and what you are happy for your child to engage with when they visit other homes. Some households may have a 'no-phones' policy, so you may need to discuss this, too.

Cybersecurity websites like those listed in the Resources (see p. 347) often offer helpful information on parental controls for protecting your child's device when they're away from home. As another measure to prevent the use of secret devices, do check any drawers containing old disused phones. You might be surprised to find one missing if you have a smart kid, as SIM cards can be relatively easy for children to get hold of and use to make an old phone into a new working one.

## The Cost of Gaming

When their children are in middle childhood, many parents buy and download games and give them permission to play them on consoles, PCs, laptops, tablets or phones. If you have a child aged between six and twelve, you'll very likely have been put under pressure at some point to buy your child the latest piece of technology-related 'merch' or gaming kit, clothing, food, music or whatever it is, because 'everyone else' has it – apparently. This is yet another manifestation of our very human instinct to fit into the tribe, squad or team.

When applied to a gaming environment, the need to fit in through buying the latest accoutrements (in-purchase items, maps, skins, downloadable content, packs, accessories, game passes, subs and various other things you may or may not have heard of in relation to games) can be something that costs you and your child daily, weekly or monthly. These are the products and purchases that can be made 'in the game' or app, and they're the add-ons, required upgrades and '*I neeeed*'s that you'll likely have to deal with on more than one occasion as the parent of a child who enjoys gaming. They're often called 'items' and represent the ways in which children fit in with their peers, so that they won't be seen as a 'noob' (internet slang for a new player, which can open up bullying and teasing behaviours). This is incredibly important to children when they begin to navigate the world of gaming. Moreover, you or your child will likely need to buy a yearly membership from the console developer or provider or for a particular game.

Children learn about all these sorts of add-ons very quickly and they'll discuss them at school – a lot. They'll often want the latest item just because their friends have it, so that they'll fit in and be liked by their peers. That's why, if you do allow a credit or debit card to be linked to games or games subscriptions, I'd highly recommend keeping a watchful eye on it. My advice is to ensure that the card has a PIN lock or requires you to approve purchases.

## *Watch Out for Gambling*

Online gambling can take many forms for children in this age group – from the old-fashioned type of 'betting' to risk-taking in environments where the outcome is to win something for themselves or others (which could also be part of a grooming process – see p. 151). It can present as an excessive need to be online, as the child tries to acquire something (such as points, accrued hours on a game or social media or the latest accessories in a game). Taking risks on downloadable content, packs, loot boxes and more is generally about wanting to be more popular or have something that is rare and makes them feel seen as special by other children, as illustrated by Ravi's story, below.

> ### *Ravi and His Football Focus*
>
> During our conversations together, eight-year-old Ravi often talked about his passion for football. He wanted to be a professional player when he was older and his favourite game to play on his console was FIFA. He excitedly told me about his team, what shirts he liked to pick for players and how, through the use of a DLC pack (downloadable content with additional material that can be added to a game after its initial release), he could win almost any player for his side. He was especially keen to get a

particular player, so his mates at school would be jealous of him for having the best team.

He explained that he spent his pocket money on gaming 'stuff' and how every week, without fail, he would buy as many packs as his pocket money would allow. When we talked about this, Ravi knew that he was 'betting' on getting a good player, but he felt sad when he got 'a dupe' ('duplicate'). Ravi didn't understand that he was losing more than he was winning. All the same, he was so keen to get the top players for his team that he would have spent any amount of money on these sorts of bets, in a bid to be popular and make his friends jealous. Ravi was unaware that he was effectively betting and also of just how much money he had spent on this pursuit.

Do keep an eye on your child's spending in games. This means keeping access to your credit cards locked and password-protected and, of course, setting up gaming systems with a pin–password combo and an approval notification linked to your phone, so you can keep up to date with any purchases. This can also help you detect if there's fraudulent activity on the card. It can be time-consuming (and heavily interrupts your day, task or patience at times) to keep approving purchases, and they can soon mount up in cost (for example 100 x £1 over 3 days is easy to accumulate or lose track of), and credit-card companies and banks now routinely ask if you have this set up on your child's gaming console or accounts. Children likely won't be keeping track of their online and in-game purchases, so you need to.

## Scam Alert

Many children in this age group can be prompted to spend money in games by other players, including their friends, or to send them money 'for favours', for items, for help or just because they're kind. I've worked with children who'll do this as a way to buy friendships because they feel lonely or unpopular. They'll often try to share or give away items that they've worked hard for, or they'll give up their passwords and usernames to people they believe to be their friends. Online, the word 'friend' can be synonymous with 'other player on the server' or 'on a shared social media feed or list'. Aside from trying to please these sorts of so-called friends, some children may be tricked into receiving codes that turn out to be scams, like the phishing emails that many of us are subjected to.

This is why we need to think carefully about the potential risks involved in children using these apps and gaming spaces, as they might be trying to make friends but falling foul of scammers who try to groom them. Head to Vodafone's website (see Resources, p. 351), where I've created some simple videos explaining this issue, and use their family online-safety hub for more information. You can also grab a fabulous free book to download about online scams, with information on how to talk about, avoid and mitigate their impact. And when you've set up notifications for purchases, you'll have an opportunity to talk to your child about the money they want to spend and what it's for – this will help them to pause, moderating the immediacy of just clicking 'yes'. As I say, 'Woah before go!'

## The Murky Waters of Meme Culture

Traditionally, the term 'meme' refers to a cultural or behavioural element that is passed on by imitation or other means. Today, however, it is better known within an online culture that's emerged whereby, when somebody makes a mistake, errs or fails, this unhappy event can then be immortalised by the creation of a meme – a picture or collage of a scene with text over the top, which often relates to it in a humorous manner (although that's sometimes debatable).

Memes are passed on by one internet user to another and can be shared many times over through different spaces online. And the evidence suggests that even young children are now sharing them with each other.[6] There are gaming memes, chat-room memes, historic and topic-specific memes and those that circulate on social media, all with the intent to ridicule, annoy and catch you out. They often relate to specific ages of the internet and can also include songs, tunes or noises. For example, you may have heard of the Rickrolling meme, which usually includes a disguised hyperlink to a video clip of Rick Astley's song 'Never Gonna Give You Up'.

The issue of memes overlaps with debates about misinformation and disinformation and even cyberbullying; sometimes we can't isolate an issue in the online space without looking beneath the surface to see what's lurking and why. Memes can also go very wrong; they can be overly sarcastic, offensive, racist and sexist, rather than funny and light-hearted. Children can find themselves exposed to lots of content this way, ranging from the mischievous to the malicious. This is often labelled as LOLs (laugh-out-louds) and bantz (banter), but the underlying intent and sarcasm can be difficult for children to understand, especially those with learning or social difficulties.

This is a complicated space and an area that adults often don't understand. Their initial reaction might be to perceive the act of sharing a meme as hateful and 'wrong' because the content is often dry, bordering on dark humour and might be construed as offensive (if taken as anything other than a joke – think of a Ricky Gervais or Sacha Baron Cohen style of humour and you'll be on the right lines). Sometimes a meme and its context may be completely misunderstood by the child and they share it, thinking it's meant to be funny (or because it is, indeed, funny – to them). This can result in reports being made to the platform about the contents of the meme (that it is racist, hateful and/or offensive), which can end in said child receiving a thirty-day ban from a game, for example, or being muted by the game administrators, which means they cannot engage with others going forward.

Quite a few of my clients have considered it appropriate because of their own sense of humour and the nature of their online friendship groups (say, squads and clans in games or messaging apps) to share a meme, and then, having sent it, have found themselves at the mercy of an online mob and a barrage of hate, trolling and cyberbullying in those same groups or games.

*TIP:* Have conversations with your child about sarcasm and offensive humour in things like memes. For example, one of the most common memes is the 'distracted boyfriend' turning to glance at a beautiful woman while he is with his partner, who looks on, dismayed and furious. The joke in this meme usually appears in speech bubbles above their heads, but what we're really seeing in the image is a depiction of feelings of betrayal in romantic partnerships and how this feels sad, upsetting and so on. As you may discover, explaining this to your child and discussing complicated things like sarcasm with them is going to be so much fun (ha, ha)! Talk to your child about when it's acceptable to say 'jokey' things and with whom, and how to consider the impact on people who may not understand that they're joking around. Explain why some people might misinterpret their attempts at fun and frolics as, say, hate speech, racism or sexism, and how these sorts of comments could actually fall foul of this. For example, people with a disability may laugh at themselves in some way, but if their friends do the same it may be hurtful. This is complex human behaviour, and I don't have the word count to do it justice here.

## *A Note on Children with Social, Emotional or Educational Needs, Neurodiversity and/or Trauma*

I will be brief here, but you can find more information on my website (on my parents' courses page). Children with neurodivergence, social and emotional difficulties may fail to read social cues relating to appropriate levels of jokiness and having fun conversations with someone in the real world, which means it can be even more difficult for them in the online space, where there are fewer visible cues. Moreover, learning difficulties can make this process even trickier, as a child might not know what some words actually mean, resulting in these being used in contexts that are inappropriate. These children may struggle to understand how other people can feel as a result of their own behaviour, and here again it can be a strenuous enough process for parents and teachers to teach them about this in the real world, let alone in digital spaces. The most common problem I deal with in children in this cohort is that they lack a theory of mind (the ability to attribute mental states to other people, or put themselves in their shoes) or empathy for others. At times, they might not care, because they don't necessarily know how to. This is a hands-on daily teaching process and one that certainly means you will need to monitor your child's interactions with others online to help them learn the social cues (which many adults don't know how to do online either).

It's important to be aware that, in some spaces on the internet, certain types of comments and memes are now on the cusp of illegality. The Online Safety Act and law-enforcement agencies such as the UK police have started to apply a set of standards according to which saying, 'It was a joke!' is no longer considered a viable excuse when posting or reposting offensive material, which is now seen as a crime under the Misuse of Electronic

Communications Act. If somebody is believed to have propagated online abuse or harassment through the use of memes, they might even find themselves accused of cyberbullying (see p. 236).

## Hidden Dangers: Grooming in the City Park

We looked at grooming earlier, in Part 1, but how do we apply what we know to this age group? Let's start with a look at Marla's story, which serves as a stark wake-up call to parents and children alike.

### *Marla's Story*

Aged eleven, Marla quite often played on her phone in her bedroom, explaining, 'It's annoying being downstairs because my little sister makes so much noise.' When she was in her room, she would open Musical.ly (now called TikTok) and copy the dances that other children were doing online. She often videoed herself and uploaded clips to the platform, where she got lots of likes and the occasional comment.

A person called Mike started to comment on her videos, telling her that she was pretty and a 'cool dancer' and that she was going to be a star when she got older. He asked her one day if she had an app called Kik and if maybe they could talk on there. Marla downloaded the app and began to chat to Mike, who said he was famous and that was why he couldn't send her an image of himself. Instead, he asked her to send a picture of herself wearing her favourite outfit. Marla did this and Mike asked her if she had any friends that they could have a video party with.

When Marla asked her friend Shannon to join her on a video call, Shannon's mum was alerted because of parental control

> settings on Shannon's phone. Luckily, in this case the contact with Mike was reported and the police acted swiftly. Marla's guardians were beside themselves at the thought that this could have happened in their home, and in Marla's bedroom of all places. They took some e-safety lessons (via their local school; you can find more in the Resources section on e-safety sites to visit) and they learned how to use parental controls (see pp. 193), which they've now put in place until Marla is old enough to use her device alone and unsupervised.

It can be difficult to explain to young children why there are issues with sharing images online, especially when some apps mean they can add funny filters to their faces or their bodies (which is what children do when they dress up in real life), and it might not seem to them like there's anything inherently problematic about letting other people see these sorts of photos or videos. However, as mentioned earlier, there are now technology programs being developed that can 'undress' pictures of adults or children using AI. It's therefore best not to share anything digitally that could be 'undressed'. So the conversation you want to have here with your child centres on *why* we don't share pictures. Unfortunately, this advice can sometimes be translated by parents as meaning, 'I'll just tell them that anything with a camera is forbidden and ban it!' (which won't work, for the reasons we saw on p. 35).

This could be the trickiest topic about which to have discussions with your child, but however you choose to broach it it's important to help them understand risk, and remind them about who else is out there in the digital city park. You need to have age-appropriate yet honest conversations, which can be difficult with this age group as they are developmentally not always ready for the conversations you need to be having. While you do need to choose words that are appropriate for your child, the conversation does need to include accurate representations of grooming and exploitation, and explain the reality of what can be done to their images. To that end, if you were to tackle this sort of conversation with a six-year-old, for example, you might say the following:

> So the thing about photographs or videos on phones and with cameras on our consoles, computers and tablets is that, when we share them with someone else, that person might have a program on their device that can 'take off' your real clothes and make you look undressed! So in our house (or family) we don't send photos or videos to people, without checking with Mum/Dad [or whoever is taking care of the child and has an awareness and understanding of what we are discussing here].

With a child aged around seven or eight, you could also ask about their feelings and thoughts on this, saying something like, 'Now, I know that you haven't really taken off your clothes for the photograph, but the AI program could, so I wonder how you'd feel about that happening to your photo?' You'd then wait for your child's reply while they think about the issue. This approach can be adapted for a more competent and mature child, too. For an eleven- to twelve-year-old, for example, you could say something like, 'What do you think of people or programs that use these apps to make children look naked? How would you react and what would you like us and/or the technology companies to do about it?'

Often, responses from children can include comments such as: 'I only send them to my friends.' This opens the way for you to have a conversation with them about who their 'friends' really are. You might ask, 'Can Mummy/Daddy/your caregiver check who these people are on your friends list?' so that you can see whether these individuals are real-life friends who you know, too. But it is also important to note that you may have to consider and convey to your child that anyone can send the pictures on elsewhere, so it really isn't just about your child sending to their own friend, it's what happens to the images next. You can also start to have conversations about body safety with technology, and about not taking devices into bathrooms and so on.

You might find that conversations like these also impact how you yourself approach sharing photos of your children online, and with whom. You can speak to them about this as well, and suggest that you both only share photos with trusted people. However, be ready to accept that your child may no longer be willing to share them at all in digital spaces.

Do be aware also that sometimes children in this age group will recruit others into visiting online spaces where a groomer might be lurking. This is often done by persuading them to join gaming or social media channels and then to invite their friends to join, too. Be aware of (incoming or outgoing) party invites, Discord links and invites to other games, platforms or apps.

> *TIP:* As I've said, the best approach is not to allow your child to send images to anyone or take images for anyone. This means you will need to set up notifications for friend requests on your phone for you to approve, so you know who your child is talking to. And, of course, have the sort of conversations we've been looking at, repeatedly and in small doses, as repetition is the same as practice. Have a narrative set up for 'if this happens' and let your child know they can come to you even if they do send images – and that you will help them, not punish them. *I cannot emphasise that last point enough* – otherwise shame can make them stay silent. They need to know it is safe for them to come to you, no matter what.

> ### *Take Five*
>
> It's disturbing to think that something as seemingly innocent as a photo of your child could be exploited in any way. Take a moment, get a cuppa – and breathe.
>
> Controlling the breath is a great way to calm down quickly and there's a practice called box breathing that you might find helpful. To do this, imagine forming a square with your breath: breathe out for a count of four, in for a count of four and repeat, until you've completed the square's four 'sides'.

## Real Friendships Online

Having looked at grooming and the dangers of bad actors in the park, I want to take a moment to consider the concept of real friendships online. Part of the criticism of digital technology and smartphones appears to have its roots in the belief that meaningful and real connections can only exist in the real world, where face-to-face interactions take place. In my view, this belief arises from a lack of understanding about how relationships can be formed and sustained online.

It's clear that 'the real world is the only way' simply isn't true when you consider the use of emojis to symbolise feelings and the shared language of online culture, as well as the dynamics of communicating both in the moment, as in gaming, and through conversations that take place over time, whether via text, email or voice messages.

Besides all that, ever since the year 2000 high numbers of romantic relationships have been formed online.[7] In fact, the internet has become the most popular way to meet a future marriage partner. So why do we think that only adults are capable of forming healthy relationships online, but children aren't? It seems a little biased, don't you think?

> ### Zac's Story
>
> Zac was eight years old when I met him as an online client. He was having problems making friends at school. He had a diagnosis of autism and struggled to play with other children co-operatively and often physically hurt them when they didn't follow his 'rules' for the game they were playing.
>
> Zac loved computer games and building computer programs, but he also had an incredible knowledge of historical figures and a fascination with dinosaurs. He struggled to make eye contact with the screen that my face appeared on, and he often wanted to show me what was on his iPad or TV, in a book or on his shelves in the house and garage. We talked excitedly about his passions, and because I could keep up with his computing knowledge we were able to build a rapport and what is known as interpersonal safety and trust, including relational processes such as taking turns and using a shared language. These processes are an important part of interacting with others and forming a meaningful connection with them.
>
> I gradually moved from being an observer into sharing games with him and, as a result, he started to refer to me by my name to explain to teachers at school how we played together online and why he was 'my friend'. In therapy language, this meant that he had 'integrated' our relationship into his world.
>
> Yet I never met him once in real life. We maintained our interpersonal bond through a screen from start to finish. Zac went on to be able to play with other children online (often in shared games like Gorilla Tag, Rec Room and Fortnite) and this then moved into his friendships at school.

What can we take from this? Corporeal interactions (i.e. in the real, tangible world) aren't everything, and real connections can take place through a screen, too. Your child may be connecting with friends in this way, and to them it really is real. Of course, all this having been said, we know that there are very valid and serious safety concerns around the connections children can form in online spaces, and these must not be ignored.

> ### *AI – Friend or Foe?*
>
> At the time of writing, AI isn't yet a known threat to children when it comes to grooming them directly, but it pays to think ahead. As I mentioned in Chapter 6, there are already AI bots inside some games and social media apps, as well as interactive apps, and I do think we need to keep a close eye on what these sorts of apps ask, talk about or indeed encourage children to share. And why. Apps that include AI may be seen as friends and confidants that may evoke a feeling of a real relationship or friendship. However, these apps haven't always been friendly, and have given mean, bullying and life-threatening advice to those who use them. So let's prepare our children for this by keeping a watchful eye on the technology and the games they are playing, who they talk to, etc.
>
> We've already talked about the risks of apps that are able to digitally undress images, and I strongly suspect that AI and interactive apps may soon become yet another problem to tackle in this area. Once again, in my view young children shouldn't be left alone with devices, and most certainly not with apps or people they can interact and share images, photos or videos with.

## Sex and Violence Online – On Devices and TV

Many parents and professionals think about viewing of violence and sex online in terms of digital devices. However, I would encourage you to remember that TV streaming platforms are 'online', too, because they are connected to your broadband. In the course of my work, I've come across children in the middle-childhood age group who've seen violent and graphic images on TVs that their parents neglected to lock down through the use of PIN numbers or the provision of child accounts. (See p. 112, for advice on TV PINs.) A similar thing applies to services like YouTube, Twitch and other platforms, where live events can and do take place alongside recorded ones, and of course social media accounts, where live events occur all the time! Bear in mind that cartoons depicting sexual activity can also appear on these platforms and in online games, where other players can make their gaming character behave in sexualised ways or draw them so they appear highly sexual.

Parental controls can serve a great purpose here, as you can limit the accidental viewing of sex and violence by setting up kids' accounts, which are available on services like YouTube. (YouTube recommend their kids' accounts are suitable until age 8, so you may find that children aged around eight start to argue for the right to have their own 'adult' accounts. My advice is to delay access to the risk of 18+ content that you cannot control.)

---

*Conversations Before and After*

The aim in this section is to help you get started on conversations with your child that will help protect them from seeing violent and/or pornographic material, and also those difficult but important conversations that may take place once they've seen it. Although a lot of this applies to teens, I'm including it here because middle childhood is when you need to lay the foundations.

Conversations should include aspects that you may not be comfortable talking about, such as gender, same-sex couples, scenarios involving more than two people, the acts that take place. Parents often tell me they would rather someone qualified had the birds-and-bees conversations with their child, and some worry they might be considered to be behaving inappropriately in raising these sorts of subjects with their offspring. But here's the thing: we just don't talk enough – in any setting – about *why we humans often have sex* (i.e. because it can be fun, it's mostly pleasurable and, yes, we do it to carry on the species as well).

Since time immemorial people have been fascinated with *it*, having *it*, seeing *it*, doing *it*, and *how* we have *it*. It is an innate part of human behaviour to be fascinated by sex, and the internet has enabled us to create huge volumes of pornographic material that has never before in our history been so accessible.

So if we want to open the way for conversations about sex *before* our pre-teens become teens and see porn, we need to speak to children about sex, sexuality and even porn *before they use the internet*. This means we must begin to have age-appropriate conversations with them about this in their middle childhood, before they start to access or stumble across porn, especially in light of the fact that avatars (characters) in 4+- and 7+-rated gaming spaces can emulate sex acts, while search engines can provide cartoon-like versions of this content and, of course, videos of the act itself can be happened upon by chance. Use parental controls to minimise accidental viewing. Also be aware that they may go looking for it purposefully if they hear words or see things that pique their interest and then seek it out through searches that lead them directly to it.

We often believe that young children are *too* young to see sex, or know what it is, or that they shouldn't know about it. And teens might be embarrassed about it, we often don't mention it to them either. But *we need to get comfortable with talking to our children about respectful relationships*, whatever their age. And that has nothing to do with porn! We need conversations about respect in relationships before they see porn, because, if that's the first time they see what happens in a relationship they may think it's the norm, or that certain sex acts constitute respect (which will be confusing for them).

Daily and weekly occurrences relating to friendships, relationships and bodily contact, such as hugs or being asked to kiss Grandma, are all moments we can use to talk about consent, agreement on body choices and what is pleasurable, such as a handshake versus a hug. Silence is not our ally on this topic, especially if there's a child or teen involved who's confused or scared about what they've seen. Creating the space for them to talk to us about any worrying or confusing things they've seen online sits at the centre of the approach taken in this book, and to achieve it we have to get past our own qualms. Sadly, times have changed since we were young, and we cannot fight this with defiance, resistance or fear.

## CPR in Action: A Family Visit to Grandma and Grandpa's House

MUM: Ok, Joe, it's time for bed shortly. You've got thirty minutes to screens off and bathtime [*consistent* with house rules, even though they are at grandparents' house].

JOE: Ok. Mum, I'm just starting a new game of Lucky Block. Scott is teaming up with me so we can beat Lewis!

[Thirty minutes pass.]

MUM: Ok, Joe, time to come off [in a tone that is neither shouty nor demanding = *consistency* again]!

JOE: But Mum, we have another few rounds to go. Just gimme another ten minutes?

MUM: No, Joe. It's time to come off. The bath is ready and your dad wants to come up for one after you. Chop-chop now.

JOE: Muuuuuuuummmm!!

MUM: Ok, Joe – I know you want to keep playing, and we agreed that it would be thirty minutes. I get that this is frustrating, and yep, I know the boys will be upset at your leaving, but we gotta get this bath in so we can all keep to the schedule [*persistent*].

JOE: Muuuuuuummmm, I just want five more minutes . . . or just two!

MUM: Joe, we have to end now for bathtime. I know you don't want to and I understand the issue. We must end now. That is the rule we have in the house. We must end [*resistant*].

JOE: Oh, I hate you doing this. You always spoil my fun. Lewis and Scott can stay on longer than me! It's not fair. [Joe is beginning to cry.]

MUM: We must end. I know it feels unfair, buddy, and you are cross with me. It's time to end and time to get a bath. You can turn it off or I can – your choice; but we must stop for tonight [*resistant*].

JOE: Fiiiine [Joe turns the console off and stomps to the bathroom].

MUM: Thank you. That was a great choice, even though you didn't want to. I'll go and make you a hot cocoa now. You want marshmallows on it?

[Later on]

MUM: How about we find a way to make the night-time endings easier? Would you like a bell, an alarm or a sand timer to help you see when time is up?

[Here, co-creation and rule setting are collaborative, and Joe may feel he has more choice if he gets to control how he sees the ending time. Also note that Mum isn't saying, 'good lad' to him for making the choice; she says, 'Thank you,' to underline the fact that it was not about being a 'good' (or 'naughty') child, but about his choices, which could be empowering.]

## Conversations around sextortion

A good way to talk to your child about material or content they shouldn't share is via stories. As an example, let's imagine a little girl called Freya, who's keen to take her phone to her room at night. When she asks her mum about it, Mum says, 'Yes, Freya, I know you want to watch YouTube or play on Minecraft on your device in your room before bed, but here's the thing: you might use another app or be talking to a friend or even a tricky person without realising it, who might even ask for you to send a photo of yourself. Some people think it's funny or silly to send pictures with no clothes on, or even just your pyjamas. We think it's really important in this house that we don't send any pictures to people without checking with me or Daddy first.

'Because you know the story of Hansel and Gretel and how the witch tricked them? Well, sometimes people can be pretending like that online, or they can get your picture and make it look like it has no clothes on – like when you take the clothes off your Build-A-Bear. So we don't want you to be tricked, and that's why we talk about sending any pictures first.

'Sometimes we might have to say no to you talking to someone or even letting you take a picture. It's not you. It's just that we know there are tricksters "in there", so we all have to be super careful when it's a picture of us or our bodies. We won't share pictures of you for this reason, either, and we will keep those images for people we can trust in our family WhatsApp group – or we might just decide it's much safer to only show them to people from our device when they come to visit us in real life.'

If the child is older than, say, ten, you can adapt your conversation accordingly, perhaps leaving out mentions of fairy tales, for example.

But it's not just about images. Kids can easily be exposed to sexual or violent language in online gaming environments, some of which can even come from other children. Here again, try to keep gaming consoles and devices within parental earshot (in living rooms, for example) and ask your child to play without headphones so you can monitor the environments that he or she is gaming in. You can help them understand that adult language consisting of swear words is inappropriate, or that it might be racist or sexist, and why. And, while it's important to monitor the activity of the child who is online, do keep in mind the little ears of other siblings and household members who might be exposed to colourful language, too.

## *What To Do If Your Child Sees Sex or Violence*

Children may have varying responses to viewing violent material. Mostly, it will be confusing and might make them worried or scared. There's lots of research to show this, which has formed part of my PhD studies and cybertrauma training for over fifteen years; mostly, this has been around (cinema) horror and slasher movies and TV shows. (My own research suggests similar effects from online spaces. This will become public knowledge in late 2025 when my thesis is publicised.) These responses can then transition into bedtime, when they might have nightmares or sleep issues. Children in this age group are often still trying to understand the difference between what's real and what's fantasy, including real or imagined threats and dangers. In my work, I've found that they are the ones who most often experience cybertrauma in response to sex and violence viewed online.

If this applies to your child, you may need to spend time helping them with getting to sleep or staying asleep. They might wet the bed, wake up sweaty and in terror, or they might start to ask questions about death and the universe and everything in between. They may go off their food and seem to need the loo more (or less) often, and some children have been known to 'not make it in time' and soil themselves more than once (signifying nervous system dysregulation) which can be incredibly shaming for them.

Be patient and answer as many questions as you can about any of the content they talk about – or about any other topic, as they may ramble about other things instead (again, this can be an effect of their brain and nervous system trying to find balance and calm). Consider reading or telling them a story with a hero in it that can help them to imagine being a hero themselves, triumphing over adversity – this can reduce their feelings of helplessness and powerlessness.

If your child is crying, rocking, not speaking or any other response that means you can't talk to them, be patient and follow the 3Rs mentioned earlier (see p. 180): regulating their emotions, relating to them and reasoning with them later, when they are calmer and able to talk to you. You can do this by holding them, rocking them or sitting near them (as some children don't want to be touched), and you can make soothing noises or say soothing words, such as, 'I know, I know, I know'.

In most cases, it's best to avoid bringing up the content with them, and to allow them to talk to you about it in their own time, otherwise you can reinforce distressing memories of it. Offer the open space to talk about it when they are ready, then wait for them to do this. They may go back and forth between starting to talk about it and then not. In most cases, children do talk about their experience; however, they might never describe it in detail. They may show signs of distress, and if this happens you should get in contact with a trauma therapist who is qualified to work with children. Cybertrauma is often overlooked as it has not yet been recognised formally as a category of trauma, but I can say with absolute confidence that it is one and it affects children more than we realise. For more help and advice, reach out and join my parenting course and group (see Resources, p. 347), as, sadly, this is a common experience for this age group.

It's also not uncommon for parents to blame themselves when their children are in this situation. But you need to be compassionate with yourself here and recognise this for what it is – a symptom of the age we live in and not your fault.

## Sorting Information from Misinformation

Nowadays, it can seem increasingly difficult for any of us, whatever our age, to differentiate between the information and misinformation that's available online. And given that AI can increasingly alter or even invent facts, events and research, how on earth can we ever expect our children to know who or what to trust online?

Much of what we've addressed in this chapter in terms of risk concerns the sort of people who children may interact with online, such as scammers and potential groomers; however, building trust in an online world differs somewhat from doing so in the real world. The truth is that we don't always get the same bodily sensations that alert us to threats when we use digital products (apart from when using virtual reality). This means our safety-and-trust system isn't running to full capacity, so it's going to make mistakes, unless we can slow down and give it more information. To do this, we need to consider how we interpret what we encounter and interact with online. And indeed, offline too.

So how do we build our child's trust in people, information and systems in the real world, so they can better assess what they come across online, while strengthening their radar for truth? We teach them critical thinking as best we can. And this involves more than saying 'that's not true'.

### *Encourage Critical Thinking*

Children often cannot begin to think about the world in a deeply critical manner till they reach adolescence (and, of course, the over-twelves are often those around whom parents have the most anxieties concerning tech and the things with which they interact – see Chapter 9). However, developing critical thinking skills is *the* backbone of online safety for us all, whatever our age; in fact, it's our superhero tool for keeping our children safe online.

To sharpen this tool, we have to slow down to speed up, as the meme goes. When we pause for a fraction of a second to assess what we're seeing, reading or hearing, we give our brains a chance to take in all the information and decide whether it represents a threat (leading to the fear response) or if we can be curious about it (non-fear response). We can look at it and say, 'I wonder...', then ask questions about the truth of the matter, rather than responding automatically from a fear-based place, which results in our need to let the 'clan' know about the danger that lurks here in this story, and a desire to 'share' or comment' before we have had time to think.*

The word 'why' is powerful and it's the most asked question by children themselves because – well, they want to understand stuff. And a spirit of inquisitiveness is invaluable to survive and thrive in a world of AI, quantum computing and the ever-increasing speed of technology.

So we really must stop avoiding the 'why' question, or trying to answer it with jargon or dismissing it with an 'I said so'. If your child asks you 'why' about the incredible park that is the internet and you're unsure of the answer, my advice is that you simply reply, 'I don't know,' closely followed by, 'Let's find out together, if we can?'

> *TIP:* Try asking your child questions in a curious and playful manner to see if you can understand more of the reasoning behind what they say and do. For example, if your child says, 'I want to play Minecraft after school,' you might ask, 'Why Minecraft and not another game?' Or you

---

* I wonder how many times you have deleted something after thinking about it and feeling it wasn't the right thing to do, or after the backlash had created that feeling from others pointing out your 'fail'? We are the adults doing this online, so what chance do our kids have if we don't help them develop these skills?

could ask, 'Why do you think children play Minecraft?' Then, 'Why do they have different play modes in it?' (Play modes refers to creative and survival modes.) For every answer, see if you can expand your discussion a little more.

Why? Because through curiosity of your own you see better into your child's world and, in the process, you can help them to understand the world they play in and to ask questions themselves about how it works.

Curiosity and a willingness to learn *with* your child will open the way for both of you to share an experience of using search engines, answering questions and doing your own research online. It can be an incredibly important exercise, as it will enable your child to learn detective skills alongside you as a way to sift through the noise online and find the signal. This is how your child will learn (once they are old enough to use social media, of course) how to check out who someone is, and to find out more about them online through their gamertags or school social spaces (if applicable) and other social media handles, accounts and pictures. It can show them how people can find out about them, too, which could be a valuable lesson. Remember, this isn't about telling them, 'Of course you can use social media to track and stalk people' (or even giving them permission to use it, if under the age of thirteen). Instead, when they are old enough, it will enable them to assess relevant information, sort through the rubbish and, hopefully, calibrate the choices they make about their online friendships. This is such an important skill for us all and it is, I believe, a requirement now, not a choice. We need to look at the posts we read, check out who shared them and maybe ask why, and what they hoped to achieve.

Let's help our children develop skills that can help them really understand the threats that exist out there and to build their own 'slow, stop and question' brains. This is the executive functioning we talked about earlier (see p. 90). It's about delayed gratification – slowing down reactive or knee-jerk responses or 'clicking' and rushing impulsively into situations, and instead first considering the impact and consequences of their reactions. Now, while the majority of children in this age group don't have fully formed executive-functioning brains, they can learn from us how to slow down before acting, although the lessons will need to be frequent.

The skill of thinking critically is a great place to end this chapter. As the world of tech becomes increasingly intense and immersive, these skills of enquiry are what children need if they're to thrive in it and stay safe from the sorts of problems we've touched on in this chapter, such as the risks of the hidden costs of gaming, scams, meme culture, misinformation, the threat of grooming and sex and violence. Critical thinking will be key to helping your child navigate the tricky waters of middle childhood before setting sail on the high seas of adolescence. Which is where we'll be heading next.

## Summary

- Use the language and level of reasoning that you think is best suited to your child, rather than a generalised approached based on their age.
- One of the biggest risks to kids in this age group is unsupervised access to gaming and the internet, which includes the use of gaming and social media sites, especially those for which they're underage.
- Join your child on an adventure of discovery, in which you can learn with them about how to navigate online spaces safely.
- Critical thinking is a crucial skill for your child (and for you) to hone, particularly when it comes to the world online.

## CHAPTER 9

# Teenage Tensions and Time Alone

I recently unearthed an old diary that I'd written as a teenager – good grief, the drama of it! The busyness! The emotion! The 'who likes who' and 'who said what' . . . It was exhausting just to read it. Although late adolescents and teenagers may seem to spend a lot of time asleep or doing very little in their bedrooms, there's usually a great deal going on behind the scenes, as it's a time for discovering who they are as individuals and how they fit in with the crowd. And of course, today, that crowd is global. So perhaps the key thing to remember when it comes to teens and tech is that they will be doing, saying and behaving . . . like teens.

As the parent of a teenager you may often feel like the least important person in your child's life, but in fact your child needs you now as much as ever, as they learn how to become an adult both in the real world and online. In short, they need your guidance, nurturing and compassion, even when it may seem like they're pushing you away or pushing boundaries.

To help them, you must really double down on informing yourself about the potential risks online and draw on this knowledge in your parenting, so that you don't find yourself feeling out of your depth. We will look at setting boundaries around tech and devices in a bit more detail later on, in Chapter 10, but here we will be focusing on connecting and communicating with teens and the sorts of problems they might face, such as peer pressure, polarised thinking, social media, obsession with body image and exposure to those familiar problems sex and violence, to name a few. This will also take us into some very challenging terrain, including issues such as sextortion, cyberbullying and self-harm, so read at your own pace and take a moment to breathe whenever you need to.

## Part of the Clan

Earlier, I touched upon how we sometimes mistake problems like addiction for the very natural drive that children and teenagers have to socialise. This can mean spending time online in the company of their mates, squad or group (as in group chat) – people they can identify and feel a sense of belonging with.

The online world has created a particular framework around the term 'friend', which means that many teens may think differently to you and me about what a friend is – or isn't. The idea that someone can join an online game for forty-five minutes without saying a word over the mic, yet be viewed by other players as a 'friend', might seem preposterous to many adults. But when we begin to appreciate the different things we all infer, the ways in which we project aspects of ourselves into cyberspace and how teens in particular can make assumptions about others based on their online behaviour, language and gameplay, it becomes easier to understand the idea of virtual strangers online becoming individuals they know, trust, understand, team up with, are in a squad with, share with and ultimately 'like' as friends.

So when we try to lecture teens about not really knowing someone and how that this means they can't really call them a friend, we're dismissing their frame of reference. This is currently where the gap sits in our understanding around how young people communicate and hang out together online.* It's why we often gauge the quality of our teens' online relationships by the amount

* See Turkle, Shirley, *Reclaiming Conversation: The Power of Talk in a Digital Age* (London: Penguin, 2014).

of time they spend in the company of others, rather than the meaningful stuff they're doing while they're there, such as hanging out together, chatting, goofing around and just being with their mates – what's known as socialising, in other words. While these relationships might seem superficial to us, in that they haven't been curated in the real world, nevertheless they concern valid connections between people who have shared interests, language and other things in common in some way, shape or form.

When teenagers get home from school or college they're going to want to be with their mates and discuss all things 'drama', 'beef' or whatever – pretty much as you might do yourself with your family, friends and your social media buddies. They will want to chat, play and be connected and learn the social norms of how to navigate their online world and the etiquette of being a teen with other teens. And, yes, when it's time to stop because it's late, they'll probably ask for 'just another ten minutes' just like you did when you were younger and out with your friends and had to come in when it was dark. When they're on a game, group chat or mic, they will want that little bit of extra time, so they don't look 'sad' in front of their friends because they have to 'go home' – i.e. go offline – early.

The fact is that in the UK we've shut down many of the real-world spaces where teens could once hang out together and just be with their mates. We move them on from bus stops and street corners and call them anti-social when they're loud, disruptive and acting like the teenagers they are. So what's left for many of them to do in the real world? And then, if they stay at home, they may have to put up with their parent or guardian telling them to 'stop shouting at the game' or 'staring at the screen'. It may sometimes seem to them as if they can't do right for doing wrong. However, in searching for somewhere to just be and a sense of belonging, they may sometimes find themselves in the grip of misinformation and algorithms online – and that is when they will need us to step up as tech-smart parents and engage with them in ways that will help them think critically about the content they come across, particularly in relation to shaping their thinking about themselves and their place in the world.

## The Teenage Search for a Sense of Self

I've talked already about the importance of teaching our children how to think critically, so that they can sift out information from misinformation both online and in the real world. Unfortunately, this is a skill that can seem to go out of the window when kids reach their teens and start to become more reactive rather than responsive to a lot of experiences. This is because of changes in the prefrontal cortex (the area of the brain responsible for skills like planning, prioritising and making good decisions) that take place over a long period of time, and the fact that the skill of responding instead of reacting takes time to develop.

If they are unsure about something or someone or don't know how to do something, they can spend time doing a lot of 'what if-ing' (which on social media or gaming looks like silence, ghosting or avoiding situations) because they're fundamentally unsure of themselves, although it might not always seem like it. Similarly, they may get caught up in online dramas because they're part of a community and fall into groupthink (thinking or making decisions as a group), in which case they may become defensive and attack others (without critically evaluating the content or their reactions). Even teens who are otherwise kind and thoughtful can end up taunting others, and believing everything they see that's shared by people they know or admire.

This sort of herd instinct can also lead to them getting caught up in the latest trends and hoaxes, becoming keyboard warriors themselves and generally behaving like irritating know-it-alls. They may also be at greater risk of following advice blindly (based on admiration rather than critical analysis) and of being tricked and coerced, scammed or hacked. They might grow obsessive about certain things or individuals, and cyberstalk without being aware that this is a crime. When taken to the extreme, obsession can even lead to them taking up certain ideologies and changing their beliefs completely, and they may even challenge reality itself (for example, there's a belief out there that space is fake).

You may find that your teen begins to lecture you – after all, what do you know, you belong to a different generation – and to impose their self-identity at home. When challenged, they will likely regurgitate much of the information, misinformation (and malformation – exaggeration of the truth) or disinformation they're encountering online (or that others share with them if they are online when your teen is not), as they may not have the critical-thinking filter of adulthood – because they're not there yet.

## Parental Concerns About Teens Online

Many of the issues that teens face are lumped together under the banner of them spending too much *time* online (though no rationale is given about exactly what this means, and we could ask, 'Too much time for what, or compared to what?'). As we touched on in Part 1, a fear of social media and how it harms teens has been brought into the limelight by social psychologist and author Jonathan Haidt and other campaigners, with claims that social media is causing changes in self-perception, body image and self-esteem, and in the way teens socialise (suggesting it can be considered abnormal if it occurs online more than offline). However, these aren't necessarily the fears of parents themselves or those of the educators who want to develop digital literacy for teens (and younger children).

In the UK, Ofcom's annual survey 'Children and parents: media use and attitudes' (which has taken place over the course of many years now) asks parents about their children's use of technology and suggests that parents of teens worry specifically that their children will be exposed to inappropriate content for their age (whether that be misinformation, extreme content such as violence or sexual content), be bullied online and see content encouraging self-harm, extreme views and spending money.* Sadly, this and other surveys don't go into much further detail when looking at parents' concerns, such as why they worry about this, what knowledge they have about the issues or where their concerns stem from.

Interestingly, children aged between twelve and seventeen often use social media as a news source. However, with the rise of AI-generated video and content filling these channels, only a third of children today trust the news on social media, which means there's a larger proportion of teens who don't trust content delivered as news on these channels. The flipside is that this could lead them to watching graphic accounts of real events and believing them to be fake. This takes us back to the fact that we need to help them develop their critical-thinking skills to navigate this tricky terrain. In situations where they may have accepted 'news' stories unquestioningly, or even acquired new values or extreme views, your role is to listen to the new information that your teen has taken on board and to create and hold the space in which to enter into dialogue with them. If necessary, do some research of your own, so you'll have the resources with which to counter their claims. You may have to challenge their evidence with your own findings, which can be tough if your child presents what looks like incontrovertible proof. (One of the most challenging aspects of being a therapist for teens is when they see or hear something, and it then becomes *their* truth. Imagine trying to persuade a rock not to be a rock any more; I kid you not – it can be that difficult.)

---

* The annual Ofcom report is available at: www.ofcom.org.uk/media-use-and-attitudes

Sometimes we adults need to tread very carefully when putting forward an opposing view.

So let's start by tackling those pesky algorithms (see p. 11) that can feed teens all sorts of content, views and information. Then we can look at what we can do to support their critical-thinking skills.

### James's Story

James was fifteen and had just started therapy with me. He was very much into fitness and began to tell me about a supplement he had read about online, and how it would speed up 'his gains'. In particular, he'd seen a podcast in which two influencers claimed that, if a person drank whey protein, it would stay in their digestive system for five years.

James didn't know about my other health qualifications that meant I was able to recognise this claim as complete BS. I respectfully challenged him about the credentials of the influencers and questioned how their information might not be quite right?

We talked about how the body worked, why he was so keen to believe what he'd heard and to become 'hench', and what that signified for him in his life. He told me he didn't want to be bullied for being small-framed and was looking to get big as quickly as possible. We spoke about how long hypertrophy (the building of muscles) takes and why there are no shortcuts, and the safety of food like whey and untested supplements.

Our conversation wasn't about me telling James that he was wrong, so much as discussing together why the claims of the influencers might not be as valid as they at first appeared to be and to help him think about them critically.

Health and body-image information – or rather misinformation – such as this could have resulted in James

> believing the hype or quick fixes about certain foods, supplements or diets. Unfortunately, this kind of content can lead to health issues that could last a lifetime, especially if young people use substances like 'injectable hormones' that may be illegal (or not even hormones) and, of course, if they don't get the right medical supervision, or understand the potential side effects, or if they undertake medical procedures that aren't available on the NHS, such as 'butt' implants for cosmetic reasons, which can impact their bone health or cause problems with infertility.

## Navigating Algorithms

Let's go back to our city-park analogy for a moment here. As our children get older, they'll start to go off by themselves more. When they first start doing this, there are generally adults around to keep an eye on them – to check which areas of the park they're going to and with whom. When they're older still, some of them may wander off to the corners of the recreation ground to hang out together. It's often in these spaces that teens learn how to navigate what's called 'street-smart' thinking and how to get along with each other (or not). They learn the rules of being in spaces together. At times, they'll be met with bullying, fighting, betrayals of trust over romantic partners and friendships; they might even experiment with drugs, alcohol and cigarettes.

Older teens will influence younger ones, pranks and jokes are played, there's jostling and tussling, and bitching and broad commonalities around the rules of engagement in that particular place and at that point in time. Different spaces have different rules; for example, teens in skate parks will dress and behave very differently to kids elsewhere in the park. And teens will look out for each other, too.

Most of us will let our teens go off into these spaces without us at some point (and we'll often try to look cool about it when we may not feel that way). This new-found freedom is a test of trust on both parts: the teen's and the parent's. And it really is a requirement for a teen to be able to learn the rules of the world, as safely as possible, and this is often why we send them off in numbers rather than alone.

Many of the spaces in which teens find themselves online are similar in structure, with players from around the world hanging out in this virtual park or youth club, but with one notable difference: there may be adults present. We need to be aware that when teens (and, as we've seen, younger children) engage in social media or in online games, or watch others in spaces like streaming sites, they may be exposed to a wide range of viewpoints, opinions and language, some of which can be vulgar, sexist, racist and the like. They'll certainly be exposed to other teens who'll be navigating similar stages of growing up. Teens will behave like teens. Yet so can any adults present.

This puts teenagers at risk of the very same fears parents have for them: of being bullied, of buying into new ideas, ideals, wants and needs, of being coerced into joining new religions (including those that are internet created, as well as established faiths) or accessing drugs more easily than you can get a new T-shirt from Temu or Shein. They can be exposed to violence, which includes abusive behaviour; they can be trolled (where someone deliberately tries to upset others online) and have their accounts recreated as fakes; they can be stalked; they can be exposed to content that traumatises them, or is inappropriate for their age and stage; and they can be harmed in many ways. All just by being in those environments. These are the risks that are generally behind the worry that they're spending too much time online, or that they're being sucked into the orbit of their peers' influence.

Sadly, these spaces don't have door staff who can spot when kids are being harmed and intervene, so it's down to the other onlookers, teens and 'bystanders' (as they are called in psychology) to take supportive action. This is why many teens act like mini therapists to other teens around the world when communicating with them online, to help them through issues like bullying, suicide ideation and depression.

However, algorithms can also rear their ugly head at this point and undo all the help on offer by sucking teenagers further into the darkness. Algorithms can lead any of us a merry dance, which means we're being targeted by marketing and organisations at a scale beyond our comprehension. So what can we do, as parents, to help our teens avoid falling prey to these? Many of us adults might change our scrolling habits (for a day or two) if we are alerted to, or noticed the algorithms and want to change our feeds in someway, only then to go about our daily business as usual a few days later without giving it any more thought – so can we really expect any different from teens?

One thing we can do is to help them adapt or change what and who they're interacting with, such as influencers or content, by having discussions with them about what they're watching (if they will do this with you). I can highly recommend the app SWAY.LY, which will be on the market by the time this book hits the shelves, which will feature guidance to help you and your teen do this.*

You can help your teen to change what appears on their feeds and what they scroll past by asking them about the types of people they see online and how they feel about the algorithm feeding them more of this content versus anything that challenges their thinking. For example, you could discuss any podcasts they listen to and ask them to tell you what they're learning from them and what might be a typical view held by somebody else who listens to that podcast. Another good approach is to ask them what opinions they have about a hot topic, such as the political landscape (and be prepared for views you may disagree with). This can provide

---

\* For complete transparency here, SWAY.LY is a service I work with and I think it can be a great addition to your parenting toolbox and can help you find balance in a world of misinformation.

an opportunity for you to discuss how they got from A to B in their thinking.

We must teach children how to think critically about the content that appears in their feeds and discuss with them how algorithms can amplify confirmation biases that promote extreme ideas about things like politics, cultural ideologies and body image.

> *TIP:* Talk to your teen about their habits when using devices and apps (which they may not be aware of). The intentional use of technology is key here, and that is going to take more than one conversation about algorithms and critical thinking. Of course, this can push teens to think you're nagging them, so keep your chats short but frequent, and vary the content of your conversations.

Sadly, it's seemingly left up to teens to report any abusive, harmful or harassing behaviour or material they encounter online – but they can only report the content itself, and cannot make complaints or report the fact that algorithms drive this content into their feed. Plus, it requires the big-tech companies to take good enough action once a report has been made, and teens often tell me that 'nothing ever happens [when reporting], so there's no point'. Tech companies must do better here – and so must we, if we can, through both the example we set with our own scrolling behaviours and consistent and ongoing conversations.

## Comparison: A Slippery Slope?

On many platforms nowadays, the most common way for teens to interact with their peers is via image-based conversations. Whether it's in Snapchat (now called Snap by most teens), TikTok videos or Insta posts, your teen will likely spend a large proportion of time seeing other people's faces and bodies online. And as they're at an age when they're still forming their own identity, they'll undoubtedly be comparing themselves, repeatedly, to others as part of that process. They'll be taking it all in: comparing themselves with the haves and have-nots, and immersing themselves in whatever admiration they receive and the crushes they themselves develop. They might even fantasise about a perfect future involving people they see online – a little bit like the crushes on pop stars that many adults of today went through as teens themselves.

But it's been suggested in the last few years, by campaigners who spend time creating content themselves and sharing it on social media, that this image and video content is occurring to a degree that's creating a body-esteem crisis in teens (and increasingly in younger children, too). This seems to be supported by figures about eating-disorder referrals, beauty interventions, such as rhinoplasty (nose jobs), and the number of older teens who are signing up for private plastic surgery. There have even been reports on social media that girls under the age of eighteen are having surgery to their labia (genital area), and some reports online have attributed this to the body ideals in porn. This might be a worry for parents, as many young adults are saying they felt this pressure growing up online but may not have told anyone about it. And, of course, the narrative about self-harm figures often centres around the comparisons of 'self to other' and how this behaviour has increased in females since 2012. This is said to be because girls are in a world of idealised body images, as cited in Jonathan Haidt's and Jean Twenge's work and in the documentary *The Social Dilemma*.

Now, whether this is true or not for all teens is difficult to gauge, because body esteem naturally fluctuates for many as they progress through puberty. For most young people, it can be like watching themselves in a slow-motion horror movie as their bodies start to change shape, size and hairiness and they transition from child to pre-teen, then from teen to grown-up. The aches and pains accompanying this can leave many in distress. Then, when they pick up a smartphone, they're confronted with lots of images of people who don't seem to be experiencing the same crisis they are and who have sculpted bodies that would make a Greek god blush. And even though they know many of these images are filtered and Photoshopped, teenagers often tell me it's hard not to be jealous when you're confronted with a beauty beyond yours, when you feel like poop, have spots galore, are big here and small there, your feet resemble those of a hobbit – and what the actual flip is going on with your voice? When presented with so much seeming perfection online, why wouldn't teenagers feel out of place and not good enough?

If you're constantly being presented with images that suggest you're flawed and lacking, at a time when you may also believe that people like your parents just don't get you, or maybe never got you or took any interest in you, then your self-esteem probably isn't going to be particularly high. Nevertheless, you may pretend that you're ok, and mask your true self and your feelings. To that end, young people often 'filter' themselves online and in the real world, so they don't feel the shame and rejection that whoosh up whenever they notice they're lacking in any given attribute, characteristic or body shape. Consequently, they upload carefully curated images of themselves and pretend online that everything is fine. Which is what their peers see. And on it goes, with young people not speaking out, and using filters to hide their faces or bodies.

The images online of perfect bodies also relate to serious problems such as disordered eating, self-harm and body dysmorphia (a form of which is orthorexia – the overuse of healthy eating/exercise and wanting to be perfectly formed). As well as related depression and anxiety, these are extensive and very complicated topics in and of themselves, which I discuss at length in my previous books, listed in the Resources (see p. 347). But for now, I'd like to keep the focus on the issues with self-esteem that many young people experience. The images they see online often suggest to them that they are not enough and if they just did this, ate (or didn't eat) that, exercised like this, took those performance-enhancing drugs, had a body like this, then they would be likeable, wanted and popular and feel less like their pubescent, disoriented self.

Today, there are so many alleged 'experts' and influencers online in the health and fitness industry, and teens are susceptible to the ideals proposed by them and by their peers – the people they look up to (who won't necessarily include their parents and guardians). What body shape should I be . . . which clothes should I wear and what make-up . . . what foods should I eat . . .? These are just some of the questions they'll start asking themselves as soon as they see images and content while they are scrolling. That's a lot of internal talk, too, as they compare themselves to what they find there.

The resulting cycle of lack – of self-esteem, self-worth and confidence – and of loneliness and feeling unwanted by society (which isn't helped by the way *we* talk about teens, either) is perpetuated online through a world filled with filters and false figures, unachievable bodies that are sold as the 'only way to be important'. It's a 'world of pretend' that insecure teens have been replicating for several years now. The pioneering psychologist Carl Rogers termed this incongruence, and it stems from the disparity between our real self and our ideal self. This gap is seemingly huge for many of us, but it can become a giant chasm for teens who don't have a clue how to bridge it. The fact is that, if we compare ourselves to unreal versions of others, then we become unreal ourselves.

This is why we adults need to be their voices of self-esteem – without being over the top and cheesy or awkward. We need to help them see their value, now and in the future, and really empathise with the fact that they're having a difficult time – and all while not appearing to pity them. Here are some ways in which you can do this:

- Celebrate your teenager just as they are, without commenting on things like their appearance or weight too often. I am aware you may need to if they gain or lose drastic amounts of weight in a short period of time or start wearing heavily laden make up, for example. (However, be aware that when you start doing this 'celebratory' stuff they will likely assume you're after something, or that you're 'being weird', as I've heard young people tell me.)
- Mention subtle things about them that you notice – things that are personality based and not focused on size, weight or make-up trends (such as their kindness, patience or diligence).
- Thank them for any small job or chore they do. Avoid any sarcasm (yes, you should rein that one in), and really thank them for helping around the house.
- Ask them for their opinion on something. You don't have to agree, but what is more important to many of us – including our teens – than someone thinking our opinion is worth hearing? Or ask them for guidance on a good TV show, or a podcast or music to listen to. And then watch or listen to it in their presence and have a conversation about it, even if you don't like it.
- Be playful. Use their language to have fun, but don't tease. This is a skill that comes from an approach by Dan Hughes called PACE – which stands for these characteristics in your parenting style: playfulness, acceptance, curiosity, empathy (see Resources, p. 350) – where we play like our children do, including computer games, just to show how rubbish we are at things they excel in. Because yes, they will be much better than you in most cases.
- Don't trivialise their understanding or feelings about any content they discuss with you (such as podcasts and opinions). If you don't agree, you can say something like, 'I like the way you think, but I disagree with your opinion

because I think differently – and that's great as we can have a discussion about stuff!' After all, who wants their children to be just another version of them?
- Talk about the long and arduous process of the teen years and empathise with them. Don't make it a competition about 'in my day . . .' but do reflect on things like how your knees or thighs may have ached with growing pains and how glad you are that there's an end to this stage for them. Give them hope!

And remember: it's ok to cry – and that goes for both you and your teen – about how long this stage of life seems to take, and how tortuous it can feel. As I write, I can remember the process of puberty and what it felt like – and I don't remember it being fun, at all. It was embarrassing, clunky and awkward all the darned time. And then there were the comparisons to all those other girls at school who never seemed to have a hair out of place, who had stunning make-up, great fashion sense . . . urgh. Our own teenagers today are navigating the most confusing, difficult and drawn-out years of their lives to date. And it's a time when even their own peers may not be making things any easier for them, by engaging in behaviours such as cyberbullying and taunting them in online spaces. Yikes. Where are the cheerleaders, memes and songs to celebrate them? Your teenager is truly amazing, even if the evidence sometimes suggests otherwise.

## Teens and Cyberbullying

Teens, especially those with vulnerabilities, may find that they're the targets of cyberbullying, or find themselves responding aggressively or offensively to someone or a group online because they feel hurt, angered or outraged by something. Sometimes children can be both the victim and the aggressor.

Teens may be targeted because of things they do or say online, the comments they make, their avatar or profile picture or, indeed, because they belong to a specific group, faith, team, culture or country themselves, or because of the colour of their skin or their gender – or, indeed, for any reason that somebody chooses to pick on them (and that somebody might even be a bot in the world we now find ourselves in).

Children who are the victims of cyberbullying may become depressed or avoidant of technology or spaces online, or feel isolated. They may complain about it to you or they may not. And they may have mood swings or trouble sleeping, so you will need to keep a close eye out for any behaviours that change in your child (mostly these changes will be rapid), in the awareness that some of these can also be simply because they are a teen, full of not just changing hormones but changing brain architecture, too. This age group needs the most observation in terms of their behaviours so that you can detect what changes occur and why. Which can be hard to do if they spend a lot of time with friends or shut away in their room.

Being a cyberbully can be intentional and repeated, but it may be a one-time response when it comes to online activity. This is often referred to as behaving like a keyboard warrior, and is mostly the result of a lack of emotional regulation in the moment, or the young person thinking that they can say certain things in public spaces or directly to someone online that they might not do in the real world. Sometimes this is because they can't see the other person, or they may not know it's bullying when they think they're being funny and 'just having a joke'. I've also found, in many cases, that something a child may say or do in the real world is exacerbated by the speed of the internet and social media, and the fact that they can't always see how their actions affect someone makes it much easier to carry it out online.

Parenting around cyberbullying doesn't involve just telling them to 'turn it off', because this isn't going to make the online space go away, won't delete the comment or post and can seem dismissive of something that's causing your child upset. Instead, consider the following:

- Help them report the bullying, if they feel this is the action they want to take.
- Help them block or mute the person or account.
- Help them understand that revisiting the post can perpetuate the painful feelings.
- Help them delete posts, where applicable.
- Help them set up a new account (this is the advice if they are the victim; however, if they are the aggressor a new account allows them to continue their bullying, as is often seen with the fake accounts they use).
- Acknowledge that they may have caused hurt or distress to another person online.
- Help them rectify or apologise if they are permitted to (if they're not blocked, for example).
- Help them understand their actions and understand why they took them (they may not have intended harm).

### *Alex's Story*

Alex had just turned thirteen. She was having a hard time at school because of issues with other pupils in the playground at break times, so she avoided going there. All the same, she was added to a WhatsApp group by a group of girls she considered friends. They talked about their classmates and goaded Alex into saying how she felt about some other girls who had previously teased her in the playground. Alex said she 'wished they were dead' and that she hated them. She used some gender slurs and said she would attack them if she could.

The girls took screengrabs of what Alex had typed in the WhatsApp group, which they sent to her bullies and teachers. Then they kicked Alex out of the group. The school called Alex's home and asked the family to come in to discuss a 'cyberbullying issue and hate speech' against the girls who had originally bullied Alex. The family included me in the conversations that followed to help the school understand the timeline and the way in which Alex had been 'set up' to say the things the teachers had been made aware of without knowing how the comments had come about.

Alex has learning difficulties and didn't know that saying something about someone's gender or sharing thoughts of wanting to harm them was hate speech. She told me she didn't know it was bad and had only meant that she hated them for teasing her. Besides this, she'd simply been using language she'd heard used by other pupils in her year. We resolved the issue with an apology from Alex to the girls (this was what she wanted to do) and the decision not to remain friends with them. Alex found some new friends in an out-of-school club, and her parents helped her develop some WhatsApp skills (which included learning to pause and ask them about language that people used in the group).

## *A Note on Children with Social, Emotional or Educational Needs, Neurodiversity and/or Trauma*

Some children and teens lack the complex thinking styles that most adults have. And children with social, emotional and learning difficulties, neurodivergence and/or trauma can repeat what they've heard others say, which can often include sexual, racist, sexist or homophobic language. And they may not consider who they repeat it to, not understanding the potential consequences of what they're saying, especially if they have social communication disorders or issues in this area. This communication obstacle can leave children in this cohort with difficulties online such as being accepted into groups, games or spaces there, as they are often bullied out of them in cruel ways, like being continuously kicked out from a game, piled on (attacked) in said game or hounded by others on social media. They may be frustrated with others when they don't understand the rules of a game, or when others don't understand *their* rules of playing the game.

In situations where text is used, children with learning difficulties or neurodivergence may find themselves confused or not understanding subtleties of language such as sarcasm. This exposes them to the taunts of others, or perhaps even exploitation for money or sexual favours, as they may not recognise this as such. Teens with relational trauma (abuse between people) or social communication presentations are at risk of blackmail and emotional exploitation, too. This age group and cohort need monitoring and parental controls that may seem out of context for children over thirteen, so seeking professional advice about the use of this tech with this age group can be helpful. Teens who use technology may want to continue to use it to calm their difficulties, for emotional regulation and because it is generally a place of predictability when it comes to the way in which technology works (which is logical). I have a resource for professionals and parents on my website for this specific topic, as it's complicated.

In today's world, anything that is said online has the potential to lead to the involvement of law enforcement agencies. Although this can sound scary and perhaps even censorial with respect to an individual's right to free speech, given that we now live in an age of online harms, which include cyberbullying, hate speech and other polarising topics online, it's best to teach our children and teens not to say *anything* that could be construed as illegal. Instead, we need to give them space in the real world, such as time in school lessons, home life and with other adults, to talk to us about things they feel angry or outraged about online. We need to be able to hear opposing views, while teaching them about the use of language and how this can form a prosecutable offence online.

> *TIP:* Whatever your own views on issues such as foul language, do talk to your child about the language that people use online. Give them the space to share and discuss their opinions and feelings with you, so they will be less inclined to vent these publicly on the internet.

## Forums, Self-Harm and Suicide Content

You may never have heard of the term 'unaliving', but you can probably work out what it means pretty quickly. Over time, younger people have changed the way they speak to each other online. With respect to a word like 'unaliving', some claim that algorithms don't promote videos or comments that use the words 'dead' or 'kill', so these have been replaced with the word 'unalive'. But perhaps young people could just be using it because, for them, language often acts like a type of social cement, showing that they're part of the gang.

Since the advent of the internet, lots of forum-based social media platforms have sprung up that are accessible via websites. Unfortunately, these sometimes propagate controversial ideas that children and teens – particularly those with vulnerabilities – may be at risk of incorporating into their own language and thinking. In these spaces, conversations about mental health and wellbeing frequently become entangled with other ideas and with internet humour and memes.

Often, children and teens with diagnoses of autism are drawn to spaces like these, for reasons we're not going to speculate about now. However, in a large proportion of these spaces, the focus is on a particular form of 'phantasy'. This isn't about a dragons-and-werewolves type of fantasy (although it might involve those characters); it's more about imagining yourself to be something other than the person you are. That can mean simply imagining yourself as a comic superhero or a gaming character, or experimenting with your identity in other potentially more significant and impactful ways, such as with gender.

In these spaces it can feel a little like anything goes in terms of conversation, and that can include discussions about sensory issues and self-soothing approaches to emotional distress, which may include self-harm or imagining that you're no longer suffering because of being 'unalive'. These options may seem logical to a person in distress; however, to a parent or caregiver reading this book they will most likely seem extreme, dangerous and very worrisome.

The fact is that sharing images and conversations in which they imagine being dead can feel calming to some children and teens, who may not fully comprehend that death is not a 'respawn' or gaming process from which they can return to restart the level or game. This is why we need to think about the conversations we have with our children and teens about the challenges of life, and how difficulties can be exactly that – difficult – but they're manageable, with professional help if needed, and, of course, time.

To give you some pointers here about the kinds of conversations to have or when to seek help for your child, it's important to note that talking about suicide doesn't necessarily increase the risk that it will occur (contrary to popular belief), but it does give the child space to talk about why they may want to unalive themselves. Often this is because in our teenage years we seek logical or quick answers (what Nobel prize winner Daniel Kahneman calls fast thinking errors of judgment[1]) and sometimes this is a teen's approach to rationalising the situation. But don't be too quick to think it is 'just' a flash-in-the-pan flirtation with ideology or thought. Instead, you might say something along the following lines:

> Feeling sad, down, fed up, desperate, hopeless, powerless or anything that feels like it lacks a solution can be normal parts of our emotional lives, and can at times feel debilitating. This can often result in us thinking about options that make these feelings go away, even permanently. Life is precious, and the feelings we sometimes have about ending life can feel scary, like a resolution and the solution to the problem – it seems to make sense!
>
> However, there is hope and things can and do get better. Some people may need professional help to support them with this set of feelings and time in their life. Is this something you would like me to help you find? I know I may not always be the person you want to talk to about these big feelings and, yes, my emotions may well get in the way here, so shall we find someone qualified to help you talk about the feelings and make sense of them or the situation?

When seeking a qualified professional, ensure they are trained to work with young people and are on a professionals' register (such as the PSA/HCPC in the UK, or, in the US, ensure they are board-certified) and part of a membership body that has trained them in understanding child development, neuroscience, the law and safeguarding, as all of these aspects are needed to work at relational depth with suicide in young people. It's also helpful if they've completed their own therapy, and it's ok to ask this question: a good professional can and will show you their qualifications, including how they've stayed up to date on training and development. After all, this is your child's mental health you are asking them to take care of.

Be aware that some teens seek out help online in forums and chat rooms or with unqualified people online. Sadly, bad actors can also be present on these forums, who may appear to encourage self-harm and suicide for 'LOLs', without realising that children with learning or social difficulties may not understand this kind of supposed humour or sarcasm. However, some bad actors will know this, and will nevertheless abuse vulnerability for their own entertainment.

In the UK online material relating to self-harm and suicide is now classified, under the Online Safety Act 2023, as being priority content that should be taken down from the internet. However, a lot of the material within this category hasn't yet been removed at the proposed rate. This is probably because of difficulties in stipulating whether or not something really does relate to self-harm, and whether it's harmful or not, or indeed how we even say that material is about self-harm unless it's clearly defined as cutting, ingesting/injecting substances, strangulation, anorexia or bulimia, for example. At present, we lack distinct ways to measure anything that doesn't fall squarely into the category of self-harm. Nor does there appear to be any consensus yet on who exactly decides what is or isn't material that relates to self-harm and suicide, or how this should be agreed upon by the different platforms, forums and online spaces.

This lack of consensus means that we need to speak to children and teens themselves about why people might want to talk about death and taking their own lives (see the above conversation starter if your child is suicidal or wants to hurt themselves), why anyone might want to hurt themselves and what this might or might not look like. We also need to ask them what *they* think about this subject matter. Asking these questions can provide some insight into the ideologies of teens on the topic, as there is a proportion of children who think harming or hurting themselves is a better option than, say, 'burdening' others with their problems; or they may not even know that there are other ways to regulate their emotions and have instead been told/guided or shown by others online that this is the first port of call. Some children believe they should punish themselves for being stupid, bad or whatever they've been called by peers and/or the adults around them at home or in school or college. What we say to our teens matters — see the guidance on celebrating your teen on p. 235.

We may think that self-harm means a particular type of activity (such as cutting). If so, we may be surprised when a child or teen talks about self-soothing practices such as biting, pinching and scratching. And we may dismiss these as just being 'silly'. I've even had adults say to me in clinic and at schools that it's 'stupid behaviour' and/or 'attention seeking', which can minimise the potential risk of escalation (whereby the teen responds with, 'I'll show you!'). This behaviour might be a way in which a child or teen seeks to have conversations with others online as well, which might, sadly, lead to them experimenting with more dangerous methods.

Monitor the conversations your child or teen has online through keeping an eye on them and chatting with them about the many different topics discussed in these pages. Also consider using parental controls, although with teens you can start to get into muddy waters around their privacy rights and freedoms and at what age this becomes an invasion of those. If you're stuck for where to start, perhaps talk about the law and legislation and ask what *they think* about the role of the Online Safety Act.

We need to have more chats with teens about this kind of content, rather than fewer, and to dispel the myth, once and for all, that talking to children or teens about these topics will lead to them trying things out for themselves. Once we open the way for conversation, it's more likely that our child or teen will talk to us about these issues, which will put us in a better position to prevent them from coming to harm.

> ### *Take Five*
>
> It can be very upsetting to imagine your child deriving any sort of comfort from online discussions about self-harm and death. And it can be even worse to consider that some bad actors might be encouraging this. So take a break now if you need to. Go for a walk, phone a friend or do whatever works for you. And breathe . . . And, as an extra tip here, go and look at a possession that makes you smile and feel gratitude – it might be something as simple as a picture, a certificate or a cup of tea. Really take in the fact that you have this thing, and what it took to get it: for example, electricity to power the kettle, running water and your favourite tea brand. Hold this feeling for about thirty to sixty seconds and drink it in (pun totally intended here).

## Sextortion

We've looked at the threat of grooming, which can occur in a variety of contexts (see pp. 151 and 202). As the age group who're most obviously forming their sexual identity, teens may be spending more time online looking at who they find attractive, exploring their sexual preferences and finding the language for this, and, of course, talking to more people online to figure it out. In some cases, this may lead to them sending images back and forth, which is how their trust can be betrayed and they can be manipulated

One form of sexual grooming can lead to the 'sextortion' of a young person, which often involves exploiting or blackmailing them into sending more images or money. This can be the outcome of a conversation that took place in an app or a game, where the teen shared something of value with the sextortioner, such as intimate images of themselves (and/or personal information about their mental health or sexuality), leaving them vulnerable to blackmail.

At the age of thirteen, some, well, most teens will be using social media (unless bans have been enforced by the time of printing), so it's important to be aware that sextortion is reported to be increasing in this age group via social media contact, according to figures from NCMEC (US) and IWF (UK) in 2024. This is why social media sites are now using what are called trust and safety measures, which prevent adult accounts from following or contacting minors; TikTok, for example, is implementing this for the under-eighteens at the time of writing.

Some unsavoury individuals can also coerce children into sharing photos of themselves that may appear innocent, such as pictures of feet (see Kendra's story, below), or they might pretend to be someone else completely in what's known as 'catfishing'. I also described earlier how there are even AI apps that can digitally undress images.

### Talking about Sextortion

While it's probably sensible not to share any photos of ourselves with other people on the internet, teenagers are at a stage when they are, at times, going to go against our best advice not to do this. In fact, I would go so far as to say good luck to anyone who tries to tell a teen *not* to post or send pictures and videos of themselves to people they know or on social media. So we need a Plan B, in the event that our teens *do* send images and they are leaked in any way by either blackmailers or a disgruntled peer or partner, so that we can support them. Let's look at what we can do or say to help them cope:

- We can sort this out together.
- No, I don't need to see the image or video.

- I get it – you wanted to feel like your friends, and this felt like a normal thing to do.
- I'm not angry with you.
- I understand that this is part of growing up nowadays.
- I can see that you regret it.

And if the images were leaked or shared or your teen wants to report them for removal, tell them:

- The disappointment and anger lie with the person who has leaked the images, but we can do something about this together. I can support you by showing you where to report the image and how to get it taken down as quickly as possible. We may need to report this to police. How would you like us to do this?

In the UK, anyone over the age of thirteen and under eighteen can report images using the 'Report Remove' tool offered by Childline; alternatively, use Take It Down, which is a free service that helps with the removal of intimate images (see Resources, p. 349). Nude or intimate image sharing takes place quite often on apps such as Snap, and as parents and guardians we may never know unless our children tell us – which likely won't happen until there is a problem. There are no easy answers to this conundrum, although, in all likelihood, we will see the creation of more online safety legislation or technology developments about this in due course.

Importantly, we really need to help our teenagers understand risk, and who is out there in the digital city park. This means that we need to keep having honest conversations about things like posting naked images, how these might be used and what this can mean for their future. And, as I said in the previous chapter, these sorts of conversations may well impact how you think about the photos you've already posted online of your teens, what ages they were in those images and with whom they were shared.

## Kendra's Story

Fourteen-year-old Kendra sadly found herself in my clinic after being groomed and exploited online. She explained that she had been approached by someone asking for pictures of her feet. She told me she blocked 'the creep' but he simply created another account and messaged her that he would keep doing this.

He offered her a substantial sum of money for pictures, and when she sent them she thought that was the end of the matter. However, he contacted her again and threatened to tell people that she'd sent the images and for how much money. He added that people would judge her for this.

Sadly, Kendra was then exploited into sending intimate images on encrypted platforms, and it was only because her mum saw one of these messages (as she said, by mistake) that the abuse was noted and reported to the police.

Teens can be enticed by money to share images, which can sometimes amount to considerable sums for pictures they feel it's ok to send (of feet in Kendra's case). Some teens are aware of the sexual behaviours and desires of others but may not understand how sextortion can take place subtly and over time, so we need to stay aware of things like sending images, or if they suddenly appear to have lots of money (you may spot this via their spending patterns – buying things like clothes or handbags or make-up, even takeaways). We need to keep the channels of communication open.

> *TIP:* If your teen is a keen gamer, you can offer to help them with the costs of playing or buying items as a form of pocket money, and – dare I say it – even as a form of bargaining chip for chores. That way, you might get a sense of how much they are spending and on what.

## Sex, Violence – and Violent Sex

It's been suggested that sexual content now makes up one-third of internet traffic, so the likelihood of your teen seeing it at some point is quite high. Young people live in a very visual world and may be exposed to extremes of sex and violence that may seem inconceivable to many adults, who probably came across nothing more disturbing than a parent's hidden stash of adult magazines when they were young. Pornography and violence can potentially be seen anywhere online via streaming platforms, social media, gaming and other forums. This can include recorded or live events, has a global reach and comes from differing times in history.

In 2013 a 'Rapid Evidence Assessment' report was carried out for the children's commissioner in the UK.[2] It was titled 'Basically Porn is Everywhere', but it pointed out that this kind of research is fraught with ethical issues, as we cannot directly ask children, usually under sixteen, but sometimes eighteen, about sexual content or activity (as in most cases ethics boards would not pass this). The report advised that it is a 'significant proportion of children who view that material' but gave no actual figures. In 2022, another report was conducted by the children's commissioner into the harmful effects of pornography on the sexual behaviour of children, where young people between the ages of sixteen and twenty-one were surveyed (and police-interview evidence of child-to-child sexual abuse was used to produce some of the report evidence).[3] The report suggested that around 50 per cent of teens by the age of thirteen and 21 per cent of children by age eleven said they had viewed pornography, and some said they had encountered it earlier than that.

To confuse matters, sex and violence often appear in combination. This can take the form of violent pornography that can be entwined with aspects of abuse and misogynistic values, or it may be a form of sexual activity that portrays aggressive acts, but which is consensual. There are many differing types and styles of pornography, but, as mentioned previously, our thoughts often go straight to the 'worst kind' (violent, degrading and misogynistic content) because the media and reports can be alarmist – at times, rightly so. Although this topic is complicated and many of us find it uncomfortable to talk about it, we need to be tooled up to have rational discussions with our teens, and to be able to manage our own fears or hang-ups, too. The need to talk about this urgently should outweigh our own reservations and embarrassment around it.

I'm aware that this can also be a taboo subject for many because of their faith or culture. Nevertheless, I want to be open, honest and frank: we need to be able to talk about pornography with young people, as we can't currently rely on age-assurance technology to protect our teens and some of them will find ways around any obstacles put in their way. This isn't helped by the fact that some of these sites claim to be social media and not pornography, or that visitors sometimes just have to tick a box ('Yes, I'm over eighteen') on a pornography website to enter it.

It's also worth noting that much of the pornography that children encounter (as they've been telling me for over a decade) is seen not directly via dedicated websites, but by being sent it or shown it by other young people in messaging apps. Moreover, accidental viewing of this material can also take place in many spaces online, because porn (of most genres) is available through searches that have nothing to do with it per se, in some instances, and is on social media and other websites that may have a tick-box entry system (at the time of writing). Plus, cartoon-style pornography can crop up in gaming or on search results online. Research suggests that children say they're aged eleven on average when they start to see this sort of content, while anecdotal reports suggest it's earlier still.[4] In fact, I've worked with children as young as five who've viewed pornographic material. That may shock you, but, perhaps worse still, in this case it was accidental in ways that could have been minimised with tech-smart parenting.

Teens (and some younger children) can find pornography exhilarating, titillating, horrifying, intriguing, exciting, confusing and thrilling all at once. And it can be traumatising, too, depending on the child, their resilience and inner resources and/or the content they see. Will your child tell you they were excited by it or liked it? Perhaps not. They may say they were shocked and troubled (because they might think that's what you want to hear), but it's likely that some aspect of it resonated with them, as most young people will be developing sexual feelings during their teen years. Will they go back to find more? It depends. Will they have a problem with it? It depends. Will they copy it? It depends. Will they rely on it? Again, it depends . . .

Mainly, it's down to how we parents and society as a whole talk to teens about sexual behaviours and the act of sex, as it's often discussed in taboo ways or not at all, and we may not even talk to our teens about the possibility of encountering it online – all of which can inadvertently steep them in the shame of then seeing it and not feeling able to talk to us about it. As education in the UK currently doesn't teach about this subject (and although the subject does still crop up, some teachers many not be ready or tooled up to talk about it), it's down to parents for now. Even if you have parental controls or have discussed the issue with your teen in passing, they may still encounter it. This is why we must now consider that parenting in a world of technology means we have to have ongoing conversations that we'd rather not have. This is sensitive territory, and educational bodies are still discussing how to provide a 'good' education to teens about sex and relationships, given that some parents don't want their children to have conversations about the online space and pornography. But this is where tech-smart parenting is important.

Sexuality is an important part of growing up and of the formation of a teenager's sense of identity. However, young people viewing pornography is complicated and reflects their age, stage and intentions; it's not always driven by sexual feelings, or even any clarity about exactly why or what they're viewing. So is it generally ok for teens to watch porn? Well, that hinges on their actual age (for various reasons, viewing pornography under the age of eighteen is classified as illegal in the UK, although the research shows that many do), as well as on the 'what', the 'why', the 'how' and with whom. For some, it really isn't a big deal, while for others it becomes quite the thing and they may become enthralled by it.

So what can we do to protect them? Yes, that's right – we can start talking to them about it. Ok, brace yourselves for how to do this, because your best line of protection is a tech-smart, open-door parenting style . . .

> *TIP:* While it's not guaranteed that your teen will view pornography, if your household has access to the internet it's highly likely to occur in some way, at some point, even with the legal process of age checks. To help prevent the viewing of this type of material by your teenager, accidental or otherwise, use the parental controls at your disposal (see p. 262) – and that includes on your smart TV. And use the pointers in Chapter 5, too (see p. 112).

### *Being Open About Sexual Content and Relationships*

Given the sexual content many teens will see online, I believe, as I said above, it's now necessary rather than optional for parents and guardians to think about this topic and broach it with their kids. However, there are ways to do so without traumatising or sexualising your children or just being 'weird' about it. In fact, conversations about online sexual content don't even need to include the word pornography. Many teens don't use that word; or, in my clinic, if they do use it they're usually talking about specific types and genres (and there are a lot of these) or they're trying to understand something they saw.

A good place to start is by being honest with our teens that some of this material is curated by professionals and some isn't (some is uploaded by people in their own homes, for example) and therefore it might not reflect what happens in the teen's own sex life – when they start having sex, of course. Some people suggest that we should tell them porn isn't real, when it actually is, even when it's acted out; although, once again, it might not reflect how sex usually takes place in real life – which is where I think we can get muddled up when trying to have these sorts of conversations. Instead, we can talk about things like the 'storyline' used in films on pornographic websites (not the 1970s' plumber one). We can say that these don't usually include conversations beforehand, consent processes, discussions about contraception or pregnancy, or the sorts of words used by real-life couples in relationships. Instead, these storylines are mostly about focusing on genitals and the mechanics of the physical act, and not the individuals involved.

We can talk to our teens about speaking up and speaking out, and what we can do to challenge the narratives we hear about harming others, such as the sexist slurs used against women online, for example. We can ask them questions about how they feel when they see or hear this happening, and we can educate teens in conversations that have a wider reach than the porn narratives or misogyny issues so readily talked about nowadays. We can learn to address these issues without blaming and shaming boys and men as well. Above all, we can begin to think about the wider picture of respect between people and how this might make for a better world all round. (For more ideas on how to start a conversation about sex and relationships, see p. 118 in Part 1 and also the box on p. 210 in Chapter 8.) We must also acknowledge that we might not have all the answers. Fortunately, the internet is a great tool for finding a professional who can help, or even books that you can buy for you and your teen to have discussions about or for them to read (and/or videos or lectures to watch if they won't read) – after you've vetted the contents, of course!

*TIP:* Conversations with your teen need to be sprinkled in among the day-to-day happenings of life. You're not looking to deluge them with life lessons, but you can show you're interested, which means finding the time to offer a listening ear. As much as tech can sometimes be a thorn in your side, it gives you *so* many topics to speak to your teen about. You can use the news, articles or videos as a starting point. For example, you could get your teen's opinion on an event like a general election (you don't have to agree with them) to open the way for conversations about other issues, by asking, 'Do you think there was fake news surrounding the elections?', and 'Why?'

### Take Five

It can be a very difficult to consider that today most teenagers will likely come across some form of extreme pornography and violence online. Take a break now if you need to. Make yourself a drink and be kind to yourself.

Take a piece of paper and pen, or use your phone, and write down five things that you love about your child and five things you've done well in parenting them so far, which can include funny moments, as well as sensible ones. Reflect for a moment on the great job you're doing so far, and remember that none of us does this perfectly, even if they claim to online. If you find that you are blaming yourself for failing to protect your child from everything that's out there, you can make a start this week by gently opening conversations with them about these and other topics. You may be panicking about this, so after your cuppa come back to this section.

## Should My Teen Be Allowed a Smartphone?

Assuming your teen doesn't already have a smartphone, this is a question you'll likely find yourself considering around now — although this also depends on the outcome of ongoing campaigns for a social media/phone ban for under-sixteens. I would love to have a simple answer to the challenges surrounding technology and children or teens, but, for the sorts of reasons I outlined earlier (see p. 35, for example), banning kids from using smartphones doesn't work — they may still find ways to access the internet that could put them at risk. However, *enabling* them to have a smartphone increases the risks, if this is given without the use of controls, conversations or tech-smart parenting. Many parents may find themselves wondering if there's a 'right' age at which to give one to their child. Of course though there isn't a one-size fits all. It really is a case of using the guidance in this book thus far to make your own decision and, if you do hand a smartphone over to your teen, you will need to think about how to parent one who may want to keep things private from you. So let's keep thinking about the digital park as a whole and the way in which teens today evolve with what always seems to be a downward-facing, eyes-down stance.

When it comes to your own child, you know them best and whether they are mature enough to use devices like smartphones safely and responsibly. You will probably also have a sense of whether they are already familiar with online spaces and know how to navigate them safely, or whether they could run into trouble if they're given freedom to roam in the city park online, especially if left unsupervised. But there are some points you can nevertheless consider when making your decision.

If we were to make a list of the risks that young people today face online and then simply remove the prefix 'cyber' or 'digital', we would be left with many of the hazards that young people have always faced in the real world, although perhaps not to the same extent to which they can now be encountered in virtual spaces. So rather than lecture or berate our teens and compare them unfavourably with our own memories of how things were back in our day, we could perhaps start to adapt our own thinking to the world we and our children find ourselves in now.

Keeping our city-park analogy in mind, as they enter their teens our children are approaching the age, in the real world, at which we can start allowing them to wander a little further away from home and spend time with their mates or with groups such as after-school clubs, so what are the rules we use for safety there? In most cases, we'll still have curfews and boundaries in place about who they can spend time with, where they can go and what they can and cannot do. And we'll also hold them accountable when they're late home or have 'forgotten' to tell us where they are. Of course, we'll get worried, angry and disappointed when they mess up. But we'll do our best not to push them away and to make sure we're there whenever they need us. And so the rules about the online city park will need to mirror this and can include things like not using tech at the table, in bed and after certain hours. It's your house, so you make the rules. Of course, you will need to know who they 'hang around with' online, which is why you should take an active interest in their online life and perhaps agree with them on ways they can show you who their friends and online contacts are.

The question about monitoring software begins to become a space for arguments that transition into my clinic regularly, and disagreements are often around the age at which a child is entitled to privacy rights, as they would be in the real world, and how you agree to this as a family. The complexities of this mirror safeguarding processes that I deal with, and getting families and teens to agree to ways they can be monitored often takes more than one session. Many parents opt for random checks of a teen's phone rather than using parental controls, but you will need to decide what to do in your home.

In the previous chapter, I said that one of the biggest risks to pre-teens is unsupervised access to gaming and the internet, and I suggested encouraging them to use devices within the earshot of grown-ups, noisy as that may be. However, getting a teen to spend any time willingly in adult company can be quite the challenge. So this is another factor to consider when thinking about whether you're happy to let your teenager have a smartphone. And if your teen does have a device, can they use it alone? What lessons or conversations have you had about unsupervised access and the risks they may be exposed to? Is yours a 'bedroom teen' or a 'living-room teen' (to use a trending social media framing of the teenage years)? The place where your teen spends most of their leisure or spare time at home will affect how you do your job of supervising their digital play. And therein lies a dilemma . . .

When teens spend a lot of time shut away in their rooms, for some families it can become a significant issue (although, let's be honest, for others it might be a welcome outcome). But when exactly is too much time on their own with technology a problem? Well, it's hard to pinpoint a specific set of hours or days of the week. It's more about what they're doing (or not) in their rooms, and it's also about the state of their emotions, rather than the time they spend in there, and whether or not there are any parental controls in place (see p. 262).

It's said that time alone is a way to decompress, yet too much time by ourselves can be isolating. And the same goes for the debate about time spent on devices and social media. Some research has suggested that time online can be beneficial for mental health in this age group, and that this cohort of teens use it most for support; other research says it's the most dangerous or damaging thing for their mental health and causes mental-health issues, as I discuss in my book *Managing Your Social Media and Gaming Habits* (see also the study 'Social Media and Mental Health: Benefits, Risks, and Opportunities for Research and Practice' for a great representation of the research as of 2020).[5] So, before focusing on gaming and devices, you need to think about your own teen and what they personally need, and that requires conversations and super-sleuth powers of detection around what's said and what's left unsaid, which is a major parenting skill – including listening to what's really being communicated by their behaviour.

We must also listen – really listen (especially when they don't talk to us, because, as I've said, their behaviour is still communicating with us all the time) – to their worries and concerns, and any deeper feelings underlying them. It isn't the easiest job in the world, but I'll say it again: you're the expert on your teenager. Most behaviours relating to distress are communicated by sudden changes that you may notice. They may also find it easier to text you than speak directly, so use technology as a way to communicate with your teen here. As mentioned earlier, offer to reach out to a professional for support, as teens often prefer to talk to someone else about their mental health – not because they don't love or respect you, but because you're their parent. (See the pointers on p. 243 about how to find that professional.)

All the same, I appreciate there's a lot of pressure in the media (and in schools, and from discussion between parents) when it comes to decisions around allowing our children to explore the real world and the world online by themselves, and whether they should be unsupervised at all, ever, with and without technology. Yet if we were to crumble under all the victim-blaming and scare stories, we'd never leave our teens alone or allow them on technology without us 'hovering' over them. So the debate rages on. When we prevent the use of technology, we ignore the fact that teens are the next generation of university students and workers who will be expected to use it, as computers and AI will be in almost every form of education and employment (more so than they are today). Instead, our teens could learn how to be competent with technology, navigating the nuances of communication online (as they will in the workplace) and the pressures of growing up in a world of tech. These are the skills for tomorrow that we cannot teach if they are not using this very technology.*

If you do give your teen a smartphone or console that they want to use in their room, but you then end up hovering over them and trying to watch every single thing they type or do with it (in what is known as helicopter parenting), well, that could end up making you feel neurotically paranoid, and you might find yourself glued to your teen's side forever more. Not a great look, and not one they're likely to thank you for right now.† The advice here is don't 'hover bovver'.

So what *do* you need to see and monitor to keep them safe? It's going to be hard to answer this in one sentence, because I don't know exactly what your teen will face online, in their feeds or on their technology. To sum up, I guess it's *every threat online* (which sounds terrifying) – but that would be impossible. So instead, let's think back to your own teenage years for a moment. You probably began closing your bedroom and the bathroom door for privacy (and still do), not wanting your parents to hear you trying to chat up a love interest, or for them to hear the terrible jokes you and your friends made, or even what you spoke to them about, which most likely included all the ways in which they got on your nerves (no? Just me?). Let's consider a couple of other scenarios, too. For example, are you able – or indeed, do you need – to see everything your child does when they go to school or college? Or when they are out with their friends? Do you have superpowers that allow you to hear every conversation they have with their peers? How

---

* Teens may be competing against AI bots or programs and they may need to develop and enhance their online communication skills even more so now to keep the advantage in their corner.

† On my social media channels I have been educated in the last year by teens (presumably, according to their profiles) that in certain countries this is the way parents often parent. So when it comes to tech-smart parenting I have to acknowledge the wide diversity and approaches to parenting globally; none of these approaches are 'wrong'.

do you manage this for their real-world safety: what rules do you have in place about being late or going somewhere other than wherever was agreed on when they left the house? What about being secretive or lying? Knowing who their friends are? What can you carry over in this thinking style to the online world they visit? It is really a case of being able to see the things they do, the places they go to, the people they talk to – and that can only really happen if you have a way to see their device. So your choice is limited to software that monitors their activity (in their words 'spies' on them), you doing random spot checks or them showing the phone to you.

The question of whether you should install parental controls on a thirteen-year-old's phone or console is much easier to answer in practice compared to, say, a seventeen-year-old's. In light of the age-and-stage model we've considered in this book, I would suggest that, as your teen develops, you will need to adapt how you approach their freedom in relation to technology based on their level of maturity and relational abilities.

Moreover, as a child begins to move into becoming a sexual individual, which can be as soon as they hit puberty, then their conversations with their peers will begin to reflect this (as was the case for every teen who came before them, and will continue to be so forever more). So if you're checking your teen's phone, are you going to be ok with any feelings that arise upon seeing sexual messages about or from your teen, who's becoming an adult, with all the desires that adults have? How will you address this, or the use of parental controls around it, if you choose to let them grow as sexual individuals? How will you have those conversations and what will they entail? And how can you filter these kinds of subjects but keep them safe from things like radicalisation, terrorism, grooming and cyberbullying, too?

There isn't room to give you all the answers here, when it concerns sexual behaviour, because families have a choice about how they parent – and it's complicated! Parental controls (see box, below) can help you with sexualised content such as porn sites by blocking them, but even then you will need to think about the age at which you feel it's ok for a developing young person to view porn, given that the age of sexual consent in the UK is sixteen. This involves ongoing conversations and adaptations, while keeping in mind, of course, any siblings in your home, and whether any controls will need to be set for the house on shared devices and not just for individual teens.

> ## *Parental Controls for Teens*
>
> I expect that some parents will zoom straight to this section looking for the names of programs and apps they can use to keep their child safe. I will not be providing these, because of the issues that can be associated with this age group – not least that they are often seen as the most tech savvy, able to circumvent controls, and sometimes referred to by professionals and parents alike as the most unruly and difficult to keep an eye on. Please see the previous chapters for guidance on some of the ways you can put controls on a device. However, the complication here is that I don't know what device(s) you have, or where you are in the world, which means I don't know who your service provider is or which controls they do or do not have. So I've provided some guidance in the Resources section (see pp. 349–51) to give you direction regarding the equipment you may need to protect your teen, and how you can access the details on the internet-service-provider system, find guidance for the router or access point in your home and place controls on each device.
>
> Of course, much of this guidance is about protecting devices in your home, but one of the biggest issues to date is that access to the internet can take place outside of the home, when controls may not work in the same way as they do in home settings. You

> may therefore need to consider installing parental controls on individual devices for when your teen takes theirs out and about, away from your home Wi-Fi and the safety net of its home-based parental controls. Your phone provider should be able to advise on this when you purchase and set up your child's device. Plus, remember that access on other people's devices may well be out of your control.
>
> With all this in mind, then, yet again, the biggest parental control at your disposal here is: conversation, conversation, conversation . . .

### *CPR in Action: When They Ask for the Nth Time . . .*

Here's an example of CPR parenting for teens (see p. 107), involving a child who's turning thirteen next month and who asks *again* to install Snapchat:

YOU: So I can hear that you want to use Snapchat, as your friends do. And I get that you want to be like them, but I said no last week and it's the same this week [*consistent*]. And yes, I know that you don't like this answer [*persistent*].

TEEN: But that's not fair! Millie and Amy have it . . . They're the same age as me!

YOU: Yep, I know, but here's my thinking: the age rating on it is thirteen and you haven't yet turned thirteen. And I don't know that you're ready just because you're almost the age where the app says you can use it. And if I'm to be a good parent and ask you to abide by rules, *I* have to do so, too, by taking care of you, and 'just because' you *can* use it soon doesn't mean it's a wise choice, yet [*resistant*].

## Finding the Right Balance

This tricky edge of parenting without intruding into the private world of their teens causes a great deal of angst in the clients I work with and the people I teach. 'But how?' is the question most often asked, and I reply that there is no handout, no procedure, no recipe book for teens as, although they have some similarities, they're all different.

The goal here is to know just enough about *your teen*'s inner life to keep them safe. So do show an interest – but don't interrogate them. Remember my mantra from Chapter 5 (see p. 111) and check in, not on. This requires you to have daily conversations with them about all subjects under the sun, while being prepared for monosyllabic responses, if any. Talking to teens can be hard for many parents as this developmental stage requires some delicate navigation, so I have provided some books in the Resources section that may help (see p. 347).

A tried-and-tested approach in navigating this dialogue between adults and teens is to 'invite' or 'request', not 'demand' answers (or instruct them to do things like chores), using a conversational framework of language called non-violent communication (as created by American psychologist Marshall Rosenberg). You can synthesise this with attachment parenting, using the approach I highlighted earlier in Dan Hughes's PACE model and the books in the resources section (which cover the work of psychologist Mona Delahooke, author Tina Bryson and clinical professor of psychiatry Dan Siegel).

To unpack that a bit, conversations such as asking your teen, 'Had a good day at school?' might start out ok, but you may find that your teen replies with little more than a grunt or replies such as 'Dunno', 'Forgot', 'Whatever', 'Meh', 'Womp womp'*,

---

* This phrase was being used by children in 2024 to mean, 'You're going on way too much so be quiet!' And that is the polite version.

'Not bothered' and 'Why are you bugging me?' Instead, think about what you would want to be asked that would encourage you to express an opinion and discuss your day. This means asking open-ended questions that invite more than one-word answers (although these too can be shut down quickly; don't think for one moment a teen doesn't know how to do that like an expert, lol).

Use phrases like 'I noticed' and then tell them *what* you noticed. For example, 'I noticed that Tara didn't walk home with you today. All ok?' Then you could leave it there, or you could risk another sentence or question at your peril, depending on the reply your teen's body language has given you, such as letting you know with a brief look whether or not it's ok to continue.

Another tack is to open a conversation with the phrase 'I wonder . . .' and then wonder out loud with them. For example, 'I wonder how the social media giants are getting us all to . . .' and then ask them if they have an opinion: 'What're your thoughts on this?'

And wait for a reply. Just wait. Today may not be the day, but one day it will be.

My main advice would be: don't give up. Do keep talking to your teen (or the top of their hoodie or earphones, if that's how they present to the world) and hold that space for them. Most importantly, hold the space for yourself when it all feels futile. The teen years can be bumpy, as these young people are going through body and brain changes, and it doesn't always seem like there's an end in sight, which can be exhausting – for you both. But I can tell you they are listening to you, by watching you, too.

### *Jared's Story*

Jared was seventeen and on the cusp of 'being an adult so I can buy my own phone'. On most days, he came home from college and went straight to his room without a word to his guardians.

He came down to get his food and took it back to his room, where he would play games and chat on the platform Discord for 'hours on end', according to the people who looked after him.

When I spoke with his guardians, I asked about Jared's interests online and what games he played. They told me they didn't know 'but they were noisy' and added that he hadn't spoken to them properly for about two years, ever since they'd given him his new phone. 'And now we have to text him for dinner,' they said. 'He's moody and just doesn't interact.'

When I met Jared, we spoke about his online life. He told me he was 'in training to be an e-sports gamer' and that he was being coached by a gamer he'd met two years ago. He explained that, if he was allowed his own account or to buy his own phone, he'd be able to collect a large amount of money within the space of a fortnight for playing in local and national tournaments.

I discovered that, while he wasn't being groomed for sexual favours, he was at risk of financial exploitation from the 'coach' who had been 'collecting' Jared's wins for the last eighteen months. (In the end, Jared never got paid for his wins.)

Jared felt ignored and unimportant, but his guardians hadn't been able to check his online life. They didn't know how or want to ask questions or have any parental controls, nor had they taken a real interest in Jared himself, and they had missed this issue. Instead, they told me they didn't know or care much about technology, 'so didn't bother to ask'.

In this particular case, Jared was at risk online because his needs in the real world were being unmet, as, sadly, his guardians were less able to care for him than was appropriate for his needs. Imagine what it might have felt like for him if they'd asked about his gaming, even if he didn't always answer them. Imagine if they'd said they wanted to see him game, but without intruding too often and while respecting his privacy, of course – if they'd

> explained that it sounded like he was having fun and excited about playing games and they wanted to understand his passion. Imagine if they'd talked to him about his hobbies, or a career, and had daily conversations with him to create that feeling of being wanted and important. And if they'd installed parental controls, would that have helped or hindered the relationship they had?
>
> When it comes to teenage online activities, the needs that need meeting in real life are often primary undercurrents to the risks taken online. There's a delicate balance between interest, intrusion, privacy, respect and monitoring.

### Avoid Extreme Measures

'But why didn't they tell us?'

Tragically, this is a sentence uttered by nigh on every parent and guardian in my clinical practice after an event of cybertrauma. It's a question asked at almost every conference I go to and at many of the presentations I give. And it's heartbreaking, because the answer is often right in front of us.

As adults, we must get better at talking to our teens and not resort to the ever-looming threat that stops them telling us anything to do with the online world – namely, removing their device or internet as punishment. It's a bit like 'you're grounded'. However, this punishment is no longer just about the street on which your teen lives, where the kids outside can jeer at them as they stare miserably out of the window. It's a server full of people; it's the squad of players who can see them being 'offline'; it's the zeros on their Snapchat streak. It is, in the words of one of my clients, 'a worldwide humiliation'. It's like telling your teen, 'You're globally grounded!'

If teens are having issues online anywhere, they will probably not tell you about them if they have the impending sense that their digital world will be taken away by the switching off of the Wi-Fi for protracted periods (we're not talking about nightly 'lights out' here), the removal of the phone or console, the cancelling of the game pass or the sudden 'reset' of their scores and progress in gaming and social media channels. For all to see, publicly. In incomprehensible numbers.

So, no, they probably won't tell you about their problems if and because it might seem easier to them to resolve an issue by themselves, rather than risk losing everything by involving you and having you remove their access to the internet. This is another golden opportunity for conversations, but remember that teens will base their approach on previous experience: so if you repeatedly take away their tech, they will take the risk of staying quiet.

It might look like I'm saying don't ever take tech away, but punishment often results in compliance but also fear – that's how most of us responded to it, too, when we were teens. So open dialogue is key: difficult conversations about friendships, betrayal, viewing porn, being scammed, cheating, bullying and isolation go hand in hand with tech-smart parenting. Conversations matter, and mattering to you matters to them. So have conversations that include them and show them you care about their welfare and relationships. And that they matter.

### *Rosie's Story*

Rosie was a teen who had been out later than her parents' curfew. As a result, they confiscated her phone, telling her this was for a full month. She told me in our session, 'My Snap score went back to zero. I hate them, they know my mates are in the WhatsApp groups and that people will see that I'm idle. They'll see the unread messages and think I've ghosted them, it's not

> fair. They could have taken my pocket money and that would have been sh*t, but at least I wouldn't be a laughing stock!'
>
> However, Rosie also knew about 'that drawer'. You probably have one, too: it's filled with all those old phones that are discarded when we adults get a shiny new upgrade. Rosie let me know a few weeks later (once it was too late for me to do anything about it) that she had used one of these phones; she'd simply bought a pay-as-you-go sim card from the newsagents and was using this to be 'back online'.
>
> You've got to admire her powers of circumvention and resourcefulness! But you can probably also appreciate the risks of a secret device, seeing as it was even less visible or manageable for her parents compared to the one that had the parental controls and was monitored. This 'second phone' issue is a risk that we all need to be aware of – so perhaps tidy that drawer if you have one!

## Time for Some Rest

While it's best not to resort to ultimatums, there may still be times when you'll need to make sure your teen comes offline, if only so that they can get enough sleep to function like a human being and do things like pass exams. However, I would advise that you try the following approach when it's not a stressful time, which taking exams is.

One way to approach this with your teen is to ask them about the amount of time they spend on their device and how they view this – whether they feel it impacts their sleep, eating, emotions, mood, mental health and so on. You may be surprised to find that the answer is yes in some cases and no in others. When it's a no, then you may have to concede, for today or this time. We must pick our battles sometimes as parents of teens, and the I-need-to-win strategy is often why strict parents get stuck. Instead, it's ok to pick another day, another time to come back to the issue when your child is regulated (and you are too). 'Small and often' win the day, so have short discussions frequently. I realise you may now be questioning whether this means they've won, or have the power, and whether, if they don't comply now, this could be permanent. But this is about a longer-term outcome.

Trust that one day of defiance isn't everything. If you get a no, you can have another go, another time and perhaps even at a different time (such as at 9pm, rather than 11pm, when patience is lower for most of us). However, if use of technology late at night is happening every single day and your teen won't come off it or get adequate sleep, seek help, because it's likely to be down to a communication problem with you or a difficulty they are facing, such as something called phased sleep shift (whereby their circadian rhythm – or internal clock – has shifted).

I talk to most of the Year 11 students I see about sleep and our brains, especially as we head towards the months of November and December and the exam season from April onwards. I'll often raise this topic in my clinic to help them understand how the brain works, and give them a lesson in neuroscience 101 before the stress of exams begins, as it's easier to communicate with lower stress levels. We talk brain health, and about how cerebral fluid washes away the 'gunk of the day' in slow-wave sleep, i.e. deep sleep. And we discuss the impacts of *not* washing away this gunk, such as brain fog, memory issues, not being able to learn new things and memory issues (joke!).

I sometimes lend them neuroscientist Dean Burnett's *The Idiot Brain* or his most recent book, *Why Your Parents Are Hung-Up On Your Phone*, and *Unlocked* by psychologist and science writer Pete Etchells, and then we talk about their contents. [6,7] We don't often discuss the blue light from devices; all the (mis)information about the effects of this is a myth, other than how it might prevent them from going to sleep, in much the same way as reading a book or painting models might do if they did it for hours on end instead of getting some shut-eye. Brain health and sleep hygiene that they themselves can be in control of through active choices seems to be the way to go with teenagers, as it gives them agency and autonomy to set their own intentions around them.

So rather than laying down the law, talk to them about the need to get enough sleep so that they can achieve all the things they want to. You could also create a set of family rules for turning the lights out and putting down devices, and discuss these with them. However, beware of what happens after you go to bed yourself, because this is the time when many of my clients go back to their devices as they think their parents won't know about it!

> *TIP:* If your teenager is prone to staying up all hours online and you wish to enforce a family 'lights out', you'll have to get wise about using parental controls, 4/5G data, your Wi-Fi and router.

Always remember: not all teens are at risk of going on particular platforms, games or websites; and even if they do, they're not all at risk all the time. They have ways to keep themselves safe, and often do, such as telling randomers to 'go away' or using private channels or parties in games. As they're not always exposed to all harms on every channel or platform, we need to think about our approach to being overly fearful – but we do need to be risk aware.

Teens are battling through one of the hardest levels in the game of life, where they are learning who they are and how they fit in. They may struggle with their self-esteem in ways that make them prone to extreme beliefs or vulnerable to exploitation, and struggle to form respectful relationships with themselves, as well as with others. To complicate matters, algorithms may lead them down wormholes and on to forums that act like echo chambers, normalising dangerous behaviours and radical views. They may find themselves mocked and ridiculed by their peers, or in bad company. So it's up to us to protect them where we can, gently guide them, support them and cheer them on each step of the way.

Much of the online safety work can be done by us in the real world by seeing the teen, not the behaviour. Many people forget to pick up their teen, metaphorically speaking, so this is a gentle reminder to do so. After all, they're tired, tall toddlers most of the time. And I say that lovingly, not in a mocking way.

Your teen is not everyone else's teen, nor are they like teens you may have known before. There will be similarities between them, but you know your teen better than anyone else does. And the truth is that you may well get it wrong at times, while at others, your relationship with them will be utter harmony. Don't automatically assume you're a bad parent or guardian if things get a little wobbly occasionally. You're reading this now because you care about getting it right for your family. If your teen spots this book, they might sniff a little at the idea that you're following the advice of some 'shrink' or social media woman. And maybe they won't talk to you about it – but they will notice.

As the adults in our teens' lives, we must create the space in which to keep talking to them – whatever their age – about the issues that exist in the park online and how to avoid them. And we can make sure that, if they do ever run into problems, they'll know that they can come to us to help resolve them.

Silence doesn't mean ignorance; our teens are some of the cleverest people I know, and they'll be running the world in a few years' time. So our job is to give them the credit they deserve.

## Summary

- Young people form friendships in different ways to older generations, and they often spend time online because they want to hang out with these friends.

- The internet can be like a wormhole when it comes to body image and image-based material; help to prevent your teen from getting sucked in by talking to them about different global ideals of beauty, filters and the way that people present such carefully curated personas online.
- Talk to your teens about bad actors, catfishing and people who may want intimate images of them (including their peers and friends) and why sending them is not a good idea. But support them if they have done this, and use the relevant resources to get images taken down quickly.
- Teens can be influenced by others' views and opinions, and we may need to hear these with an open mind before we challenge them.
- Teens can encounter sexual material and not be sure about their feelings towards it; you will need to consider 'the talk' sooner than you might want to, but you can do it!
- Use parental controls to limit opportunities for your teen to view material you'd rather they didn't.
- Teach teens about the importance of respectful relationships.
- Do express an interest in your teen's personal life, but don't expect to know every detail.
- Avoid threatening extreme measures, like cutting off the internet for extended periods.
- Listen to what is being communicated by what they say, but also by their behaviour.
- Adopt the CPR parenting approach: consistence, persistence, resistance.
- Discuss how being online might affect your teen's health and brain, especially when it comes to sleep.

CHAPTER 10

# Boundaries – How to Create and Implement Them

Healthy boundaries are an important part of any relationship, including yours with your child. A healthy boundary is clear and firm, so that you both know where you stand. Yet it can also be flexible to a degree, so that you can revisit it in a timely and considered manner together to adapt to changing circumstances. And it's respectful, too, rooted in open dialogue that takes into account everybody's feelings, which means that you and your child both feel heard and understood. Boundaries like these can help to create a structured and consistent environment for your child in which they can feel safe and supported, able to turn to you if they do run into any problems.

However, none of this is to say that putting boundaries in place is a piece of cake. When you try to implement them, you will likely encounter rebellion and resistance along the way, which is why in this chapter I'd like to share some practical tips and strategies to help you whatever the age and stage of your child.

## The Early Years

Psychologists and child-development experts around the world are still debating the recommended screen/device time for very small children, with much of the advice for under one year of age being that it should be 'very limited'[1] (yet not giving an actual temporal number such as sixty minutes or less, for example, which is the advice for toddlers).[2] Also still under debate is exactly what sort of screens they should be allowed to use, which may include either watching TV or having it on in the background, and whether technology really is causing issues with language acquisition and/or impacting cognitive understanding or any other area of development in small children. Moreover, organisations such as the APA (the body in America that regulates psychologists) don't always explain the reasoning behind their recommendations, because of the issues discussed in Chapter 7 about the research and its findings, which can often be inconclusive and complicated by other factors. And so they tend to opt for precautionary advice along the lines of 'we're not fully sure, so let's not exceed X amount of time'. Which, of course, is sensible.

That being said, when our little ones face a screen – unless that screen has a video of a loved one with whom they are interacting – it's worth being aware that they'll be missing out on the cues that relate to how the world around them really is. You may struggle with conversations and CPR parenting if they don't interact with you face to face. They'll miss the crinkles and wrinkles on our faces as we talk to them, which are incredibly important in helping them develop connections to others. And this might impact their ability to understand the people with whom they interact online, potentially putting them at risk of falling prey to scams and exploitation. So we need more of a 'phones-away-and-face-towards' approach – at any age, but especially with this age group, so we can form those spaces in which to have conversations that matter. Placing boundaries here may be easier with infants because we can wrangle a device away merely because we're bigger than them, and can quite easily pop them into their cots or playpens while distracting them with something else. In comparison, it's not so easy to pop toddlers with the skills of Houdini in playpens and distract them, so do dip back into Chapter 7 for advice about taking away the shiny toy using CPR parenting (see p. 179).

## *CPR in Action: Boundaries in the Early Years*

When applying boundaries about technology with the under-fives, remember the principles of the 3Rs (regulate, relate and reason), as well as CPR parenting:

- *Consistency*: show up consistently with the same attitude to parenting, and hold your own emotions in check if you're out in public, say, and people are watching you with your young child, who may be screaming about the removal of the device. Use the model of regulating and relating before reasoning, and always give yourself enough time to approach the 'stop point' calmly before taking back a device.
- *Persistence*: stick predictably to that approach no matter what setting you find yourself in. However, you can pre-agree flexibility in your rules and boundaries for certain situations, such as car rides. Be persistent in the conversation about the technology time and stick to your initial end time.
- *Resistance*: don't give in to pleading, screaming and tantrums. If you've made a rule that's in your child's best interests, stick to it and explain your reasoning behind it. Repeat your rule verbally (more than once, if necessary). This age group are still learning to regulate their emotional responses. You will need to consider the longer-term consequences for them, as they're not always able to make associations between different events once they've calmed down and are emotionally regulated.

## Middle Childhood: Five to Nine Years of Age

Parents with younger children might find it useful to draw up family agreements, in which you decide rules and boundaries together. To that end, you can create a document or chart with pictures, such as using images of clocks or the sun and moon to show the time of day. There also needs to be a discussion about the consequences of not following these rules, which can be along the lines of reducing or removing a privilege. This means adapting your boundaries to suit your child's age and stage, so the consequences for a five-year-old would have to be different from those for a nine-year-old, for example.

When I use the word 'boundaries' here, I'm referring to a set of context-dependent rules. They are not necessarily fixed or permanent as demarcations, like iron railings. There's a degree of 'give' to them, and you can be flexible without breaking them. This sort of flexibility allows you to put rules in place to which you can then make specific and short-lived changes that fit the circumstances (this may because you are on holiday or it's the weekend, for example, and you can have a more flexible approach then compared to school nights). However, you'll have to communicate any changes beforehand and the subsequent return to the more rigid rules to enable your child to understand the days of the week, or how rules might vary according to specific circumstances.

Rules and boundaries entail making decisions together as a family, which you need to talk about together so you can create an agreement. Besides teaching your child about democracy and voting rights in this way, negotiation can be key here in building trust and in understanding your child's motivation about their tech use. And this will help to build language, thinking, reasoning and social skills, too.

## CPR in Action: Boundaries in Middle Childhood

When discussing security measures and rules around technology (at home, for example), remember the principles of CPR parenting:

- *Consistency*: show up consistently with the same attitude to parenting, but be willing to listen (although you don't have to agree). Remember to regulate and relate, as this age group often cries out about unfairness or 'just one more minute' and will begin to compare their rules to other children's (sometimes making things up to get what they want in the moment).
- *Persistence*: stick predictably to that approach, no matter what setting you find yourself in. However, you can pre-agree flexibility in your rules and boundaries for certain situations. Hold your rules in your mind, regardless of how much your child cries, has a temper tantrum or even threatens to run away.
- *Resistance*: if you've made a rule that's in their best interest, don't give in to pleading, crying or even violence if this emerges. Explain your reasoning behind the rule and repeat the rule verbally (more than once, if necessary). This age group are still learning to regulate their emotional responses. Hold off speaking about the consequences until you and your child are both regulated (which might be much later in the day).

## Pre-teens and Teens: Ages Ten to Thirteen and Then Thirteen+

When children reach their pre-teens and then teens, they'll very likely start to push for greater independence and less supervision when it comes to online life. Many ten-year-olds in my clinic tell me they are grown up now, as they're heading towards their final year in primary school and their first real academic tests. They're also usually now able to think in more rational and abstract ways and, of course, this conveys to them that they are able to understand 'everything' (as I am often told) and they really are adults!

Similarly, teens feel they are more grown up than their years because they are making choices that may impact on their future careers (such as choosing options in schools for their exams) and they also have brains that encourage them to think they are older, wiser and, of course, better than many of the (stupid/old/annoying) adults around them. This is also a regular conversation in my clinic, where they often tell me they can be trusted, they aren't stupid and they understand 'all about the internet, games and people cos they ain't a kid no more'. I am sure that some readers will be chuckling here, as this is a common narrative among this age group, and it gets even more embedded in the 'I-ain't-stupid' discourse of the sixteen- to eighteen-year-old cohort.

When this growth from child to adulthood happens, you may well have to rethink your strategies around tech-smart parenting and how much freedom you are going to allow when it comes to tech and digital devices, negotiating realistic boundaries and talking about the pitfalls to avoid. Given they will be required to use technology for homework, exam prep and applications to college (or jobs), you will need to consider that this is about internet access writ large rather than 'just' social media.

Don't get me wrong – I'm not saying it's going to be easy.

# BOUNDARIES — HOW TO CREATE AND IMPLEMENT THEM

I've yet to meet a single parent or guardian who's told me that their pre-teen or teen has been compliant with all their boundaries, always. Whether it concerns boundaries around mealtimes, tidy bedrooms, time and money spent on devices or gaming, or the homework a pre-teen or teenager needs to do (or didn't do), virtually every parent or carer says this is where conflict, disagreements, discord, fights and arguments occur.

When you're wrangling with a furious developing pre-teen or teen, it can come as small comfort to learn that it's considered a normal part of human development for this age group to push back against their carers or the village that raised them and to move into a new arena of 'I'm becoming a grown-up now', the inference being, 'so you can't tell me what to do, help me, understand me or tell me *anything* because I already know'. This is all part and parcel of reaching puberty and the brain changes of adolescence (the onset of puberty has changed somewhat in the last decade or so and is now occurring at younger ages; hence why I'm discussing pre-teens and teens together this section). So buckle up – it might be a bumpy ride, but I'm here to help you survive the turbulence!

When it comes to protecting your teen at home, the best you can do is to defend your castle and all those in it by installing age-appropriate parental controls, using a combination of discussion with your teen and tech-smart parenting. Considerations for this age group are similar in nature to those for younger children, in that it's important to be aware that teens mature at different rates and that you'll likely be the best judge of the extent to which yours understands the world, and whether or not they'll be able to take your advice on board; and if they can't, won't, or need another adult to help them, do reach out to a professional.

The nature of the adolescent brain as puberty begins means they are more predisposed to lots of changes in their thinking, reasoning and risk-taking behaviours, and so boundaries here need to be fluid to match these changes. Sometimes they need a gentle guide or stricter coach, like you (or another adult), to help them consider and make 'sensible' choices within the boundaries they have. Similar to an athlete who's keen to progress to the next step in the belief that they've mastered the current one ('I know!' is the cry of most teens at this stage), they may need steering towards repeated practice to become adept and skilled in their executive functioning, behaviour and performance. And so it is with the online world: you may need to prevent, delay or control access to spaces and places online until they are mature enough to visit them. And this may sometimes involve the repeated removal and reinstatement of a restriction until they have mastered this process.

It's likely that teens will argue for any reason they can logically think of to push you into conceding and giving them 'ultimate freedom online'. With technology, of course, this will be based in the rhetoric that they're skilled enough to manage this space, or almost old enough, and so on. In these instances, your most-needed skill is resistance. You might hear phrases like: '... but I'm nearly fifteen, I can stay safe', 'I won't look at A, B, C' or, 'I promise I won't X, Y or Z...' And so on. All the while, you'll need to resist the temptation to seal your own argument with the immortal refrain 'Because I said so', as that often sets in motion the gremlin of circumvention that all teens have sitting on their shoulders. Perhaps if we had the powers to see this gremlin and how it operates, we might say things differently, so as to more successfully put in place the boundaries they seek to work around. After all, it's often our own diminishing levels of patience and tolerance and our embarrassment in that moment that make us resort to 'Because I said so'.

All that said, if you do find yourself shouting, 'Because I said so!' it's not the end of the world. In fact, welcome to the club – I've been there, too, and it's nice to meet you! It just means you're human. You can work around it, although you may well have to swallow some pride and admit later, when you're regulated and calm, that this wasn't the best response. This will help to rebuild your teenager's trust in you.

## CPR in Action: Boundaries and Teens

When discussing security measures like parental controls and TV PINs with your pre-teen or teen, remember the principles of CPR parenting:

- *Consistency*: show up consistently with the same attitude to parenting, but be willing to listen (although you don't have to agree with them). Use examples in advance to explain why the rules are in place and what the boundary violations mean in terms of consequences for them, so they know what to expect if they break them.
- *Persistence*: stick predictably to that approach, no matter what setting you find yourself in. However, you can pre-agree a degree of flexibility in your rules and boundaries for certain situations. Hold your own emotional regulation here, as they can now debate and argue with reason.
- *Resistance*: if you've made a rule that's in their best interest, explain the reasoning behind it and don't give in to pleading, comparisons or slurs against you. And repeat the consequences for violations of the boundary. You may need to become a broken record and repeatedly address this, as boundaries can be regularly challenged in some cases.
And have your wits at the ready for tackling those occasions when they don't violate the boundary fully but 'bend the rules a little'. In some respects, we have to admire this new level of thinking. It shows a developing mind that is independent and critically analyses things like rules.

## *A Note on Children with Social, Emotional or Educational Needs, Neurodiversity and/or Trauma*

This cohort of children often don't see risk, danger or issues as clearly as other children do, so your approach to any rules and CPR responses will have to reflect the needs of your own child, as the advice given in this chapter is generic and not tailored to any individual. Depending on the stage and development needs of your child, you may have to use some of the ideas from the early years sections, in particular; but, if suitable, you could have conversations and put in place practical measures along the lines described for children who belong to the pre-teen and teen years, too.

It's advisable for this cohort of children to have stricter boundaries in place, such as parental controls and notifications on your phone, so you can keep them safe. The general consensus between academics and practitioners in the space of online safety is that this cohort is the most at risk of online harm, and I've witnessed this consistently myself in my clinic for over fifteen years. They need guidance in their online interactions and, most importantly, until they are over the age of thirteen or fourteen unsupervised access isn't recommended (as outlined in UK safeguarding measures known as the Gillick competence and Fraser guidelines, which consider a child's functional ability to make a decision). However, this is your call as a parent – as ever, you know your child best. For example, you may have a neurodivergent twelve-year-old who is capable of playing games and being civil, and knows how to report issues and can talk openly with you about them.

This cohort will not, in most cases, be able to understand the long-term effects of the issues relating to online harms, nor perhaps why they need to be protected from these through boundaries. In some instances, they may resort to verbal or physical violence towards you when they're asked to come away from a screen or stop playing a game, or aren't allowed go on a device or platform. In these circumstances, CPR parenting often reflects the approach taken for the younger years, and you may need to access professional help to create parental controls that can't be circumvented (in my experience, it's often the children who fall into this cohort who have the highest tech skills from the age of seven or eight).

## *Self-Care Break*

Phew . . . this parenting stuff can be full of moments when we realise we might not have taken the best approach, or the approach recommended by professionals in this space, and this can bring up feelings of inadequacy, failure or even denial. I've been there myself, and frequently had to engage in self-compassion when yet another 'do-gooder' on social media highlighted various things I didn't do as a parent. So this self-care break is slightly different to the others – it is a self-compassion exercise that I've adapted to share with you here:

- Place your hand on your heart area. Hold it there for a few minutes and feel the warmth of your hand through your clothes. Notice how you feel doing this.
- Notice your breathing and notice your heartbeat, if you can feel it.
- Place your other hand on top of the hand on your chest and notice the warmth.
- Now say to yourself, out loud, 'I'm doing the best I can with the tools I have as a parent and at times I can find it difficult. I am a good-enough parent.' (Repeat as many times as you like or want to!)

- Stay here for a while.
- Breathe in, and sigh out.
- And yes, you *are* a good-enough parent.

## *Being Flexible*

In Part 1, I explained how taking a flexible approach to boundaries is an aspect of tech-smart parenting. This will especially be the case for pre-teens and teens, and can be part of your ongoing conversations and negotiations with them around your household's rules for safe tech use. For example, during school holidays many may want to spend more time on their devices (or stay up later or in bed for longer on said devices) because the usual rules of getting up early don't apply. If you allow changes and exceptions, this doesn't mean you're weak; it means you're being flexible and can adapt to the changes of the calendar, your family dynamics and much more.

Some adult readers might be saying, 'But surely this sort of flexibility means our kids can manipulate us whenever they want, and they won't respect us. They'll walk all over us.' And then I'd ask just what it is that parents think they're trying to achieve by sticking to rules that aren't flexible in any way or adaptable to changed circumstances.

I'm not saying that we must pander to an adolescent's wishes or agenda every time; nor do we have to negotiate anew on every occasion. After all, we're still the adults in this situation, so by default that puts us in charge. To use a gaming metaphor, it's totally your house, your castle and your rules, because you're the one who's completed childhood and levelled up to being an adult, and then 'prestiged' (a gaming term meaning the best level) into parent mode. You're the boss.

All the same, discussions about technology and boundaries are the most active (and sometimes loud) conversations I hear between parents and adolescents, and the ones that cause the most dysregulation about fairness, rebellion and comparisons. As I like to say, with little children you can literally pick them up and put them in a safe space, like a crib, but teens, well, they're just too heavy and tall – too independent. So your words and actions have to build their boundaries and create a safe space in which they can speak to you about any issues they face with technology. And that's a skill you only really learn when you have a teen. Of course, these boundaries will also act as their guide when they use technology and you're not there to oversee their interactions.

For CPR approaches to renegotiating boundaries around tech, I suggest we remind our teens of the contract or any ground rules we've already set before trying to revisit them. When it comes to the original negotiation, you will now have a date and a baseline of then versus now to refer back to, and with which to compare any potential changes as part of a renegotiation.

On a related note, the most common (and sometimes uncomfortable) conversation I have in my clinic is around safeguarding issues – where a boundary and my duty of care are implicated. I have to remind clients of the agreement we made on a certain date that, if a particular issue arose, I would need to take action, and that I now have to act in line with that, irrespective of the client's age and any vulnerabilities or difficulties they may have (although language must be adjusted accordingly). On the outside this can resemble behaving like a harsh parent, but I know it is ultimately about taking care or protecting my client, although at the time they may not see it that way (and they tell me so). Yet I still use the CPR approach, with empathy, compassion and understanding about their response. Because I get it – by putting myself in their shoes. This is the best piece of advice I can offer here: when dealing with a pre-teen or teen who is renegotiating or angry with you or wants you to change your mind, then *time travel*. Go back in time to your own teenage years and remember how terrible it was to have boundaries, even if you can now, as an adult, appreciate their value.

Be aware that the closer this cohort is to the age of 'being allowed' to do something (such as use social media, have sex or be treated as an independent adult when approaching thirteen, sixteen and the grand old age of eighteen, respectively), the more appealing to them the next stage of growing up becomes, and the more likely they'll be to test the waters. On the other hand, the further kids are from the age of consent to do things like drink or have sex the less likely they are to push the boundaries – because what's the point in saying 'I'm almost old enough' if it's patently not true?

However, I'm aware that some children may be more mature at earlier ages – for example, your twelve-year-old may have more social or reasoning skills than many fourteen-year-olds and you, as their parent, may believe they are ready for social media based on this. In such cases, moving the goalposts isn't always driven by the child, but by the observations of the adult who believes their child is ready for a particular experience.

A point to note here is that, as mentioned earlier, you may make these decisions only to find that your pre-teen or teen wasn't quite ready for an experience after all, and you may need to dial back the parameters of this new freedom. This is ok and it's exactly how many of us learn in life by trial and error. By staying aware of the risks online and through technology, you will be better placed to see when you can try moving the goalposts and when you might have to move them back again. 'Scaffolding' is a term used in psychology, and in practice it looks like a bit like stabilisers on a child's bike: it allows your child to try things and experiences (in line with the law, of course), but if they 'fall off' you can pop the stabilisers back on again.

With this in mind, imagine there was a ban in place prohibiting under-sixteens from using social media: what would happen when a fifteen-and-a-half-year-old began to ask to access it in the run-up to their sixteen birthday, arguing, 'I'm almost old enough – what's a few months or weeks?' What risks might they take in relation to this sudden freedom, especially if they or their parents hadn't really considered or discussed those risks before? Or perhaps the parent isn't even aware of them, because they didn't need to worry previously about a space their child couldn't visit till now? If this happened to you and your child, would you – or they – be fully informed about the risks from Day 1 on the device?

In my clinic, the moment a child reaches twelve or thirteen they'll often start filling their devices with apps, games and social media, because they tell me they're 'allowed now' (or a parent said they could, and so they did) and, of course, in some cases they meet the threshold of being 'old enough'. Yet does a chronological date like a birthday mark a difference in the development of their social, emotional and psychological skills compared to the day before? Or should we be thinking in terms of scaffolding and learning, rather than handing over the online world to children at a particular age? And what flexibility should be applied to those kids who are approaching thirteen versus those who are over this age and what this means in terms of their safety online? As always, you will have to take a nuanced approach in relation to your own child and their unique personality and needs when making any decisions.

## Contracts

As I work with many children with vulnerabilities, we sometimes hit a touchy part of our therapeutic relationship when we discuss maturity and risk in the online world (and this can be the case with their parents and guardians, too). This involves a discussion with the child and carers about ages of access, the abilities of the child to assess risk online and the harms they may encounter and, of course, safeguarding conversations should anything arise (which is mostly what I work with as a cybertrauma clinician).

As part of tech-smart parenting, it pays to pre-empt situations. This means *you* may need some e-safety and cybersecurity lessons, as well as reading books like this, and signing up for e-safety newsletters to keep on top of trends and risks online. It seems like a lot to take on as part of your parenting role, but to be honest in a world of technology it's now a necessary part of parenting.

If you talked to your child when they were younger about the world online, and informed yourself about it, too, you will be in a much stronger position to reason with them when they are older. If you have armed yourself with knowledge, you can keep those Batfink ears on standby and be alerted to issues early, and with this book you'll now have options, strategies and ways to assist your pre-teen and teen as they head into social media and gaming spaces.

Written contracts or agreements can be a great way to work with children between the ages of five and ten, but it's important to be aware that as they get older children will start to think about the world differently. According to the psychologist Jean Piaget, it's in adolescence that they begin to understand and apply the concrete and abstract rules of life, and to challenge what they hear and see, especially if rules are imposed on them that seem unjust in any way.

'Hypocrites!' This is among the words most frequently uttered in my therapy room by children and young people, along with: 'How come they can and I can't?' and 'It's not fair'. The word 'hypocrite' is used by some (ok, most) clients when referring to the 'they' that is their parent, guardian or other adult, such as a teacher, using devices. So if you're going to use contracts with children and you wish to avoid conflict, here are some guidelines to follow, particularly with older kids:

- Discuss the terms of the agreement with your child first, explaining the reasoning behind them (especially if they apply to some but not all members of the household), and also allow for a degree of flexibility.

## BOUNDARIES – HOW TO CREATE AND IMPLEMENT THEM

- Use images, timers, dates or days on the contract or calendar for quick reference points and for children with learning difficulties. Keep the contract in a shared area, visible for all to see (on the fridge door, for example).
- Separate flexible rules out in an 'If . . . then . . .' format.
- Have regular updates and renegotiate as your child grows and moves into new phases of life; for example, when they start going to an after-school club or acquire new friends.
- List the consequences on a separate sheet for each individual in the family and include parents on this sheet; and be accountable if your child pulls you up on one of these moments, just like Claire did in the case study in Chapter 5 (see p. 109).
- Print out the logos of apps that you allow versus those you do not, and update as necessary.
- Include a regular check-in with your child about how they're getting on with the online space and what progress they are making. Discussions shouldn't always be about rules or 'don't's'; let them see they have some successes.
- Ask them for feedback on *your* technology use. And don't judge (see the social media videos about this process called 'We listen and we don't judge'; they can be hilarious).
- Agree together clearly that your contract can be extended to include the households of other family members (or clubs/social events), so that visits to these places are still following the rules and your child knows this is the case before they visit.
- Most importantly, discuss your contract with other parents before sleepovers or visits (at theirs or yours – see box below).

> ### *Agreements with Other Households*
>
> If your child is a member of a blended or separated family, you may need to talk to the heads of other households about any rules or boundaries you put in place as part of your family agreement, so there is some consensus across the board.
>
> Also talk to other households and family members about what you consider inappropriate content before your child visits or sees something on *their* devices or TVs. In the case of other children visiting you, it can be helpful for other parents to know your take, too (as above). You have the right to stop your children viewing material you deem unsuitable or using online spaces that you've said no to in your home. While some children may not be fazed (they say) by inappropriate content, growing children and teens will remember – in both their brains and their bodies – content that is emotive and graphic. My career as a cybertrauma clinician and PhD researcher is testimony to this issue.

*TIP:* It is helpful to distinguish between those boundaries you intend to keep to rigidly, ones that can be flexible and ones that are 'for now/this weekend/this social situation' (for example, no devices when you visit family members, but your kids can use phones and tablets in the car on the way there and back).

## Testing Boundaries

So why do our children push the boundaries, and what else can we do when this happens?

Here, it can be helpful to understand why children do the things they do online. For kids, it's often just because they can, or because they want what they want right now. However, some children will push boundaries because it's forbidden (in much the same way that some young people drink alcohol or have sex underage). It can also be because they don't understand or consider the consequences, in much the same way that a small child under the age of seven might steal biscuits from the cupboard because they are hungry right now and don't think about the consequences of you finding out and just hope that somehow their answer about the dog eating the biscuits will be believable when you ask them about it.

Some children might break house rules and spend a lot of time online because they are busy socialising and having fun, or they feel a compulsion to be with their friends, or they've got themselves caught up in a drama or are watching one unfold, or they're taking part in an event . . . like most of the other things they do when in the real world. And when it comes to your online rules being broken, thinking about this can help to temper your response.

If possible, we should aim to meet challenges, when they arise, from what is known as 'the window of tolerance' (a concept developed by neuropsychiatrist Dan Siegel and others). This is a zone in which our own emotions remain balanced and controlled, where we're experiencing neither hyperarousal (such as feelings of anger, flight or fight) nor hypo-arousal (such as depression and numbness). This zone of tolerance supports the brain's and body's capacity to deal with any stressors, both on our own behalf and on behalf of somebody else, which is why learning how to get into this zone is a master skill in online safety and tech-smart parenting. This is what clinicians mean by being regulated and it involves: the recognition that you have emotions rising that can be big (like being angry), but you are able to feel the emotion without using it on others (anger or aggression, for example) and you know it will pass and have exercises to help you manage it, such as breathing techniques. When you are regulated and using the CPR approach you may find a situation like the following occurring:

You are sitting in a café and it's time to leave. You ask your child to put the tablet away and get their coat on.

They refuse, saying, 'Just one minute, I gotta . . .'

You acknowledge this is repetitive behaviour from them; you also know it's a tactic to carry on playing in the hope that you will give in. Older children may notice that you get embarrassed in public spaces, and based on previous experiences they'll be aware that this could turn into a bit of a show if they push to disobey the request.

You ask again, and this time you say, 'I know you're having fun, and it's disappointing to end the game, but we've got to catch the bus or we'll be stuck in the rain walking home.' In this moment, you might be feeling exasperated or annoyed with the behaviour, thinking, Why do they always . . . or, Are they pressing my buttons? But you don't say these things or show your feelings, and maybe you practise some box breathing (which we looked at earlier – see p. 206). Like a broken record, you repeat your request and talk through the consequences of them not doing as they are asked.

This back and forth may go on for several 'rounds', with more exaggerated behaviours from the child (such as getting louder, shouting or trying to lash out). You may even need to take the tablet from them physically to end it, all while feeling annoyed with your child and their behaviour, yet holding your s**t together, using CPR and not losing your temper. This is not an easy task!

With practice, you can feel your feelings and still remain regulated. It can take time to learn this new art of 'zen', but it is possible. However, we do need to accept that sometimes this battle around technology is because we just want our kids to 'do as they are told', no questions, because it makes our lives easier in the moment – and we forget that this is a two-way relationship requiring an agreement between us (even if we don't say it out loud).

## BOUNDARIES – HOW TO CREATE AND IMPLEMENT THEM

In the Resources, p. 347, I point you to some great software and books to help you with this; I also invite you to watch my 'polyvagal motorway of wellness' video online to grasp the analogy of driving in the middle lane and being able to manage the traffic of life.

> *TIP:* The quickest self-regulation tool is coherent breathing. This is where we create harmony between our breath and heart rhythms. Now, breathing practices are often pooh-poohed, as people can't believe that a few rounds of box breathing (see above), the yogic practice of pranayama (perhaps using a four-seconds-in, seven-second-hold and eight-seconds-out technique) or a physiological sigh (big breath in, another sip of inhale and one long, loud, drawn-out sigh) can do the trick. But they most certainly can, and learning how to do this automatically when pushed to your limits is the best free parenting hack on the market.

It's down to us as our children's parents and guardians to be their first line of defence, and not the tech industry or 'the powers that be'. Straightforward bans simply don't work, as children will often find ways to circumnavigate them, which may, ultimately, place them at greater risk. So we need to teach them how to use online spaces safely as part of their education in a world in which tech is going to be part of their future.

Parental controls and cybersecurity products are important, as ever, as is learning how to use them in ways that suit your family circumstances and work for you and your children. However, before harnessing any controls or other cybersecurity measures, you'll need to start talking to your child about these and any family rules or boundaries that you'd like to set in place, to explain your thinking, as discussed in this chapter. And be prepared to meet with challenges, in which case the CPR approach to parenting may come in handy whatever the age or stage of your child.

While it's not especially easy to create boundaries or contracts and to keep them in place, and they can result in friction, verbal fights and (intentional?) forgetfulness about them, it's worth weathering the storms and persisting. They're one of the best ways to protect your child while ensuring that your relationship with each other is one of mutual understanding and respect. Remember, a healthy boundary isn't rigid and uncompromising; it can be flexible and adapted to suit changed circumstances when appropriate as part of your ongoing exchange of views and opinions through talking and listening to your child, which is what we'll be looking at in Chapter 11.

## Summary

- Don't impose outright bans, but do discuss boundaries with children, including why they are needed.
- Consider family contracts or agreements about technology use and access. Sit down as a family and talk about rules around using technology that work for your household.
- Ensure that agreed rules are in place for families that are separated, blended or where children are in care.
- And breathe . . . you've got this, and you're now better informed to make decisions that can protect your child. That is an amazing part of your parenting love for them.

CHAPTER 11

# Let's Keep Talking

By this point, you may well have started to piece together a clearer picture of what kind of parent it's best to be in a world of technology. It requires us to be with our children, not just as a physical presence but really 'with' them by leaning into the emotionally hard bits and showing up when we feel like running away. To learn and develop with them, and to know that we won't always get it right but we're doing our best . . .

There are no quick fixes in tech-smart parenting, because what you do now may need changing in a few weeks', months' or years' time, as your child matures, or if they circumvent your digital parenting strategy, and as the landscape of technology itself changes, too. Because, as we know, artificial intelligence has already altered some of that landscape, so it pays to remain aware that the terrain online is ever-evolving, which means our approach to it has to be as well. We have to be prepared for what could occur, rather than lamenting, 'Oh, we weren't ready!' after the event.

Parenting in a world of technology requires that we are active in our children's digital lives from many perspectives. We don't have to be a presence haunting their feeds or hovering over their devices 24/7, but we do need to take an interest in what they get up to online, who they interact and speak with, where they 'go' and how they do this. All the while remembering to *check in, not on*.

We also need to think about the age- and stage-appropriate methods of monitoring them in that online city park in the same ways that we would in the real world, and to consider our responses if things do ever go wrong – all of which is discussed in these pages.

But, above all, we need to keep talking. Which is why, in this chapter, I'm coming back to this subject one last time, and will be offering some general guiding principles for supporting your connection and conversations with your child or teen, and how these can apply in even the most difficult scenarios.

## Start Young

Begin to have conversations about challenging topics such as sex and violence when your child is still young, if possible. How do we do that? Well, we start with what we have at our disposal (and, yes, tech is going to help here) and we go at the pace of our child's development. Let's think about some potential routes to starting any of these talks. (I'll be including examples that you can adapt for your own age- and stage-appropriate conversations.)

### *Chats in The Early Years*

You might ask a small child about what they've been watching. For example, 'When you were watching *Peppa Pig* today, what did she do? And what did you think when Peppa pushed George down the hill? Do you think he got hurt? What did Peppa say to him and why do you think she did that? What if she'd taken photos of him like we do with our phones – do you think that would be kind?' You could then chat about filming people and taking selfies (of course, young children do this and parents do upload them to the internet).

You can always talk about your technology use, too, to help them understand that it has many modes of use; for example,

'Daddy is sending an email, which is like a letter, and he has to type out some words and then he sends it. Would you like to press the little icon to send it?' Then ask your child to show you where they think the icon is, or you could show them the mouse and or trackpad, for example. But good luck explaining how email works to a five-year-old, who may well ask you!

If you want to talk technology and body health, then rather than saying things like 'your eyes will go square', you could describe how our eyes get tired from looking at the screen all day. You can talk about sitting all day in front of a screen and not getting some stretches in and how that isn't good for a growing body. Your reflections to them about their body and its needs can help them see that we all need to move, stretch and relax our eyes, so that when you ask them to take a health break, you are not stopping them using tech because you're mean, but looking after them. (Just remember to do this for yourself too!)

Any topic that has been discussed in this book is suitable to discuss in an age-appropriate and relevant way with your tiny person and to adapt to the task in hand. So if, say, you want to approach topics like sexualised content online, such as in twerking videos or models in skimpy clothes, you can carefully move the discussion to people not wearing clothes and being 'naked' or undressed on videos online. But please don't use the word 'rude' to describe nakedness, as this can be confusing when we also tell children that sticking your tongue out is rude, or slamming a door. (If you need more help with this, see the Resources, p. 347.)

Remember that small children are curious and will be watching you as well as wanting to chat (a lot) about everything you do and have.

## Talking to Children in Middle Childhood

Choose a TV show, game or video viewed online that's of interest to your child and talk to them about it. I'll use the game platform Roblox as an example:

'You know how on Roblox there are tons of games that are designed by other people? . . . Have you ever seen any that are scary-looking or that other kids say are scary?'

Or

'Why do you think developers make scary games for kids your age, and why do you think kids play them?'

You can also ask questions when your child is playing games like Minecraft or Fortnite: 'You know you can't do [insert an action like a 'headshot'] in the real world? I wonder what you think about being able to do that to other players?'

And/or 'Why do you think adults make games where you can [kill/shoot/push/bash/use a sword/crossbow]?'

And, 'What about games where the players are wearing weird outfits like they have no clothes on? Have you ever seen anything that's weird when you're gaming, or using your device/phone/computer?'

Listening to your child here may give you some insight into the way they think about these games, videos or other online content. But more importantly, they'll see that you're taking an interest, too, besides just having a lecture from you. Questions like this show you care because you asked about *their* opinion or experience openly and allowed them space to tell you about it all, whilst approaching issues of risk, harm and inappropriate content. .

Often, children aged between seven and twelve will tell me they know about nudes and using sexual language (which they may call 'dirty minded'). These sorts of conversations indicate that we need to be discussing the moral, legal and ethical aspects of this with them, and asking what they would do if they saw it; would they report it to the platform, or to you?

Kids in this age group also say they're 'well aware' that violence is illegal, but they 'love to do it in a game, 'cos it's not real, and you can be really mean and not get in trouble'. So have conversations with them about empathy, too, and about how actions in a game such as flying, falling or coming back from the dead (respawning) aren't something we can really do or achieve in real life, although it's fun to do in a make-believe way in a game.

This age group is likely the first to begin to understand that cyberbullying can take place online, as they may find in gaming there are players who 'wind them up', who hack (cheat) and who kick them out of the game or harass them. (Some children tell me it's more about those who camp out 'on purpose', with 'camping' being a dodgy strategy in gaming.) You can talk to them about kindness online and how to report players who are bullying, and how to let you know so you can help them.

If your child doesn't want to engage in conversations about online safety, technology or any of the topics here, then my advice is to seek professional help or ask their school to help. I would also question whether they have the resources yet to be on technology safely, so you might want to consider removing it until they can engage with you about it.

## Conversations with Pre-Teens and Teens

I had a chuckle to myself when considering what to write here, because invariably this age group typically doesn't want to talk to parents. (In the 1990s, Harry Enfield gained a great deal of success with his character Kevin the Teenager for precisely this reason).[1]

So let's begin with what we *can* talk about and why they might engage in this topic. Ready . . .? It's technology! Tech is often a topic young people who come to my clinic absolutely *will* talk about, non-stop. But why are they willing to do this? And how do I get them to? Firstly, it's more than likely because I'm not their parent, but it's also because I've learned and continue to learn about the trends and turns of technology; I know the difference between a controller and console, and whether PC gaming supersedes other forms, for example. Now you don't have to become a 'tech speak' guru yourself, but I would suggest that you use all the information in this book / on my socials and look to the safety companies and technology-related spaces on social media (such as the PlayStation channels, Xbox Facebook group or TikTok trends) for more information about the newest updates, challenges or changes taking place. Chat with other parents and family about technology, too, and – most importantly for our purposes here – show an interest in your pre-teen or teen's interests with tech. If they want to buy a game for their console, ask about it, search YouTube to learn what it is, and ask them to show you the reasons why they want it. If they want a VR headset, a new speaker for their Spotify playlist or a headset, check this out online and in stores so you can have an informed conversation about what they are asking for.

Topics that relate to online safety can take the form of conversations about something else entirely – see the James Bond mini-script in Chapter 5 as an example. When it comes to violence online, there are plenty of videos, topics and debates you can use to kick-start conversations. For example, in the summer of 2024 there were riots in the UK. Events like these can be strong starting points for discussing things like empathy and tolerance and the capture of violence by phones and the media.

When considering the risks that pre-teens and teens face online, head back to Chapter 9 and think about how you would approach a topic like terrorism content, racism or misogyny with them. With respect to misogyny, you might ask whether they think that this specific topic has resulted in terms like 'toxic masculinity' (a contentious and potentially unhelpful label because, although it's about the fact that some males behave in toxic ways, it can teach boys to believe that they are toxic just because they're male). These subjects can lead to very heated debate, so please get as much information about a topic as you can before embarking on a 'let's discuss X' session with a pre-teen or teen, as they can become very animated in such conversations. Which leads me to the conversations you can have about people in technology, such as Elon Musk. Again, hold regulated conversations and space for views you may not agree with.

It helps to remember here the regulation exercise I pointed to in Chapter 10 (see p. 293). The more adept you become at this, the better equipped you are to show your teen how to have a disagreement, stay regulated and make a point without losing it. If this happens, wait for them to calm down before engaging with them about much else, as they can be like a pot of boiling water with a lid on. Lifting the lid just a little too soon can result in the steam coming out fast! Teens often need some decompression time, so learning to notice what this looks like is your best tool here. Also, revisit Chapter 9 for a refresh on why this age group wants to have their own voice and sense of self (see p. 224).

---

*A note on conversations with children with social, emotional or educational needs, neurodiversity and/or trauma*

Children in this cohort vary, and, while they may be a specific age in terms of the number of years they have been alive, at least one of their domains of development will likely not be in line with this. For example, you may be talking to a twelve-year-old who presents as a five-year-old in their emotional skills, or perhaps a seventeen-year-old who is cognitively delayed and understands the world as a seven-year-old would. You know your child better than anyone and you know how to have conversations about daily tasks such as getting dressed, washing themselves or reading a book. So your conversations with them about the online world are going to be a variant of chats you already have with them – say, about people, relationships, friendships and even kindness – and you can rest secure in the knowledge that you are the best person to do this with your child. Still, it is important for me to give you a guide to help with this.

The most crucial piece of advice I have been able to pass along to parents, guardians and adults around children with these difficulties is to tell your child the age-relevant truth in respect of this online space and its content. There will always be someone in the online world to do this for you if not. This is the most challenging aspect of today's world for you and for them, as children who are facing the information overload online are more vulnerable in that space if they are not adequately prepared to do so. You do not have to charge in on topics like sex if you already have a way to talk to your child about this, but it will be an inevitable component of the online world, and such conversations will probably be ones you never envisaged having with your child until they were ready to leave school and perhaps in romantic relationships. It might have felt very far in the future, yet here I am centring this back at your feet now. The feedback I get from children in this cohort is that, while they are often technically minded and able to navigate the online space because it is logical and linear, and therefore safe and predictable, people are not. Please bear this in mind, as it is the most important aspect of both their online safety lesson and their conversation with you, and tailor it to them and their level of understanding.

Many spaces online, like gaming, have etiquette, social norms and rules (and the same can be said of social media), so it can be helpful for you to play games *with* them so that you can watch

> and learn, and feed back to them where you can see those rules, in much the same way that you would when explaining a cricket match, ludo or snap, say, in the real world. As for social media, help them to understand that these are spaces where people interact, and monitor and feed back to them as you might with a social gathering. It's slightly different, but in most cases people are still people, and you can support your child in these arenas and help them learn how to behave there.
>
> It might help here to use the chapters and thinking for younger age groups when having the necessary conversations and to give you some reassurance and confidence in doing so. As I've said throughout the book, you really have got this. And for extra help and information you can always check out my website and the resources section there.

## Discuss, Don't Dictate

When debating an issue with a child or teenager, don't slam down your points, but ask open-ended questions like, 'I'm curious that you think that. How did you get to that conclusion?' Also use phrases like 'I wonder' before asking questions. For example, 'I wonder who said that and what qualifications they may have?' or, 'I wonder if that's because they are a popular person online?' or, 'I wonder how many other kids/players might think/say/do that and why?'

Another helpful approach is to ask your child to explain something, such as a piece of information or video that they've found online: 'Can you explain it to me, so I can understand it?' While the answer they give may have some logic, it might not always conform to accepted facts about the world (such as the laws of physics and the Earth not being flat, for example). Whatever their reply, listen closely and take your time in responding. If necessary, let tempers cool down, agree to disagree and revisit the topic another day. In the words of American brain coach Jim Kwik, be their thermostat, not their thermometer. Don't react to their 'temper'-ature, but regulate them instead, so they don't boil over in heated mode. This means you need to be regulated first.

If necessary, and if safe to do so (if no other children are present, for example), take yourself off to a different room for at least five minutes to reset your own emotional temperature setting and to give them time to do the same.

## Navigating Real-World Spaces

We now live in a society where we need to think about the real-world spaces children visit and what, who and how many other children may be there with devices of their own. We may need to consider whether those children have protected devices, tech-savvy parents or even just parents who care at all about keeping kids safe online. The risk of access and exposure to the sort of content and dangers discussed in this book are highest in the real-world spaces where children can be subjected to content on someone else's device.

That's why giving our children a 'get-out plan' can be really helpful. For decades, we've been teaching kids to walk away from strangers who offer sweeties in the park. In the same way, it's useful for our children to have a script they can use when a friend wants to show them something inappropriate on a device when they're not with us. It could go something like this:

FRIEND: 'Hey, wanna watch this?'

YOUR CHILD: 'What is it? I don't want to watch something that might upset me, or is horrid, so I'd rather not, thanks.' [An older child or teen could say: 'If you think it's ok for me to see, why don't you text it to my mum and I can watch it later?' Said with a little sarcasm, this challenges and highlights the fact that most wouldn't send it to the mum.]

If your child feels uncomfortable, they can now text or call you or another trusted adult to inform you. Texting can be done in silence, with muted keys and notifications, so the other person is unaware that your child is requesting help; or they can prank call you (so the phone rings only once, just enough for the call to register on your phone). You can even set a code word or phrase your child can use to indicate that they need you; I work with some children from separated families, and, when they are in need of being picked up (perhaps because they're uncomfortable with something at the non-resident parent's house), they text the resident parent with an icon/emoji or word that's been decided beforehand to mean this.

Similarly, a child might overhear inappropriate material in a public space if somebody (such as an older child or teen) has it open on a device. Sadly, our online safety acts cannot stop what happens in public spaces, so this calls for real-world parental controls, whereby you may have to think about where you allow your child to roam and whether you let them be around others who have devices.

If your child does see or hear something distressing, they need to be able to tell you about it. Again, you can establish a code word they can use to let you know they've been subjected to viewing something that has upset them. Decide on a way for them to let you know this, follow the 3Rs (see p. 180: regulate, relate and reason) and discuss it with them later. It can be more distressing for a child to recall the material immediately after an event, so you want to be their emotional-regulation tool (i.e. their emotional thermostat – see p. 306). They may have recurring memories of the viewing, and this may show up as bodily function issues like restlessness, sleep, toileting problems and wanting to be near you a lot. Be patient and, if needed, seek professional help.

*TIP:* Be curious but not intrusive. Asking your pre-teen or teen any question can always be interpreted by them as though they've been arrested and are now in the dock at court. (I see this so often in my clinic.) Wondering out loud about something can be a good way into a conversation. However, if you give the impression you have zero knowledge about a subject, it might seem like too much hassle for them to teach you (again, another common response in my clinic), so aim for the middle ground of having just enough knowledge to pique their interest and ego. Yes, I suppose this sounds like a manipulative technique, but it's been successfully used by many practitioners over the years as a way to begin a conversation – because this age group loves to feel an element of mastery over us. So let them! They don't get to enjoy that feeling very often, as they claim they're always being told what to do, think and know by us old fogies, so it's nice for them to have a chance to educate us.

Every relationship has its up and down – times when we agree, we agree to disagree or we simply can't see eye to eye with each other. In our conversations with our children, it's down to us, as the adults in their lives, to keep the lines of communication open whatever happens and to meet strong emotions such as anger and despair with kindness, compassion, reason and understanding. In turn, let's learn from our kids to keep our minds open and to stay curious about the world online and around us. We won't always have all the answers (even if we sometimes think we do) and we can join them on a journey of discovery as their guides, guardians and travel companions, so that they know we will always be there for them whenever they need us.

## Summary

- When discussing an issue with a child, ask questions that can't be answered with a simple 'yes' or 'no'. Use open-ended ones that will encourage them to engage in a conversation with you.
- If you disagree about a topic and tempers are getting frayed, take some time out to let things calm down.
- Agree a 'get-out plan' with your child in the form of what to say and do if somebody tries to share inappropriate content with them, or if they feel uncomfortable in a situation and need help.

## CHAPTER 12

# Troubleshooting – How to Respond When Things Go Wrong

It can be exhausting to be a parent in a world of technology, can't it? Despite our best intentions, life happens, and things do go wrong. Kids will make mistakes, whether intentionally or otherwise.

Sometimes children do these sorts of things simply to get round our rules and regulations, which is totally normal; and of course, nowadays, given the existence of parental controls, it can entail the thrilling challenge of matching their skillset to yours. This sort of boundaries-pushing behaviour is very much a part of being a child or teen. Can you remember breaking adults' rules for the sheer sake of it? And what was it like when they found out and perhaps – to paraphrase the words of so many of my clients – lost their s\*\*t at you? It's something that many children describe to me in my clinic. And I admit that I've been a parent who's had a very similar reaction when I discovered my own children had circumvented the parental controls I'd put in place. When I look back, I wonder whether I would have tech-parented differently if more controls were available, as they are today. My children tell me to this day that they would *still* have circumvented the controls just to see if they could. For them, it was a battle of tech-savvy wits.

Whether your child is a toddler, teen or in between, whether they have a vulnerability or not, whether they're similar to or entirely different from other children, the relationship they have with you is the one of the most important factors in their online safety. You are indispensable in all this. That's why this whole book has focused on the role you play, the conversations you have with your child and your reactions to their behaviour. Yes, we're back to our old friends, connection and open dialogue, which hold the key to tackling all manner of circumstances, including situations when things start to unravel.

So what do you do when . . .? I'm now going to share several scenarios (some are intentionally quite extreme) and consider how best to respond to them. You will see that I don't use the words 'catch' or 'caught' in any of these, and that's because, if we talk about a child as having been 'caught' doing something, the implication is that we're somehow playing a game of 'gotcha!' with them, as though we view them in the same light as a criminal and that we're waiting to catch them out, to punish them.

Understanding that the digital age is a space in which problems can be exacerbated, exaggerated and escalate very quickly is key to being able to deal with issues that arise. We need to remember that a child has fewer emotional regulation skills than an adult, and may well do, say, post or react to something faster, in ways that can end up hurting them or result in them being ostracised, rejected or attacked when online. Relationships can be littered with fall-outs, disagreements and hiccups – or what we call ruptures. Our children have to learn from us that rupturing moments can be repaired, and, for them to learn this, we must be the ones to repair any ruptures in the relationship we have with them.

This is sometimes difficult because our children will want to punish us when we try to repair rifts, and it can hurt when they kick back at us. We may need to learn how to self-soothe in these moments. But repair the rupture we must, for our children to be safe, seen, soothed and secure (the 4Ss we looked at earlier), so they can take this behaviour and learning into their activities online.

The stories that follow in this chapter are intended to be examples only, not precise directions about what you must or mustn't do in these situations. They are for guidance, so that you can see regulation, empathy, compassion, CPR (see p. 107) and non-violent communication in action. They offer examples of providing the conditions for your child to be safe, seen, secure and soothed by your parenting. The intention is to help you see below the surface 'presentation' of the behaviours to their deeper significance, and what is being communicated by them, which has been the line throughout this book. Remember that you are always the parent in all situations with your child, and that my hope in sharing these examples isn't to undermine your approach but to provide you with some more tools and new ways to think, which you will also find in the books listed in the Resources on pp. 347–9. This can expand your window of tolerance, helping you to stay regulated and creating that much-needed open channel with your child. Whatever age they may be.

These stories reflect conversations or consultations from my clinical work. Names and identities have been protected to uphold the integrity, confidentiality and ethics of my work. A few are taken from events that I have permission to share (including one involving my own child) and they are all told in a way designed to help you understand the complexities of cybertrauma, which I've lived with personally as well as professionally, and which is why I'd like to emphasise the personal attachment I have to this chapter and, of course, the book as a whole, as this is a major part of my work with children, teens and adults who are online and live in a world of technology.

### *Playing Games Underage*

Billy is twelve. You've told him no when he's asked to play Grand Theft Auto. He goes to his friend Matthew's house after school and, when he gets back, he tells you he played the game with Matthew and his older brother, and he had a great time.

Billy tells you Matthew's older brother laughed when he explained he wasn't allowed to play the game, and said it would be ok. He put on the game and let Matthew and Billy play, too. There was a scene in which the car ran over a pedestrian. Billy thought it was funny, but he knows you can't do things like that in the real world. He enjoyed the game, but realises you'll be mad at him for playing.

*What do you think?* You could tell Billy he's never going to Matthew's house again. And in the heat of the moment this could be exactly how you feel. But what if, instead of rushing to ban Billy from visiting his friend, you were to ask him about the game – why he played it, what he saw and how he felt about that?

*What to do:* Does Billy's description tell you something about his thinking about hurting people? He knew you didn't want him to play the game, and he explained that to Matthew's brother. Can you use this as an opportunity to discuss the situation with him and explain that the game has elements in it that are inappropriate, which is why you don't want him to play it? Perhaps you can mention the PEGI rating and why it applies. And is there anything you'd like to say to Matthew's parents about what happened?

*What does a child like Billy need?* First, consider why Billy told you about playing the game in the first place? In telling you, he trusted you would talk to him – not shout, ban or punish him. Perhaps he even hoped you could deal with the situation involving the older brother because, after all, Billy is still only twelve and might not have been able to leave the house when the older boy put on the game. Can you think of a way to get Billy to agree to communicating with you if a similar situation arises in future and what you could do in the moment? What do you think Billy would have wanted you to do if you'd known?

## HOW TO RESPOND WHEN THINGS GO WRONG

### *Seeing Something Inappropriate, Scary or Illegal*

Sophie is five and loves cartoons, so you've set up YouTube Kids on her tablet and now she's busy watching her favourite one. It's nearly bedtime and she takes her tablet upstairs to carry on watching the cartoon while she gets ready for bath and bed. You let her because you're trying to make the other children their supper. At bedtime, she insists she sleeps in Mummy's bed because there are scary things in her room.

On the first night, you let her sleep in your bed, but by the tenth night you're exhausted, and put her to bed in her own room. However, she begins to wake up her siblings with her night terrors, and wets the bed regularly. You can't understand it.

When you're busy in the kitchen one day, you suggest that Sophie watches her tablet with her siblings to keep them occupied. She breaks down crying, saying she doesn't want to watch it. You discover through her search history that one of the videos she watched alone in her bedroom is completely unsuitable for children. It only made it through the filters as it was developed by an adult who made it look like a 'normal' version of the cartoon, but it includes scenes of violence and sexual themes.

When we see something that contains violence, we may identify with the feelings of someone else in pain, which can result in our own bodies feeling a level of 'ewww', 'yuk' or fear of some kind. This can affect how our nervous systems respond. In the case of Sophie, she suffered with anxiety about bedtime because of the association with where she had seen the content. As a result, she had nightmares and lost control of her bladder.

*What do you think?* You might think the best option is to remove YouTube from Sophie's tablet and never let her use it again, or to stop her using it till she's reached the age of eighteen and can make her own decisions. You might think you failed her in some way and feel a lot of guilt or shame.

*What to do:* Five-year-old Sophie is clearly very affected in many ways by what she's seen. (However, the advice here is applicable to a child of any age who sees something that scares them, is traumatic or includes interpersonal violence or injuries.) It's important to realise that, when we see something violent, scary or even horror based, our bodies and brains can respond to it and our nervous systems can go awry. It's therefore very likely that, if your child has seen something like 'war gore' or violence online, their nervous system is going to become dysregulated. They may show signs of fatigue, dissociation or, at the other extreme, excitability and distress, which means they could find it difficult to sleep or stay asleep, eat or visit the loo regularly – all kinds of behaviour that might annoy or worry us. We need to understand that there's often much more going on beneath the outward behaviour. Perhaps you can discuss with Sophie watching television downstairs in the future, where you can play YouTube together and you can keep her safe?

In this scenario, bedtime becomes a very difficult process for you, so in this case I would be encouraging you to make the routine around this time of day about energy release – such as running on the spot, star jumps and jumping into a pillow on the bed – followed by a warm bath to slow down and soothe Sophie's nervous system. You could also use the opposite approach if she' is already very energetic: slowing down first, then having a warm drink and a story about being 'a hero', so the memory areas of her brain learn to associate the bedroom with triumph. A night light can also be helpful.

*What does a child like Sophie need?* When we discover that our children have seen something upsetting, it's important to remember that our own nervous systems help to regulate theirs, too. So if we get angry, shout or tut, we'll send them a message that things aren't safe. This is why it's crucial to keep ourselves in check as far as possible when we care for our children in the wake of this type of cybertrauma and the viewing of inappropriate material and content online. Use parental controls where possible to minimise access to violent content, and have those uncomfortable conversations with people in any other places that your child may visit to reduce the likelihood of this occurring there as well.

### *Bullying Online*

Fifteen-year-old Emma is quite a lonely child at school. She has friends at her dance class, but she only goes there twice a week. You've learned that she recently didn't get the main part in an upcoming dance event (Emma's classmate Jackie got the starring role), and you're concerned that she'll be devastated. When you talk to her about it, she says she's not bothered, really, as she's still part of the event.

One Sunday evening, Jackie's mum phones you up to ask why Emma is being so mean to her daughter. You're taken aback and decide to 'sneak' a look at Emma's social media accounts. To your dismay, you discover she's been commenting on all of Jackie's posts, saying what an ugly, horrid person she is. And it seems that a few of Emma's other friends are making similar comments, too.

You're mortified that Emma is behaving like this online. She's such a quiet and sweet girl at home and at school. You suddenly feel like you don't know or understand your daughter.

When Emma gets home from dance class, you ask her to explain. She tells you she has a group of friends on the message service Discord who really 'get' her, and they think that Jackie isn't as talented a dancer as she is, so they've been encouraging her to say mean things. They've also used an AI program to change how Jackie looks and created a video of her dancing stupidly. Emma shared this to her social media account and her new friends have been commenting on it with laughing emojis and nasty insults about Jackie.

Then Emma tells you that Jackie started it all by laughing at the school photos of Emma that you shared online and tagged her in. Jackie used AI on these photos to turn Emma into a hippo, an elephant and an anteater. The girls at dance class shared the pictures on their social media accounts and lots of other people commented and adapted the images, too. This has been going on for months. When Emma joined the group on Discord, they encouraged her to get her 'revenge'. This is what Jackie's mum called you about.

*What do you think?* At first, you might not understand your daughter's behaviour and you might label her as a bully both in your mind and when speaking directly to her. You might wonder where you went wrong, how you failed or who it is that's teaching your daughter to behave like this. You might also wonder if this could result in her being banned from or kicked out of any of the relevant environments, or if the situation will now escalate and result in your daughter being bullied, too.

*What to do:* The best response is to think about CPR parenting (see p. 107) and to show up for your daughter in an empathic way, whereby you try to connect with her frustrations and why she took the action she did. However, accountability is key here, too, so you can discuss online behaviour and what might happen should a report be made to the police. You can also explain that information relating to behaviour like this online can be collected by other people who might use it against her, including future employers.

You may need to think about how you can ensure the offensive content is removed and how to have a conversation with Emma about her online access, monitoring and online behaviour in terms of your role as her parent and why.

This situation is also likely to require a conversation with Jackie and her parents. Unfortunately, uncomfortable conversations like these may be a constant yet necessary part of parenting in a world of technology. But we must step up and have them all the same. Gulp!

*What does a child like Emma need?* You have been wrapped up lately in personal and finance matters at home. Emma tells you she had to deal with this situation on her own because she could see you were busy and she didn't want to add to your problems. Can you make the time for her now, even if you feel disappointed by her behaviour? Many issues that arise between friends in the real world can transition into the online space and vice versa. Emma has tried to fix this situation herself and has engaged in behaviour that you might not be happy about. However, can you try to understand it? Often, this sort of behaviour is a reaction to being bullied, which is how issues escalate. And online situations can do so at an accelerated rate, compared to in the real world.

## *Your Child is Still on a Device at 3am!*

Cara is fourteen and has autism and learning difficulties. She often tells you that she struggles to go to sleep and that using her iPad to listen to music can help her drift off. Most nights, you wander to bed around 11pm and nip into her room to turn off her technology and bedside lamp, as she's usually asleep by this time. But lately she has been complaining that she's tired and struggles to regulate her emotions during the day; she tells you there's no point in taking her night-time medication (to help her feel sleepy, as she can stay awake for the whole night) as it doesn't work. One night, you wake up around 3am to go to the bathroom and as you head past her bedroom you see she's playing on her iPad. When you enter the room to take it off her, she tells you this is what she has been doing for over a week, and that she's already told you her medication is useless. Rousing her in the morning for school is becoming more difficult each day and she has recently fallen asleep in class, too.

*What do you think?* At first glance, you might think this is indeed a medication issue, or that Cara is being obstinate or there is something wrong with either your parenting or her body clock. You might even think about turning the Wi-Fi off at 10pm so that she can't go online, and try to work out ways to take her technology from her in the evening.

*What to do:* There are several actions you can take with the technology, and, while the idea of turning the Wi-Fi off might prevent access to the internet using your router, if there is another way that she can access data she may do this instead. And, of course, it won't prevent her using any apps on the device that don't require internet access. You could also take the device away from her at a set time and discuss with her why the iPad must be handed over at 10pm, for example. In this scenario (neurodiverse/learning difficulties), conversations about brain health and sleep hygiene may or may not be understood or actioned by Cara. This is one situation where you may now need to adapt your evening and night-time schedule to accommodate Cara's particular issue with technology use, and her ability to understand why you're taking the device or taking control of what she can access and when. Taking the device is certainly going to bring up emotional turbulence, so this is a CPR moment of repeated communication about the device being handed over at 10pm to enable her to get sufficient sleep. Or you may need to lock apps on her device or find a CD player that she can play music on to get her to sleep instead.

*What does a child like Cara need?* Often, young people in this age group can phase-shift their circadian rhythm and sleep later, or not at all in some cases, especially young people who are neurodiverse. Sometimes their sleep schedule can change and result in sleeping in the daytime rather than during the night. In this specific situation, Cara is on medication to help her sleep, so you may need to monitor her intake of this and implement some evening-routine sleep-hygiene tips to shift the time she falls asleep back from 3am to a more reasonable time of 10 or 11pm. This might take a few days, a week or more, as you may need to reduce her waking hours by approximately fifteen to thirty minutes per day by waking her consistently in the morning and creating a schedule that down-regulates (i.e. slows and calms) her in the evening. This could include lower lighting levels, less noise and maybe interventions like a bath and even a story or music. (Audio books can be a great help here, with locked devices that can access this app only.) One of the most actionable steps is to concentrate on the waking-up time and getting some sunlight/daylight into the eyes within the first few hours of the day. This doesn't mean staring at the sun, but does mean being outside for approximately two to twenty minutes.

### *Sexual Content is Being Accessed or Shared By Your Child*

Elizabeth is eleven and recently another parent contacted you to say that she had shared a video with her son that was of a sexual nature. Elizabeth had also been taking screengrabs of material that was being sent to her by another child in her direct messages on Snap and Instant messaging (IM) and she was sending this on to other children as well. Elizabeth doesn't have a strong friendship group and when she's talking to you about her friends she regularly mentions different names and tells you she's fallen out with the previous group. Elizabeth says the content she received was 'funny' and it was only a joke that she sent it to her peers. She can't understand what all the fuss is about, because it was only a screengrab, and she can't see that she did anything wrong. Elizabeth is usually quite mature for her age and this recent behaviour doesn't seem to make much sense, because you've had conversations about accessing material where people are naked and she promised to tell you if she ever saw anything like this.

*What do you think?* You might be wondering whether your daughter is heading into puberty and beginning to find sexual material exciting, or whether an adult or perpetrator is sending her the videos. Or perhaps she is lying and hiding something from you? You might start to wonder what else she's been hiding in terms of her online activity and so begin to feel scared at this point about what you might find on her device; perhaps your imagination starts to run wild about the kind of content she has been accessing. You might also be thinking about what other parents think of your parenting and you might begin to worry about taking your daughter to school. You might also consider that you need to get help from a professional and/or that now is the time to revoke Elizabeth's access to chat-based social media apps such as Snap, IM and WhatsApp.

*What to do:* In this scenario, a conversation with Elizabeth is needed and may have to take place over a few hours or days, via small and frequent references to the situation. It may be uncomfortable for both of you, and having the right words, tempo and cadence to your voice will be your super skill here, being calm, and understanding that she may feel shame, even though you are intentionally trying not to make her feel this.

A check of Elizabeth's devices would certainly be warranted. Given she is underage for accessing social media and well under the age for accessing pornography, checking her device is a very wise move indeed. Implement and ensure that parental controls are in place in future to prevent her accessing this sort of material online, and perhaps even include parental controls to prevent her accessing social media. Upon checking her phone, you will need to assess who is sending the videos to her in the first instance, and you may need to report this to the police and the platform (see Resources, pp. 349–51, for guidance). I say 'may need' to report it to the police as the videos may not have been sent to Elizabeth; she may have been accessing them herself – or perhaps you find the sender may have deleted their account. However, reporting this issue to the police could protect other children, so this is a decision you will need to make based on what you find. It may also be other children who have sent the videos, so this becomes a safeguarding issue and, in this case, the police, perhaps the school and other parents will all need to be notified. Yes, this can be hugely uncomfortable, but it's necessary for dealing with content relating to porn, sex and intimate images of naked people.

Go slow and steady but do be sure to have the necessary conversations about checking her phone and reporting the process. A helpful tip is to communicate that you know she doesn't want you to carry out these actions, but that you must – all while acknowledging her discomfort and desire for you not to.

*What does a child like Elizabeth need?* During your search of her device, you find that she is also being sent this material on WhatsApp, which previously you hadn't previously considered as being a form of social media. In this scenario, a conversation with Elizabeth is absolutely a requirement. However, when young people access sexual material, it can bring up feelings of shame and embarrassment, which will have an impact on whether she wants to talk to you or even listen to you. Nevertheless, a compassionate, empathic and curious enquiry about who she speaks to online is a priority, so have a conversation about this. Another priority for discussion is the fact that this sexual material is illegal for her to watch and send on to others, and that you will now have to action some changes around her technology use and internet access to keep her safe. This is a sensitive but necessary part of this issue and she needs you to be compassionate to her feelings and the issue, but firm, using CPR. It is serious and has lots of big, awful feelings attached to it as a topic; you might even be feeling some of those yourself on reading this.

The actions you take next, whether contacting the police or school, will depend on what you find on Elizabeth's device and who it was sent by. She will need you to be transparent about your actions, even though she may not like them. She will need connected parenting from you in this moment, which acknowledges her shame or embarrassment and, of course, her not wanting you to contact the police, school or other parents. She will likely plead with you not to do this!

Elizabeth will need time to process what's happened and

she may exhibit punishing behaviours towards you for being firm and reporting the issue, because she will be scared, sad and ashamed. She may stop speaking to you for some time, tell you that she hates you, or engage in physical violence, abuse or destruction of property in the house, which are all ways in which children often express difficult feelings. In each of these circumstances, applying CPR parenting is key, while also ensuring that no one else is physically hurt in the house and maintaining your own emotional regulation around her emotions. Reporting the behaviour and the accessing of this material isn't going to be comfortable for you either, so you must take care of you as well. You can use any of the self-care breaks in the book as a way to be self-compassionate here. This is one of the trickiest topics in the book.

### *Your Child Won't Talk to You About Their On- or Offline World*

Romeo is sixteen and quite an independent young man who likes to play cricket, rugby and football after school. He is due to take his GCSEs soon and is often in his bedroom, where he tells you he's revising while playing music. He also plays his console games later in the evenings. Sometimes this carries on beyond midnight, which can interrupt his younger siblings' sleep, as he is chatty with his friends, and yet when you try to talk to him about his hobbies, his sports, his technology use or his exams he just grunts at you and walks off. When it's dinnertime, he comes to the table when called and eats his meals in silence with his hoodie up, barely making eye contact with anyone else, before heading back to his room almost as soon as the last morsel enters his mouth. His younger siblings try to talk to him, and he often tells them to shut up and get out of his room. He tells them they are annoying. He is still washing and showering, and he wears aftershave and combs his hair. He gets to

## HOW TO RESPOND WHEN THINGS GO WRONG

school on time, and he is prompt for all of his team matches and is considered a team player. He just won't talk to you.

*What do you think?* You might have lots of thoughts about Romeo, which can include the belief that he's ignorant, he's a teen, he's disrespectful, he's rude, he's emotional, he will get over it, he's accessing pornography, he's at risk online, he's not at risk online, he's lazy, or he has lots of friends and lots of interests. And surely he must be doing ok, otherwise he would tell you. You might think he's just a normal teen; you might think he's a bully to his siblings. In fact, you might have lots of different thoughts, which sometimes include the fact that you're thankful he stays out of your way of an evening, because that's the only time you get to clean the house.

*What to do:* In this scenario, I see major positives in Romeo's behaviour through his taking part in family mealtimes, attending school, practising self-care and taking part in sports. Often these positive behaviours are missed, because we tend to focus on what a boy like Romeo is *not* doing. What you can do in this scenario is to keep the channel of communication open by telling Romeo verbally that it is open. To do this, you might use reflective and rhetorical statements rather than firing questions directly at him, which he may find difficult to answer. Remember the discussion in earlier chapters about 'wondering' and 'noticing'. Of course, one line of questioning that may be pertinent here (without expecting a full answer) is: 'What's happening?' or, 'How's it going?' rather than 'What is wrong?' Even a response in the form of a 'meh' or ''s alright' is progress in these situations (or a shrug of the shoulders).

You could also remind Romeo that you know you're his parent and that he probably finds you intrusive, but you just want to let him know that you're here and you don't want to be nosy, but you do want to know he's ok and safe. And that's why you check in with him. This can be a simple way to let him know that you care, and that's why you're asking questions.

Even though he may already know this, some teens need to be told, repeatedly, that we care. In many cases, I also need to explain to parents in therapy situations that we humans aren't mind readers and our assumption about what our children 'ought to just know' is a false friend. We have to tell them verbally. (And tell our partners, pupils and/or friends that we care about them, too.) In some instances, you might want to ask if he would like to talk to anyone else (rather than you), such as a professional, and allow him to reply about this later (via text, for example), rather than creating a scenario where he feels pressured to give an answer on the spot – other than *I don't know*, perhaps. And one last piece of advice that could be helpful here is that, if you haven't gone to his sports matches to watch and celebrate him in these endeavours, do so (remember my point earlier about celebrating our teens). Find the time to go to see him perform. Although many young people claim they're not bothered about their parents or caregivers attending these events, they express a wholehearted wish for it in my clinic. Yet another time when you need to be a mind reader as a parent.

*What does a child like Romeo need?* Romeo is clearly indicating that he finds it difficult to communicate with you verbally, yet he is also communicating that he *can* sit in your company, albeit only for the time it takes to eat the food you've cooked for him. What Romeo needs more than anything is verbal communication from you to let him know that you are there and open to talking to him whenever he is. You may also need to let him know that you can help with any issue he faces, and, while you may not have all the answers, you can work things out together. You may need to provide him with this knowledge in small chunks, and often. You can even do it with occasional texts or small notes (like Post-its), remembering to be curious but not intrusive or over the top with your enthusiasm. Be reflective through your out loud 'wonderings' rather than accusative in your communication with him, and show that you notice things about him. But don't necessarily try to do all of this at once, which could be overwhelming.

Romeo might also need professional help, and you may need to ask him about this directly. Patience is required when one side of the relationship is struggling to communicate, tempered with the knowledge that you may need to intervene occasionally with questions to ascertain what he wants to do.

A child's preferred communication method when they were a toddler (for example, whether they needed a cuddle or space, reassurance or encouragement) can give you some insight into how to handle them now as a teen. We replay our need-seeking behaviours in later life very much as we did as tiny toddlers. The teenage years mark a very sensitive period, with exams, stress, adolescence and puberty; and, of course, online behaviours often occur out of our sight, so words and language are our only resource. Yet this is a scenario where they aren't being used by your teen. Pay close attention to their non-verbal communication and to the way they speak to their friends, without obviously listening in. This can include cadence or tone and monitoring whether you feel they are struggling in any way.

Context is key here, too; it might be the case that Romeo is trying to keep his brain free of anything other than his exams. There is no magic wand to this situation, or any approach other than to wait and watch and intervene. While Romeo's is a completely individual scenario, my aim here is to give you ways to handle interactions with *your* teen that seem less intrusive or aggressive in their approach. And remember that they also need celebrating in small and big ways.

## TECH SMART PARENTING

### *Your Child is Buying Drugs, Knives or Other Goods Illegally Online*

Richard and Dave are best friends and both fifteen years old. They are beginning to exert their authority in school on other children who come from a rival neighbourhood. The school has called you as they are 'concerned about some of the language that is being used by the boys as it sounds like gang culture talk', but you're not sure what they mean by this. You call at the school to collect your son, Dave, and are told that Richard has been buying knives and 'edibles' (cakes and sweets laced with cannabis) online and that the two have threatened some other pupils with the use of knives. As you leave school with Dave, he tells you that he hasn't done anything wrong. When you search his device, you find that he has been looking at content that relates to these issues and has arranged with a Snap contact to buy knives later this week. He would have used your credit card to do this, if the problem hadn't been picked up by the school today.

*What do you think?* Most parents would be devasted to learn that their child was considering buying knives or drugs and threatening other kids in school. You might think they are absolutely taking the biscuit with this behaviour. You might think about grounding them for life and keeping them locked up in their bedroom till they learn to be nice! You might worry that they could be stabbed in retaliation, or that they are involved in other crimes. You might be thinking how disappointed you are in them. You might also think you have completely failed as a parent. You might be concerned that they are in a 'gang', and fear for their life.

*What to do:* It seems that the school has been appropriately active in this situation and jumped on a potential issue before it's escalated into real-world violence. It's likely that they would have involved the police and perhaps even Prevent officers (the programme in the UK that gets involved in these sorts of situations) as well. The school will likely discuss with you how they want

Dave to begin to re-attend school from this point, or whether he will be managed in some other way – such as attending alternative provision or a scheduled timetable – and what they expect from him (and you) going forward. Given he has been picked up from school after this event, there is an expectation from him (and possibly some readers) that he is going to get a lecture/get shouted at and more, as this might seem an appropriate response to being sent home under these circumstances. What Dave needs from you, however, is a regulated conversation, later. Leaving a gap can be helpful for regulating emotions, which are probably running very high at this point. You can explain to Dave that this time-gap is going to happen by telling him, 'We will talk about this, but not right now, because I have lots of emotions and thoughts going on, and it's best I find a time when I am feeling and behaving my best. This will also give you time to do the same; you will need to let me know when you are ready, although this cannot go on for days and we will be having that conversation.' This conveys that you are aware of both your own and Dave's internal state and that you want both of you to be regulated before speaking. Then pick a time to talk when you can hold your window of tolerance (even though you may not want to right now and would really love to just let Dave know how you feel).

*What does a child like Dave need?* We often need time in to reflect on our behaviour and this needs to be managed by you in this instance, to give the fifteen-year-old in this story some time out from discussions, and from where you are at right now, to consider their actions. However, don't prolong this for days and weeks. I'm sure you can regulate yourself within a few hours, so the conversation about this event with your child can take place, in most cases, on the same day or the very next one. Dave's needs are to be understood, but this doesn't mean that you don't impose consequences, such as the removal of technology or privileges in relation to technology, as this is an incredibly serious matter.

Discussions about behaviour will need to lean into why Dave

was considering buying knives. You will need to ask why he thought this was appropriate and why he felt it necessary to have, own or even consider using a knife.

He needs your empathic and compassionate ears while offering his explanation; however, as already mentioned, that compassion also includes warranted consequences. You will need to decide what these are as a family and to discuss what they are and why and how they will take place. You may also want to discuss his ongoing friendship with Richard. If you give Dave some space to discuss his thoughts in this process, now you are away from school and the big feelings have subsided somewhat, you may find he comes up with acceptable decisions about his future behaviour and actions, such as finding new friends.

Again, this is a tricky topic fraught with real-world consequences and law-enforcement considerations. It's also one that can bring up many feelings of shame and failure for both you and your child. Shame is a tricky emotion for many of us and we try to avoid it at all costs. And why wouldn't we – it feels horrible! However, your robust nature as the adult in these scenarios is what's needed most, and that requires you to be in charge of your emotions.

## We Can Only Do Our Best

So just what *can* we do to keep our kids safe online? We can do our best. First and foremost, this means accepting that it's our responsibility to protect them; as I've said, we can't trust that social media sites, digital corporations and the gaming industry will look after them on our behalf. Instead, we may have to do some research into the cybersecurity, data protection and parental controls that are most suitable for our own households and the children or teens in them.

However, we should also remain aware that, whatever

protective measures we install on the systems in our homes or on devices, kids can often find ways to circumvent these. As we've discussed, it's a natural part of growing up to test boundaries and push back against adults – to venture into questionable spaces, whether that's trespassing in a neighbour's garden in real life or exploring the far reaches of the digital park online.

Things will sometimes go wrong, and, when they do, we may need to take a moment to compose ourselves and try to see things from our child's perspective. Bad behaviour usually has an underlying cause. And to help bring that cause to light, we must do our best to respond in a way that opens up conversations with them, rather than closing them down.

# Conclusion

As I said right at the start of this book, I know you're a good parent and that's why I'm cheering you on – because you *are* a good parent, but you might just need to say it to yourself a bit more often! There are people who'll never pick up a book like this one because they believe they're doing it all right and don't need help, and there are those who simply don't care. This is not you. *You are the best thing for your child and – equipped with all that you've found in these pages – you'll be a tech-smart parent, too.*

In a world in which technology is evolving at an incredible rate, it's natural to feel overwhelmed, scared and confused at times about how best to keep your kids safe online. Fearmongering headlines in the media and political rhetoric aren't any help; they provide little in the way of soothing advice or informed analysis of the real issues. As a parent or guardian, you may feel stuck in the middle – told to control your children's tech use (or hide it deep in a well, oubliette or cave somewhere), when screens are becoming an ever-growing and more necessary part of our lives as we evolve with the technology.

Being tech-smart means knowing the existing risks and dangers and that the changing landscape online will likely bring new worries and concerns – all while being aware of the tips and takeaways in this book. Yes, there are bad actors who want to steal identities, bully, harass, exploit and manipulate children online. Even our kids' peers can be mean and use technology to bully each other, and AI may now be a threat in many ways (we just don't know the full extent yet). However, this is the playground our children are growing up in. This also includes immersive

## CONCLUSION

spaces I haven't even discussed in the book, but which have similar issues, such as virtual reality and other types of tech that are yet to become mainstream and used by many children. Nevertheless, you will now be better informed about how to talk to your child about technology, and this will set you up for the future as it evolves. And do keep up to date by using the Resources section – see p. 347 – and, of course, by following my short videos on social media to get ahead of some of the harms.

The dangers are real, and we need to be well versed in them – all of them. But online is also the place where all those cute kitten videos can be found, where kids can get support from their friends and use the space to expand their knowledge and education. And it's the place where they will learn the skills that they need for tomorrow's world, when they are the adults running the world and making decisions about us in our old age!

Your connection with your child is the most important aspect of their online safety. And being tech-smart means that you can be connected with them in the real world, too.

They need to know and trust you'll be there for them in good times and bad; and you need to be aware that you might sometimes behave in ways that make it look and sound like you don't want to be, especially when tempers are frayed. Being a parent is hard at times, and we sometimes get it wrong. Underneath it all, our children need that feeling of solid connectivity with you.

Children will make mistakes, but knowing you are there for them, regulated and able to listen and empathise, will be an important aspect of keeping them safe online, as they'll know that they can turn to you if things do go wrong. That's what parenting is all about: prevention where possible, hoping and then helping, before and during the moments when they take risks and have the potential to get hurt. And I can say with confidence that as parents and guardians we're going to be the ones who must do the most work in this arena as, sadly, the online space is not. Big tech doesn't parent or protect children in the way that we can.

## CONCLUSION

Think of yourself as accompanying your child or teen into the wonderland of the city park online. There may be a few dark corners, but there will also be incredible opportunities for amazing experiences and advances as technology continues to evolve, bringing with it fast-moving AI, immersive spaces and even new ways to produce food and beat disease. It's exciting to consider the ways that tech could help solve the problems facing our children, such as climate change, and play a part in their economic futures.

I hope this book has helped to shed a little light on how to navigate this world together with your child, whatever their age. By embracing technologies safely and helping them to do the same, you will be giving them the best start in life.

Good luck! You really are a superhero parent, and maybe one day your child will come back to you and point this out, too. Maybe they will see this book as the cape you wear because you care. They will feel it and know it, but they might not say anything about it for a few years. So hang on in there. You can and you are doing this, and for that I honour your parenting approach.

You've got this; I know you have.

# Glossary

*Addiction:* a psychopathological diagnosis of continued abuse of a substance or specific behaviours, despite negative outcomes (according to the diagnostic manuals, specific symptoms must be present for a specific time).

*Algorithm:* a computer program that is specially aimed at identification and pattern recognition of the 'inputs' it receives and is often used to measure the interactions of users on specific websites or platforms or on social media sites. This is often then used to drive specific patterns to the users based on their previous interactions.

*Artificial intelligence (AI):* the 'evolving intelligence' of machines programmed to learn and think like humans. Many of these programs/algorithms are based on large numbers of transformers (no, not the robots in the cartoons or films) and can also be called large language models (LLMs).

*Attachment theory:* psychological theory relating to an infant's relational bond with a caregiver (usually a parent).

*Avatar:* a figure that represents a player in the computer game, which can often be designed, updated or enhanced by the player.

*Blue ticks:* the ticks often used in WhatsApp to denote when the message has been opened and read.

*Cyberbullying:* online abuse, bullying and other behaviours intended to cause harm or distress.

*Cyberspace:* often called the online world; the space in which you are connected to the internet via your cellular device, internet connection or Wi-Fi.

## GLOSSARY

*Cybertrauma:* the proposition that trauma can occur, via or mediated by any internet-ready device, to a person using a device or machine learning application.

*Desktop device:* often kept on, under or next to a desk and often means a personal home computer.

*Digital immigrant:* an older person not born into the digital age who uses technology.

*Digital native:* a young person who has grown up with technology in the digital age.

*Disinformation:* propaganda and mistruths conveyed to create confusion among the population.

*Emotional regulation:* the capacity for a child or adult to notice and manage their emotional state.

*E-safety:* education about the safe and responsible use of the internet and technology.

*E-sports:* electronic sports and tournaments similar to those in the real world (e.g. the Olympics).

*Gamer:* term used to identify a player online.

*Gaming disorder:* recently added pathological disorder with specified characteristics present for over a year in the sufferer.

*Misinformation:* non-truths often shared without malice (i.e. disseminators not knowing it's untrue) or shared to create confusion (although the actual intent in sharing the information can be difficult to know without further enquiry).

*Neuroplastic/neuroplasticity*: the lifelong ability of the brain to change and create new connections.

*Platform*: a space (often social media) that many users can visit and interact with other users on/in or through.

*Respawn:* the ability to start again or reincarnate in a game that doesn't require the gamer to go back to the start.

*Screen time:* time spent on devices.

*Social media:* a very broad term used to denote any platform, application or program where users can socialise in some way.

## GLOSSARY

*Trauma:* an event that creates an impact of psychological, emotional and sometimes physical injury; often confused with the event itself, this is more the story a person tells themselves about the event and how it has changed or affected them (or not).

*Virtual reality:* immersive technology that produces a computer-simulated, 360-degree world that you can interact in and with.

# Notes

### INTRODUCTION

1. Broccoli search on pubmed: pubmed.ncbi.nlm.nih.gov/?term=broccoli&filter=years.2020-2020

### CHAPTER 1

1. Buller, R. (2023) 'Their kids died after buying drugs on Snapchat. Now the parents are suing'. Available at: amp.theguardian.com/technology/2023/oct/18/snapchat-sued-overdose-deaths

### CHAPTER 2

1. Knibbs, C. (2024) *Black Mirror Spyware, Smother Mother or well intended not so great parenting?* Available at: www.childrenandtech.co.uk/blog/black-mirror-spyware-smother-mother-or-well-intended-not-so-great-parenting
2. US Department of Justice, 'Department of justice's review of section 230 of the communications decency act of 1996'. Available at: www.justice.gov/archives/ag/department-justice-s-review-section-230-communications-decency-act-1996
3. United Nations (2021) 'General comment No. 25 (2021) on children's rights in relation to the digital environment'. Available at: www.ohchr.org/en/documents/general-comments-and-recommendations/general-comment-no-25-2021-childrens-rights-relation
4. Twenge, J. M. (2017) 'Have Smartphones Destroyed a Generation'. Available at: www.theatlantic.com/magazine/archive/2017/09/has-the-smartphone-destroyed-a-generation/534198/
5. Wagenaar, A. C. and Toomey, T. L. (2002) 'Effects of minimum drinking age laws: Review and analyses of the literature from 1960 to 2000'. *Journal of Studies on Alcohol, Supplement* (14): 206–225

NOTES

CHAPTER 3

1. World Health Organization (2022), *ICD-11: International Classification of Diseases* (11th revision). Available at: icd.who.int
2. Kumar, R., Mitchell, E. and Stolerman, I.P. (1971) 'Disturbed Patterns of Behaviour in Morphine Tolerant and Abstinent Rats', *Br. J. Pharmac.* 42: 473–84
3. Alexander, B.K., Coambs, R.B. and Hadaway, P.F. (1978) 'The Effect of Housing and Gender on Morphine Self-administration in Rats', *Psychopharmacology* 58: 175–9
4. Kaufman, Scott Barry, (2021) *Transcend: The New Science of Self Actualization.* (Sheldon Press)
5. Revealing Reality (2024) 'Children's Media Lives 2024. Ten Long years of Longitudinal research. A report for Ofcom.' Available at: www.ofcom.org.uk/siteassets/resources/documents/research-and-data/media-literacy-research/children/children-media-use-and-attitudes-2024/childrens-media-lives-2024-summary-report.pdf?v=367549
6. The Cybersurvey by Youthworks (2023) 'Real or Fake: The report of the Cybersurvey 2023'. Available at: www.thecybersurvey.co.uk/real-or-fake--cybersurvey-2023
7. Harlow, H.F. (1964) 'Early Social Deprivation and Later Behavior in the Monkey', in A. Abrams, H.H. Gurner and J.E.P. Tomal, *Unfinished Tasks in the Behavioral Sciences:* 154–73
8. The Cybersurvey by Youthworks (2023) 'Real or Fake: The report of the Cybersurvey 2023'. Available at: www.thecybersurvey.co.uk/real-or-fake--cybersurvey-2023

CHAPTER 4

1. The American Psychiatric Association (2020) 'New Survey Shows Increasing Loneliness, Including on the Job'. Available at: www.psychiatry.org/news-room/apa-blogs/new-survey-shows-increasing-loneliness-on-the-job
2. Office of the US Surgeon General (2023) 'Our Epidemic of Loneliness and Isolation: The U.S. Surgeon General's Advisory on the Healing Effects of Social Connection and Community'. Available at: www.hhs.gov/sites/default/files/surgeon-general-social-connection-advisory.pdf
3. Johnson, S. (2023) 'WHO declares loneliness a "global public health concern"', *Guardian.* Available at: www.theguardian.com/global-

development/2023/nov/16/who-declares-loneliness-a-global-public-health-concern
4. Šimić, G., Tkalčić, M., Vukić, V., Mulc, D., Španić, E., Šagud, M., Olucha-Bordonau, F.E., Vukšić, M. R. and Hof, P. (2021) 'Understanding Emotions: Origins and Roles of the Amygdala', *Biomolecules*, 11 (6): 823
5. Zych, A.D. and Gogolla, N. (2021) 'Expressions of Emotions Across Species', *Current Opinion in Neurobiology*, 68: 57–66
6. Siegel, D. J. (2014) *Brainstorm: The Power and Purpose of The Teenage Brain*. (Scribe UK)
7. James, W. (1890, revised in 1918) *The Principles of Psychology*, vols. 1–2, (Pantianos Classics, 2017)
8. Briener, F. and Gadsden (Eds, 2016) *Parenting Matters: Supporting Parents of Children Ages 0–8* (National Academies of Science, Engineering and Medicine)
9. Radesky, J., Miller, A.L., Rosenblum, K.L., Appugliese, D., Kaciroti, N. and Lumeng, J.C. (2015) 'Maternal mobile device use during a structured parent–child interaction task', *Academic Pediatrics*, 15: 238–244
10. Department for Education (2013) 'Statistics: Special Educational Needs (SEN)'. Available at: www.gov.uk/government/statistics/child-development-outcomes-at-2-to-2-and-a-half-years-april-2023-to-march-2024-annual-2023-to-2024/child-development-outcomes-at-2-to-2-and-a-half-years-2023-to-2024-statistical-commentary
11. Ibid.
12. Donnelly, L. (2022) 'Covid lockdowns left toddlers unable to speak or play properly', *Telegraph*. Available at: www.telegraph.co.uk/news/2022/05/16/covid-lockdowns-left-toddlers-unable-speak-play-properly
13. Alamri, M., Alrehaili, M., Albariqi, W., Alshehri, M., Alotaibi, K. and Algethami, A. (2023) 'Relationship Between Speech Delay and Smart Media in Children: A Systematic Review.' *Cureus*, 15
14. Brushe, M.E., et al (2024) 'Screen Time and Parent–Child Talk When Children are Aged 12 to 36 Months', *JAMA Pediatr.*, 178 (4): 369–75. doi: 10.1001/jamapediatrics.2023.6790. PMID: 38436942; PMCID: PMC10913002
15. Brushe, M.E., et al (2024) 'Screen Time and Parent–Child Talk When Children Are Aged 12 to 36 Months', *JAMA Pediatr.* 178(4): 369–75. doi: 10.1001/jamapediatrics.2023.6790. PMID: 38436942; PMCID: PMC10913002
16. Zhou N, Qin. W., Zhang J.J., Wang Y., Wen J.S., Lim Y.M. (2024)

'Epidemiological Exploration of The Impact of Bluetooth Headset Usage on Thyroid Nodules Using Shapley Additive Explanations Method'. *Sci Rep*, 14(1)

17. Uzefovsky, F., Paz, Y. and Davidov, M. (2019) 'Young infants are pro-victims, but it depends on the context', *British Journal of Psychology*. doi: 10.1111/bjop.12402
18. Florinauzef 'Victim Video (Uzefovsky, Paz & Davidov, 2019)'. Available at: www.youtube.com/watch?v=7Fwd3t3xTNQ&feature=em-share_video_user
19. KD 'Little girl crying while watching an animated film about a #Dinosaur'. Available at: www.youtube.com/watch?v=YI9inwHC62k

## CHAPTER 5

1. Knibbs, C. (2022) *Children, Technology and Healthy Development* (Routledge, 2021)

## CHAPTER 6

1. Salter, M. et al (2023) 'Identifying and understanding child sexual offending behaviours and attitudes among Australian men' Available at: www.humanrights.unsw.edu.au/research/current-research/understanding-online-child-exploitation-practices
2. Me too toolkit '25 Things Parents Should Know About Sexual Abuse'. Available at: metoomvmt.org/wp-content/uploads/2020/05/1.4.1_25-Things-A-Parent-Should-Know-About-Sexual-Abuse_V2.pdf
3. Children's Commissioner (2013) 'Basically Porn is Everywhere'. Available at: www.childrenscommissioner.gov.uk/resource/basically-porn-is-everywhere
4. Children's Commissioner (2023) 'Information Sheet: Pornography and Young People'. Available at: www.childrenscommissioner.gov.uk/resource/information-sheet-pornography-and-young-people
5. Children's Commissioner (2016) 'The impact of online pornography on children and young people'. Available at: www.childrenscommissioner.gov.uk/resource/an-examination-of-the-impact-of-online-pornography-on-children-and-young-people

NOTES

CHAPTER 7

1. Alamri, M., Alrehaili, M., Albariqi, W., Alshehri, M., Alotaibi, K. and Algethami, A. (2023) 'Relationship Between Speech Delay and Smart Media in Children: A Systematic Review.' *Cureus*, 15
2. Roxby, P (2024) 'One in three children short-sighted, study suggests', *BBC News* website. Available at: www.bbc.co.uk/news/articles/como99zm4wyo
3. The Vision Council (2023) '2023 Annual Report'. Available at: thevisioncouncil.org/annual-reports
4. Zhang, S. (2022) 'The Myopia Generation: Why Do So Many Kids Need Glasses Now?', *The Atlantic*. Available at: www.theatlantic.com/magazine/archive/2022/10/kids-glasses-vision-increased-nearsightedness-myopia/671244/
5. Perry, B. (2018) *The Neurosequential Model in Education: Introduction to the NME Series: Trainer's Guide* (The Child Trauma Academy Press)

CHAPTER 8

1. Ofcom (2024) 'Children and Parents: Media Use And Attitudes Report 2024'. Available at: www.ofcom.org.uk/media-use-and-attitudes/media-habits-children/children-and-parents-media-use-and-attitudes-report-2024
2. Pew Research (2020) 'Parenting in the age of screens'. Available at: www.pewresearch.org/internet/2020/07/28/parenting-children-in-the-age-of-screens
3. Pew research (2021) 'How parents' views of their kids' screen time, social media use changed during COVID-19'. Available at: www.pewresearch.org/short-reads/2022/04/28/how-parents-views-of-their-kids-screen-time-social-media-use-changed-during-covid-19
4. *Primary Times* (2020) '10 – The Official Age Children Should Own a Smartphone', *Primary Times*. Available at: www.primarytimes.co.uk/news/2015/09/-10-the-official-age-children-should-own-a-smartphone
5. Donovan, J. (2016) 'The Average Age for a Child Getting Their First Smartphone is Now 10.3 Years', *TechCrunch*. Available at: techcrunch.com/2016/05/19/the-average-age-for-a-child-getting-their-first-smartphone-is-now-10-3-years
6. Kelly, H. (2023) 'Young kids are bringing TikTok memes to the playground', *Washington Post*. Available at: www.washingtonpost.com/technology/2023/03/09/tiktok-memes-kids

NOTES

7. Rosenfeld, M. J., Thomas, R. J. and Hausen, S. (2023) 'How Couples Meet and Stay Together 2017–2020–2022 combined dataset.' *Stanford, CA: Stanford University Libraries*. Available at: data.stanford.edu/hcmst2017

## CHAPTER 9

1. Kahneman, D. (2012) *Thinking Fast and Slow* (Penguin)
2. Children's Commissioner (2013) 'Basically Porn is Everywhere'. Available at: www.childrenscommissioner.gov.uk/resource/basically-porn-is-everywhere
3. Children's Commissioner (2023) 'Information Sheet: Pornography and Young People'. Available at: www.childrenscommissioner.gov.uk/resource/information-sheet-pornography-and-young-people
4. Children's Commissioner (2023) 'Growing Up with Pornography: Advice for Parents and Schools'. Available at: www.childrenscommissioner.gov.uk/blog/growing-up-with-pornography-advice-for-parents-and-schools
5. Naslund, J.A., Bondre, A., Torous, J., Aschbrenner, K.A. (2020) 'Social Media and Mental Health: Benefits, Risks, and Opportunities for Research and Practice.' *J Technol Behav Sci.* Sep;5(3): 245–57.
6. Burnett, D. (2016) *The Idiot Brain: A Neuroscientist Explains What Your Head is Really Up To* (Guardian Faber Publishing).
7. Etchells, P. (2024) *Unlocked: The Real Science of Screen Time (and how to spend it better)* (Piatkus)

## CHAPTER 10

1. American Academy of Pediatrics, 'Screen Time for Infants'. Available at: www.aap.org/en/patient-care/media-and-children/center-of-excellence-on-social-media-and-youth-mental-health/qa-portal/qa-portal-library/qa-portal-library-questions/screen-time-for-infants
2. Healthy Children.Org, 'Beyond Screen Time: Help Your Kid Build Healthy Media Use Habits'. Available at: www.healthychildren.org/English/family-life/Media/Pages/healthy-digital-media-use-habits-for-babies-toddlers-preschoolers.aspx

## CHAPTER 11

1. BBC Studios, 'Kevin Becomes a Teenager'. Available at: youtu.be/dLuEY6jN6gY?si=FG0VTcG4y_5LO8Rk

# Further resources

*Catherine Knibbs*

*Home page:* www.childrenandtech.co.uk

*Books:*
*Children, Technology and Healthy Development: How to Help Kids be Safe and Thrive Online* (Routledge, 2021)
*Online Harms and Cybertrauma: Legal and Harmful Issues with Children and Young People* (Routledge, 2023)
*Children and Sexual-Based Online Harms: A Guide for Professionals* (Routledge, 2023)
*Managing Your Gaming and Social Media Habits: From Science to Solutions* (Routledge, 2024)

*Blogs:*
Black Mirror Spyware, Smother Mother or well-intended not-so-great parenting? www.childrenandtech.co.uk/blog/black-mirror-spyware-smother-mother-or-well-intended-not-so-great-parenting
The 'Human algorithm' that schools and parents feed through fear concerning social media 'trends'
www.childrenandtech.co.uk/blog/the-human-algorithm-that-schools-and-parents-feed-through-fear-concerning-social-media-trends
*Level-Up Course for parents:* www.childrenandtech.co.uk/courses-for-parents

*Podcasts and Videos:*
'Polyvagal "motorway of wellness" – updated version with brain and body visuals'. Available at: youtu.be/QGBv1KrJ5Pk?si=FvQvdm6PIRYYrpku
'Bodies, Brains and Technology – The real social dilemma', TEDx Doncaster (2022). Available at: www.youtube.com/watch?v=lRX_DW03KPs

FURTHER RESOURCES

## *Books and Articles*

American Psychiatric Association (APA), *Diagnostic and Statistical Manual of Mental Disorders* (2013) 5th ed.

Anti-Bullying Alliance, 'Cyberbullying definition' (2022). Available at: https://anti-bullyingalliance.org.uk

de Botton, Alain, *A Therapeutic Journey: Lessons from the School of Life* (Penguin, 2023)

Burnett, Dean, *The Idiot Brain: A Neuroscientist Explains What Your Head is Really Up To* (Guardian Faber Publishing, 2016)

Children's Commissioner UK. 'The things I wish my parents had known: Young people's advice on talking to your child about online sexual harassment' (2022). Available at: www.childrenscommissioner.gov.uk/report/talking-to-your-child-about-online-sexual-harassment-a-guide-for-parents

Clear, James, *Atomic Habits: An easy and proven way to build good habits and break bad ones* (Random House, 2018)

Delahooke, Mona, *Beyond Behaviours: Using Brain Science and Compassion to Understand and Solve Children's Behavioural Challenges* (John Murray, 2020)

Delahooke, Mona, *Brain-body Parenting: How to Stop Managing Behavior and Start Raising Joyful, Resilient Kids* (Harper Wave, 2022)

Etchells, Pete, *Unlocked: The Real Science of Screen Time (and how to spend it better)* (Piatkus, 2024)

Fortune, Joanna, *Why We Play: How to Find Joy and Meaning in Everyday Life* (Thread books, 2022)

Gerhardt, Sue, *Why Love Matters: How Affection Shapes a Baby's Brain* (Routledge, 2014)

Gilbert, Paul, *The Compassionate Mind: A New Approach to Life's Challenges* (revised edition) (Constable, 2010)

Goldacre, Ben, *Bad Science* (Fourth Estate, 2008)

Goleman, Daniel, *Emotional Intelligence* (Bloomsbury, 1995)

Goleman, Daniel and Davidson, Richard, *Altered Traits: Science Reveals How Meditation Changes Your Mind, Brain and Body* (Avery, 2017)

Haidt, Jonathan, *The Anxious Generation: How the Great Rewiring of Childhood Is Causing an Epidemic of Mental Illness* (Penguin, 2024)

Hanson, Rick, *Resilient: Find Your Inner Strength* (Rider, 2018)

Kaufman, Scott Barry, *Transcend: The New Science of Self-actualization* (TarcherPerigree, 2020)

Martin, Holly-ann, *Somebody Should Have Told Me* (Safe4Kids Books, 2018)

Siegel, Daniel, *Brainstorm: The Power and Purpose of the Teenage Brain* (Tarcher, 2014)
Turkle, Shirley, *Reclaiming Conversation: The Power of Talk in a Digital Age* (Penguin, 2014)
Walker, Matthew, *Why We Sleep: The New Science of Sleep and Dreams* (Penguin, 2017)
Zuboff, Shoshana, *The Age of Surveillance Capitalism* (Profile Books, 2019)

## *Apps for Emotional Regulation Skills*

Headspace app: www.headspace.com/cath For 30 days free
Heart Math app: www.heartmath.com
Insight timer app: insighttimer.com/en-gb
Othership app: othership.com Use CATHKNIBBS at checkout for 30 days free
Syntropy States app: www.syntropystates.com

## *App for Digital Wellbeing on Social Media*

Pro Parenting, Pro Child, Pro Family, Pro Safety, Pro Tech App: www.sway.ly

## *Websites*

*BBFC age classifications for films:* www.bbfc.co.uk
*Boys-2-men:* boyz-2-men.org.uk
This company supports young men and boys with support around their masculinity and opportunities for developing emotional regulation and resilience as they grow up.
*BT parental controls:* www.bt.com/help/security/how-to-keep-your-family-safe-online-with-bt-parental-controls-an
*Child exploitation and online protection:* www.ceop.police.uk
Those worried about online sexual abuse or the way someone has been communicating online can make a report here to one of CEOP's Child Protection Advisors.
*Childline:* www.childline.org.uk
Childline is there to help anyone under nineteen in the UK with any issue

they're going through. Information about their Report Remove tool can be found at this link: www.childline.org.uk/info-advice/bullying-abuse-safety/online-mobile-safety/report-remove

*Childnet:* www.childnet.com

An organisation that works to make the internet a safe place for children and young people.

*Dan Hughes and the PACE approach:* www.danielhughes.org/p.a.c.e..html

*EE Telecoms parental controls:* ee.co.uk/help/broadband/getting-started/using-parental-controls

*Get Safe Online:* getsafeonline.org.uk

Provides practical advice on how to protect yourself, your computers and mobile devices and your business against fraud, identity theft, viruses and many other problems encountered online.

*Giff Gaff parental control advice*: www.giffgaff.com/blog/internet-safety-parental-controls

*Internet Matters:* internetmatters.org.uk

Supports children's safety online.

*Internet Watch Foundation:* www.iwf.org.uk

Report online child sexual abuse images and videos here anonymously.

*LGBT Health and Wellbeing:* www.lgbthealth.org.uk

Scotland's health and wellbeing charity for LGBTQ+ adults (16+).

*Mind:* www.mind.org.uk

Support for mental health issues.

*NSPCC:* www.nspcc.org.uk

Child protection charity.

*O2 parental controls:* www.o2.co.uk/help/safety-and-security/age-restricted-content-and-age-verification

*Ofcom: UK Online Safety Act:* www.ofcom.org.uk/online-safety/illegal-and-harmful-content/enforcing-the-online-safety-act-platforms-must-start-tackling-illegal-material-from-today

*Parent Zone:* www.parentzone.org.uk

An organisation working towards a safer digital world of opportunities.

*PEGI:* pegi.info

Age classifications for video games.

*PlusNet parental controls:* www.plus.net/help/broadband/how-to-use-plusnet-safeguard

*Samaritans:* www.samaritans.org
Charity dedicated to reducing feelings of isolation and disconnection that can lead to suicide.

*Sky TV parental controls:* www.sky.com/help/articles/sky-go-parental-settings

*Stop It Now:* www.stopitnow.org.uk
Support for anyone with concerns about child sexual abuse and its prevention.

*SWGL:* www.swgfl.org.uk
Charity dedicated to empowering the safe and secure use of technology through innovative services, tools, content and policy, nationally and globally.

*Talk Talk parental controls:* community.talktalk.co.uk/t5/Articles/How-to-use-HomeSafe/ta-p/2205196

*Tesco Mobile parental controls:* www.tescomobile.com/help/safety-and-security/parental-controls-and-content-settings

*Three Mobile parental controls:* www.three.co.uk/support/mobile-broadband/parental-control-software

*UK Safer Internet Centre:* www.safeinternet.org.uk
Guide to staying safe online.

*Virgin Media parental controls:* www.virginmedia.com/help/security/parental-controls

*Vodafone online safety tools and digital parenting advice:* www.vodafone.co.uk/newscentre/smart-living/digital-parenting
Scroll down for the free Digi-Tales book and the videos about scams mentioned in Chapter 8 p. 198.
www.vodafone.co.uk/help-and-information/nspcc-phone-safety-toolkit/03-how-to-online-safety-tools

*WeProtect:* www.weprotect.org
Global alliance for protection against child abuse.

# Acknowledgements

To my children – you keep me grounded and in check every day. I love you beyond words and thank you for holding me accountable for all my actions and deeds. Yep, even the not-so-great Mum moments, which I hear are quite numerous. Allegedly . . .

I want to give a nod to my sweary and down-to-earth PhD supervisor Mark Widdowson, who died in 2024 and whom I ignored when he told me, 'no more f***ing books till you hand in the thesis'. This one, Mark, is for the parents (and professionals). Our extensive talks on this subject mattered greatly, and I am not sorry I ignored you. This will make a difference, and I know you approve really.

To my friends, thank you for being there when I needed you. Writ large and for knowing me so well which is always conveyed in the cards you send me. You are my laughing buddies and that is priceless.

To Leah, Sue, Anne and Jacqui. Thank you for the questions, guidance and edits in the process of the book.

To the reviewers and testimonials, thank you. I was moved by your words and this has challenged my internal script for sure.

Thank you to you the reader, the parent, the grandparent, the guardians, the aunts and uncles and the extended family around the children. I really do hope this book does help you, without shame, judgement and castigation. To mirror what Marie Curie (allegedly) said: 'Nothing in life is to be feared, it is only to be understood. Now is the time to understand more, so that we may fear less.' I hope this book helps you understand your child and the technological, digital and real world landscape in which they now navigate their development towards adulthood. And if they become parents, may they then pass on the baton of knowledge to their children with confidence.

# Index

3Rs (regulate, relate and reason) 180, 216, 277, 307
4 Cs (content/contact/conduct/commercialism) 29–33
4Ss (safe, seen–soothed, secure) 27, 56, 70, 72, 91, 111, 312–13

abuse, child sexual 127, 143, 146–8, 250
accountability 318
addiction 63–70, 73, 80, 84, 93
  behavioural 68–9, 71
  bio-psycho-social model of 70, 74
  diagnosis 67–8
  psychological 69, 76
  substance-dependent 68–9, 71, 76–7, 84
  *see also* tech addiction
advertising 29–30, 89–90, 150
age of child 5, 14, 24, 32–3
  *see also* middle childhood; teenagers; tweens; young children
age ratings 186, 188
age-appropriate open dialogue 5, 28, 82–3, 121, 136–7, 203–5, 209–11, 213–16, 264–72, 275, 295–309, 312, 314, 322–3
  refusal to participate in 324–7
age-assurance checks 41
age-restricted products 46
agreements 107–8
algorithms 136, 149–51, 227–31, 241, 271
anti-virus software 54, 55
anxiety 37, 87, 233, 315
artificial intelligence (AI) 8, 22, 126, 218, 226, 297, 333, 335
  changing identity with 127
  chatbots 153, 208
  and content regulation 39, 41
  and cyberbullying 317–18
  and exploitation 153
  and middle childhood 189, 208

and online violence 140
and teenagers 259–60
'undressing' 128, 203–4, 208, 214, 247
attachment 66–70, 73, 75, 81, 122–4, 153, 183
attachment theory 3, 68–70
attention 92–5, 174–5
attention deficit hyperactivity disorder (ADHD) 87, 93
attention-needing behaviour 93–4
attunement 3, 62
autism 47, 83, 93, 207, 242, 319–21
avatars 152, 210, 237

bad actors 3, 117, 127–32, 190, 206, 244, 333
  *see also* perpetrators
Barrymore, Drew 36
bedtimes 57–8, 270, 271, 319–21
belonging 70–1, 75, 76, 81, 122–3, 195, 222–4
Berne, Eric 62
big tech 22, 38, 39–42, 134, 191
bilateral stimulation 174
bio-psycho-social model 70, 74, 98
biofeedback 8
biological model 68, 71
*Black Mirror* (TV show) 37
blackmail 128–9, 240, 246–8
blame 42–4, 65
  *see also* self-blame
blended families 292
blue light 23, 103, 169–70, 270–1
'blue-tick distress' 115–16
Bluetooth 45
body dysmorphia 233
body image 221, 225, 227–8, 231
body posture 102
body weight 235
body-building 227–8
body-esteem crisis 232

355

# INDEX

boundaries 5, 13, 14, 58, 107–8, 275–96
  fluid 281–3, 286–90, 292, 296
  testing 280–2, 287–8, 292–6, 311, 331
Bowlby, John 3, 122–3
brain 4, 270–1, 320
  development 87, 90–1, 96, 174
  effect of tech on 14, 87–106, 183
  language-acquisition device 96
  and puberty 90–1, 281, 327
  reward system 72, 74, 185
  'slow, stop and question' approach 219–20
  teenage 224
breathing, box 206, 295
browser histories 182
Bryson, Tina 3, 264
bullying 328–30
  *see also* cyberbullying
Burnett, Dean 270

cancel culture 120
carers, young 56
case studies 14–15, 49–51, 79–80, 108–9, 121–2, 128–9, 148, 163–4, 166–7, 196–7, 202–3, 207, 227–8, 238–9, 249, 265–7, 268–9, 313–14
catfishing 247
'checking in' (not 'checking on') 27, 111–12, 164, 291, 297
child development 3, 22, 30, 32–3, 58, 62, 82, 87, 90–1, 96, 98, 160–3, 165–8, 173–5
  milestones 14, 33, 101–5, 160, 168
child sexual abuse 127, 143, 146–8, 250
child-centred approaches 82
Childline, 'Report Remove' tool 248
children's needs 3, 123, 314, 316–21, 323, 326–7, 329
  parents who ignore 266–7
  and tech 'addiction' 66, 81–2
children's rights 42
children's viewpoints 14
choice 213
Chomsky, Noam 96
circadian rhythms 172, 270, 320
'city park' framework 1, 23–4, 30, 42, 44–5, 52–3, 57–8, 126, 202–6, 218, 228–9, 248, 256–7, 297–8, 331, 335
CO:RE 29–30
co-regulation 4, 82, 164
cognition, under-fives 174–5

collaboration 28, 58–9, 213
commercialism 29–30
communication 14, 24, 27–9, 58–9, 107–24
  children's preferred method of 327
  co-created interpersonal 28
  failure 61–2
  non-verbal 327
  and tech 'addiction' 85
compassion 82, 104, 123, 287, 313, 323, 330
compulsions 68, 83, 93, 165
computers 49–50, 54–5, 193
conduct 29
confirmation bias 150–1
connection
  children's search for 61, 66–7, 70–1, 73–7, 107–24, 188
  connecting with children 3–5, 10, 14, 24, 27–9, 58–9, 334
  human need for 81
consent 117–20, 211
contact 29, 30
content 29, 30–1, 315–17
  adult 24, 38–40, 47–8, 188
  and algorithms 149–51, 227–31
  how to decline 306–7
  tailored 39, 149–51, 227–31
  ways of sharing 46
  *see also* pornography; sexual content; violent content
context 30
contracts 107–9, 289–92, 296
Covid-19 pandemic 22, 99, 125, 171
credit cards 328
critical thinking 136, 186, 217–20, 224–6
curiosity 218–19, 323
cyberbullying 13–14, 88, 154–5, 188, 194, 200, 202, 222, 226, 229–31, 236–41, 301, 333
  when your child is the bully 237, 317–19
cybersecurity 107, 194, 290, 295, 330
Cybersurvey 43, 76, 81
cybertrauma 6, 8, 13, 30, 84, 148–9, 215–16, 252, 267, 292, 313, 316

death, premature 23, 30
Delahooke, Mona 3, 264
Department of Eduation 55
depression 233, 237
desire 68, 70

356

# INDEX

*Diagnostic and Statistical Manual of Mental Disorders*, Fifth Edition (DSM-V) 64
digital distractions 87, 92
Discord 13, 188, 189, 205, 266, 317–18
discussion 305–6
dominant approaches 28–9
dopamine 67–8, 69, 71–4, 185
drugs 30–1, 328–30
dumbphones 45–6, 50, 115
dysregulation 61–2, 114, 123, 146, 180, 287

e-safety 82, 177, 183
  lessons 189, 203, 290
eating-related issues 38, 232
echo chambers 150–1
education 3, 43
  educational devices 47
  *see also* schools
emotional co-regulation 4, 82, 164
emotional regulation 4, 62, 123, 216, 240, 244–5, 270, 277, 306–7, 312–13, 319, 324, 329–31
  parental 82, 176, 180, 270, 293–5, 303, 306, 324, 330, 334
  *see also* dysregulation; self-regulation
emotional thermostats, acting as your child's 306–7
empathy 14, 83, 87–8, 91, 104–5, 120, 123, 153, 168, 184, 301–2, 313
  parental 234–6, 287, 318, 323, 330, 334
end-to-end-encrypted (E2EE) 134
Etchells, Pete 270
executive function 90–1, 219–20
exergames 188
exploitation 84, 117–20, 152–3, 188, 194, 204, 240, 266, 271
eyesight 103, 168–74, 183, 299

Facebook 8, 141, 188
FaceTime 171
facial recognition software 39, 40–1
fads 38
family agreements 278
'filtering' software 2, 31–2, 182
filters, body 233, 234
firewalls 54, 55, 182
flaming 154
flip phones 2, 45, 50, 137
foetal alcohol spectrum disorder (FASD) 96

Fonagy 3
forums 241–5, 271
Fraser guidelines 284
friendships 206–8, 222–3, 257, 306–7

gambling 196–7
gaming 8, 16, 22, 330
  add-ons 195–8
  'addiction' to 65–7, 74–5, 78–80
  age ratings 186, 313–14
  and AI chatbots 153
  and the brain 93
  conduct in 29
  costs of 195–8, 249
  and cyberbullying 154
  delaying access to 47
  and etiquette 304–5
  and memes 199, 200
  and middle childhood 186–90, 193, 195–8, 207–10, 214, 218–19, 300–1
  and real friendships 207
  sexual content 209, 210, 214
  taking to children about 300–1
  and tech bans 45, 47, 57–8
  and teenagers 222, 249, 258–9, 266–7
  time spent on 57–8
  underage play 313–14
'gaming disorder' 65–6, 67
gangs 328
Gen Z ('digital natives') 21, 125
gender identity 41, 76, 121–2
geolocation services 115–16
Gillick competence 284
Goldacre, Ben 169
governments 38–9, 43
Grand Theft Auto 313–14
grandparents 211, 212–13
grasps 102, 160–1
grooming 23, 31, 151–3, 182, 188, 202–6, 246, 249, 261
groupthink 224

hackers 31
Haidt, Jonathan 42, 45, 225, 232
Harlow, Harry 81
hate speech 122, 200, 238–9, 241
headphones 102–3
hearing 102–3
herd instinct 224

# INDEX

holistic approaches 33
homophobia 50, 239
Hughes, Dan 235, 264
human algorithm 136
human rights 40, 42
humour, sarcastic 199–200, 240, 244

identity 81–3, 225, 232, 252
illegal activity/material 30–1, 83, 120, 143–4, 147, 152, 188, 201, 228, 241, 253, 301, 323, 328–30
images of your child, shared 127–32, 151–2, 181–2, 202–6, 214, 247–8
immersive spaces 333–4, 335
incongruence 234
Instagram 9, 188, 231
Instant Messaging (IM) 137, 155, 188, 321–2
internet 2, 6–7, 21–2, 25, 254
  and boundaries 280
  and critical thinking 218
  and cyberbullying 237
  extent of use 76–7
  and forums 241
  and memes 199
  and middle childhood 187
  and parental controls 110
  risk of unsupervised access to 189–92, 208, 258
  and sexual content 210, 253, 323
  and tech 'addiction' 64, 76–7
  and tech bans 35, 38, 40, 44–7, 51–2, 54, 267–8
  and 'therapy speak' 64
  usefulness of 51–2
  violence on the 139
Internet Matters 190
internet service providers 53–4, 117
  blocking services 193
internet-safety companies 43–4
interpersonal neurobiology 9
iPhone 8, 45–6, 54
iTunes 154

James, William 94

Kahneman, Daniel 243
Kaufman, Scotty Barry 72
Kik 202
knives 328–30
Kwik, Jimi 306

language
  acquisition 14, 95–101, 165, 167, 183
  delays 98
  pathologising 22, 63–7, 73, 84, 93
  use of inappropriate/abusive 83, 154, 214–15, 239, 240–1
  *see also* hate speech
learning 14, 104–5, 167, 174–5
learning difficulties 47, 98, 174, 201, 239–40, 244, 291, 319–21
Level Up club 53, 141
loneliness 81, 87–8, 234
love 122–3
lying, about time spent online 76–7

masculinity, toxic 302–3
Maslow, Abraham 72, 80–1
mastery 78–80, 188
maturity levels 3–4, 288
medical model 69
'memes' 198–202
mental health 9, 38, 63, 241–3, 247, 258–9, 269
middle childhood 14, 185–220, 278–9, 300–1
millennials 125
Minecraft 57, 213–14, 218–19, 300
misinformation 217–20, 223–7, 270–1
misogyny 142, 250–1, 254, 302–3
modelling behaviours 124
'Momo Challenge' 135–6
money mule-ing 152
money transfers 152
money-making 80, 84, 128, 152, 249, 266
monitoring software 51, 115–16, 214–15, 257
monkey studies 81
motor skills 160–2, 173–4
  fine 102, 168, 174, 183
  gross 168, 174
motor-movement learning 167
music 154
Musk, Elon 303

National Center for Missing & Exploited Children (NCMEC) 127, 247
needs
  hierarchy of 72, 80–1
  *see also* children's needs
needs (body-and brain-based) model of online safety 3

# INDEX

needs-based approaches 3, 62, 68–70, 72–7, 80–5
neologisms 64
neurodiversity 6, 32, 93
  and boundaries 284–5
  and cyberbullying 239–40
  and memes 201
  and online safety 116–17
  and pornography 142, 144
  self-diagnosis 93
  and tech 'addiction' 83–4
  and young children and tech 165
  *see also* autism
neuroplasticity 89, 94
neuroscience 89, 270
neurotransmitters 71–2
  *see also* dopamine
night feeds, using tech during 178–9
nutrition 173

obsessive thoughts 68, 83, 93, 225
Ofcom 38, 43, 190, 225–6, 765
online landscape 14, 21–34
'online lives', loss of 37, 48–9
Online Safety Act (2023) 38, 39, 150, 201–2, 244–5
online safety/security 83–4, 109–20, 247
  needs (body-and brain-based) model of 3
  practical guide to 157–331
  *see also* e-safety; parental controls
online skills, lack of 47, 137–40
'out and about', accessing tech when 113–14, 138, 194, 262–3, 292, 306–7, 313–14
overprotection 42–3, 63, 111

PACE model 235, 264
parental controls 2, 31, 54–5, 58, 84, 107, 202–3, 295, 330–1
  and child sexual abuse 147
  getting around 311, 331
  how to approach with children 109–14, 117
  and middle childhood 192–4, 209, 210
  real-world 307
  and sexual content 146, 209, 210, 252–3
  and teenagers 245, 252–3, 257, 261–3, 266, 271, 281, 283–5
  and violent content 133, 209
  and young children 175–6, 182, 183, 316–17

  *see also* geolocation services; monitoring software
parenting styles
  CPR (consistency, persistence, resistance) 107–9, 114, 124, 179–81, 212–13, 263, 276–7, 279, 283–5, 287, 293–4, 296, 313, 318, 320, 323–4
  'dragon/helicopter' 37
  intrusive 111, 325, 327
  soft 29, 59, 82
  using technology 175–7
parents 333–5
  affirmations for 17
  authoritarian 29, 123
  bad choices of 176
  blaming/shaming 28, 42–4, 100–1
  common tech-related questions 11
  and emotional regulation 82, 176, 180, 270, 293–5, 303, 306, 324, 330, 334
  empathy 234–6, 287, 318, 323, 330, 334
  as experts 259
  failure to keep up with tech 137–40
  'I-need-to-win' strategy 269–70
  integral role in your child's online safety 311–12, 334
  lack of support for 16
  overprotective 42–3, 63, 111
  and peer pressure 190
  role modelling 124
  and self-blame 216, 255
  and sleep deprivation 178–9
  and tech 'addiction' 65
  tech savvy 12, 51–3, 58, 221, 223–4, 302, 308
password protection 183, 193, 197–8
peer pressure 190, 195–8, 221–4, 245, 272
PEGI age ratings 186, 314
perpetrators 47, 129, 152
  *see also* bad actors
Perry, Bruce 180
personal data, children's 39
Pew 190
phantasies 242
'phone boxes' 36
physical exercise 173–4
Piaget, Jean 290
pincer grasp 160–1
pinch grasp 160–1, 174
PINs 112–14, 183, 193, 196–7, 283
Pinterest 13

# INDEX

plastic surgery 232
play, learning through 174–5
PlayStation 191, 302
polarised thinking 221
police 201–3, 248–50, 322–3, 328
pornography 118–20, 141–6, 148, 209–11, 232, 250–5, 262, 322–3
posture 173–4
power struggles 28–9, 123
powerlessness 123, 216
prefrontal cortex 90, 224
Prevent 134, 328
privacy issues 40, 78, 257
proxy networks 36
psychological craving model 68
puberty 90–1, 232–3, 236, 281, 327
public spaces 307

queerness 121–2

racism 50–1, 120, 229, 239, 302
radiation exposure 102–3
radicalisation 134, 261
'rage quitting' 79–80
Rat Park experiment 69–70
reading 98
real-world spaces 306–8, 328–30
rebellion 46–7, 111
regulation, lack of 35, 134
relational ruptures 312
respectful relationships 120–23
Revealing Reality 75–6
risk-taking 2, 24–7, 83, 90–1, 196
risks of tech 188
  biggest 189–95, 258
  blanket advice regarding 125–6
  identifying 29–32, 125–56, 256–7, 288, 333–4
  inability to see 284
  who is your child communicating with? 127–32, 188–9
Roblox 300
Rogers, Carl 234
romantic relationships 206
Rosenberg, Marshall 264
rule-breaking 36, 41, 43

safe spaces 4–5
safeguarding 126, 143, 257, 287, 289, 322
'safety by design' 42

safety/security, sense of 27, 70, 72
  *see also* online safety/security
scaffolding 288, 289
scams 197–8, 225
schools 50–1, 55–7, 189, 203, 322–3, 328–9
screen breaks 171–2, 269–70
screen time
  and child development 58
  heavy use 24, 57–8
  late at night 319–21
  limits 168–72
  for young children 275–6
screengrabs 128
scripts 4, 62, 306–7
secretive behaviour 47, 50, 76–8, 321–2
Section 230 39
secure relationships 3, 27, 70, 74, 183
self 4, 224–5, 234
self-blame 216
'self-care breaks' 14–15, 141, 147, 154, 168, 172, 206, 246, 255, 285–6
self-esteem 233, 234, 271
self-harm 23, 38, 46, 150, 222, 226, 232–3, 241–6
self-regulation 82, 83, 90, 180, 306
  tools for 295, 303
  *see also* dysregulation; emotional regulation
sex 38, 146
sexism 120, 229, 239, 254
sexology 142, 144
sextortion 128–9, 213–16, 222, 246–9
sexual abuse 127, 143, 146–8, 250
sexual consent, age of 262, 288
sexual content 31, 117–20, 143–6, 182, 188–9, 315–17
  children who seek out 321–4
  and middle childhood 209–16, 300–1
  talking about 298–9, 300–1
  and teenagers 222, 226, 229, 250–5, 262
  violent 250–1
  what to do if your child is exposed to 215–16
  and young children 251, 298–9
  *see also* pornography
sexuality 261
shame 28, 46–7, 78, 323, 330
  cycle of 42–4, 65
shared experience 162–3, 164–5, 167–8
short-sightedness (myopia) 169, 170
Shrier, Abigail 63

# INDEX

siblings 50, 192
Siegel, Dan 3, 27, 90, 264, 293
SIM cards 194–5, 269
sleep 270–1, 319–21
  deprivation 178–9, 319
  phased sleep shift 270
smart TV 50, 112–14, 253
smart-watches 56
smartphones
  blanket advice regarding 126
  and the CPR approach 109
  and middle childhood 190–1, 194–5
  in schools 55–6
  secret/hidden 36, 269
  stealing old 194–5, 269
  and tech bans 36, 38, 40, 44–51, 55–6
  and teenagers 256–63, 266
snacking 173
Snapchat 13, 50, 57, 72–3, 75–6, 134, 141, 155, 188, 231, 248, 263, 267–8, 321–2, 328
social comparison-making 231–6
social, emotional or educational needs, children with 6, 32, 47, 48–9, 83–4, 116–17, 141–2, 165, 201, 239–40, 284–5, 303–5
social, emotional and mental-health difficulties (SEMH) 98
social media 2, 9, 13, 16, 19, 22, 330, 334
  'addiction' to 65–7, 75–6
  and age restrictions 188
  and AI chatbots 153
  blanket advice regarding 126
  and boundaries 288, 288–9
  and the brain 93
  and children with additional needs 305
  conduct and 29
  and curated feeds 39
  and cyberbullying 154–5, 237, 240, 317–18
  delaying children's access to 43, 44–51
  and memes 199
  and middle childhood 188, 189–90, 193, 208
  as news source 226
  and parental controls 112
  and resetting algorithms 122
  and self-diagnosis 93
  and sexual content 321–3
  and tech bans 35–8, 40, 43–51, 57–8
  and tech scare stories 26
  and teenagers 221, 225–6, 247, 251, 258
  and 'therapy speak' 63–4
  time spent on 57–8
  uploading images to 131–2
  and violent content 133, 135, 141
social norms 223
social processes 70–3, 75, 76
  see also connection
socialising 3–4, 183, 207, 223, 225, 293
South West Grid for Learning 138
special educational needs (SEN) 98
Spotify 112, 154, 302
stimming 165
streaming sites/apps 112–14
suicide 38, 129, 150, 153, 230, 241–5
SWAY.LY 230

taboos 146, 251, 252
Take It Down 248
talking to children 146, 205, 213–16, 247–9, 253–5
  see also age-appropriate open dialogue
tech
  access delays 43, 44–51, 282
  at different ages 14, 24, 32–3
  see also middle childhood; teenagers; tweens; young children
  benefits of 188, 334
  and boundaries 5, 13, 14, 58, 107–8, 275–96
  'dark side' of 14
  'demonising' approach to 177
  effect on the brain 87–106
  removing from children 285
  troubleshooting 14, 311–31
  see also risks of tech
tech 'addiction' 14, 19, 61–85
  and children's search for connection 61, 66–7
  and craving more time online 77
  focus on 63–7
  and hiding the extent of internet use 76–7
  in middle childhood 185
  needs-based approaches to 68–9, 72–7, 80–5
  and preoccupation with being online 76
  and secretive behaviour 78
tech bans 14, 16, 22, 35–59, 194, 288–9
  children's circumvention of 36, 41, 43–6, 50, 58
  and governments 38–9
  inefficacy 295

# INDEX

tech bans – *cont.*
  and lack of regulation 35
  managing with tech 53–5
  outside the home 37, 44–5
  and teenagers 267–9
  *see also* 'out and about', accesssing tech when
tech landscape 14, 21–34
tech scare stories 22–3, 26, 28
teenagers 14, 221–73, 317–21, 324–30
  bedroom vs living room 258
  and boundaries 280–9
  finding balance with 264–9
  lack of real-world spaces for 223
  and the necessity of being tech smart 259–60
  need for their parents 221, 223–4, 272
  parental concerns about the online activity of 225–8
  and privacy 257, 260–1, 264
  seeking the opinions of 235–6
  and sexual abuse 147
  and sexual content 146, 211
  talking to 301–3
terrorism 134, 140, 261, 302
text messages 46, 50, 72–3, 137, 307
'therapy speak' 63–7, 73, 84, 93, 207
tics 93, 165
TikTok 9, 188–9, 202–3, 231, 247
touch screens 163–8
Transactional Analysis 62
transgenerational transmission 62, 147
trauma, children with 6, 32, 83–4, 116–17, 140–1, 142, 144, 148, 165, 201, 239–40, 284–5
  *see also* cybertrauma
trends 38
troubleshooting 14, 311–31
trust issues 110–11, 115, 123, 136, 207, 217, 229, 247, 278, 314
trust and safety measures 247
TV 175, 193, 209–13, 276
  smart 50, 112–14, 253
tweens 185–220, 280–9, 301–3, 313–14, 321–4
Twenge, Jean 232

'unaliving' 241–2
United Nations Convention on the Rights of the Child 2021 42
URLs 46, 137

victim-blaming 28
violent behaviour 62, 79–80, 93–4, 120–1, 285
violent content 31, 132–41
  and middle childhood 209–13, 300–1
  talking about 298–9, 300–1
  and teenagers 222, 226, 229, 250–5, 302
  what to do if your child is exposed to 215–16
  young children's exposure to 315–17
virtual proxy networks (VPNs) 36, 54
virtual reality (VR) 8, 102, 334
Vision Council 169
vitamin D 173–4
Vodafone 198

'war gore' 31, 133–4
WhatsApp 13, 134, 141, 154–5, 188, 188–9, 238–9, 268, 322–3
Wi-Fi 50, 54, 268, 271, 319–20
window of tolerance 293, 313, 329
Winnicott, Donald 122
worldwide web 22

X (formerly Twitter) 112, 133–4, 135, 188
Xbox 54, 191, 302

young children 14, 24, 159–84
  and boundaries 275–7
  development 102, 160–3, 165–8
  exposure to disturbing content 315–17
  issues to avoid 181–4
  and screen time 58, 168–72
  taking technology off 179–81, 276–7
  talking to 298–9, 305
  and touch screens 163–8
YouTube 13, 104, 112, 118, 143, 166–7, 182, 188, 209, 213–14, 302
YouTube Kids 133, 193, 315